I CANNOT COME DOWN

Answering God's Call To Serve

The Constitution hangs by a thread

CHRISTOPHER DAVID BORCIK

Paperback ISBN: Paperback
EBook ISBN: 978-1-962570-12-1
Hardcover ISBN: 978-1-962570-22-0
Ingram Spark ISBN: 978-1-962570-14-5
Library of Congress Control Number: 2023918979

Cover Design:
Images: Adobe Stock

Cover Design: Angela Ayala
Editor: Marguerite Bonnett
Interior design: Marigold2k

Published by Spotlight Publishing House –
www.Spotlightpublishinghouse.com

https://RestoreAmerica.Today

ENDORSEMENTS

Chris shares with the reader valid points supporting the causes of the current political and economic situation we find ourselves in. Chris and I have been friends for many years. Our country is suffering more now than at any time during my life. There is little doubt that forces have chipped away our Constitution for some time now. I first heard in the late 1970s that there will be a time when this country is in a position that the Constitution "hangs by a thread." At the time, I thought if this were to happen, it would be a physical confrontation. May God guide us back to a safe course individually and as a country.
—Gary Moore, retired airline pilot and USAF pilot

I have known Chris and his family for many years. We share many common formative experiences that include similar yet different military training, long family separations, investigations into the meaning of life and development of strong faith in the Lord and His plan for His children. Chris' devotion to God and to His instrument, the Constitution, is deep and abiding. His points about turning back to the original document and the intent of the framers of the Constitution are spot on. In an age where wisdom is dependent on fads and transitory pleasures, it is refreshing to engage in a discussion of eternal truths. I suggest that all Americans read and digest the arguments found herein.
—Michael W. Cannon LTC, AUS (Ret.)

Chris' well-written book provides an in-depth exploration of the shortcomings of our financial system while highlighting the deficits in our federal government's efforts to be true to our country's Constitution. It also alludes to the innumerable characters throughout

our nation's history who have wittingly and unwittingly contributed to the severe problems we have today."
—Anonymous Friend September 25, 2023

Chris writes a compelling story of his personal journey of faith and inspiration while simultaneously searching for answers to our nation's most serious issues. His explanation of the Fed and monetary policy is outstanding, a must-read for anyone who wants to know about the Fed. Additionally, his introduction to the Constitution is outstanding. If you are looking for solutions to our nation's problems this is a must-read.
—Mike Spain: 1978 US Air Force Academy graduate, USAF pilot & Retired Delta Air Lines Pilot

Our nation is in desperate need of being Restored. The principles and standards that have made this country the greatest nation on earth and the beacon of freedom throughout the world have been trampled down in the name of progression and modern enlightenment. These important principles and standards have been viewed as outdated and old fashion and out of touch with societal trends. However it is in these founding and transcendent principles that this restoration can be achieved. It is always in the wisdom of the ages we can find the best solutions to the complexities of our modern issues. In Chris' book I Cannot Come Down he perfectly identifies the issues facing our nation and a clear plan for restoring America to sound and correct moral, financial and electoral practices that build this nation from its founding. Chris takes a deep dive into many factors facing our nation. His ability to research and articulate the important factors and histories which caused much of the decline in our nation is extraordinary. I have known Chris as a devoted husband, father and friend, a man of faith and courage. I would recommend I Cannot Come Down as a great resource and course for our nation and I would recommend Chris as a great messenger of these important truths he speaks in his book.
—Michael Brosnan, Former Asia Pacific President of ViaViente, CEO of BellaVita Group LLC, and Founding Partner of Viaggio Resorts

I CANNOT COME DOWN

Answering God's Call To Serve

The Constitution hangs by a thread

CHRISTOPHER DAVID BORCIK

SPOTLIGHT
PUBLISHING HOUSE

Goodyear, Arizona

CONTENTS

PROLOGUE

As I approached this book's conclusion, I struggled to produce a captivating title when the perfect inspiration suddenly struck me. After relocating to Georgia in March of 2022, my wife and I were quickly called upon to teach a Sunday school class that consisted of precious youngsters who would be turning eight years old during the calendar year. We were teaching our class of eleven students about the Old Testament with the help of materials and ideas provided by our church. On that given Sunday in July, we were learning about Nehemiah.

Nehemiah isn't a well-known biblical character. In fact, I didn't know anything about him before our preparations for our students. After studying him for the week and providing the lesson tailored for our students, the inspiration came for the title of this book. I'll share what I learned about Nehemiah and let you decide if the title is appropriate.

Nehemiah's story comes well after famous biblical characters such as Abraham, Isaac, and Jacob, or Moses and Joshua, or David and Solomon. Let's pick up our story after the southern Kingdom of Israelites (mostly consisting of the tribe of Judah, or Jews) fell to Babylon about 587 B.C. Their capital, Jerusalem, was destroyed and many citizens were carried off into captivity.

Babylon's power waned as a new regional power emerged. Persia, under the leadership of Cyrus, conquered the region including Babylon. Cyrus' reign over the conquered people was uncharacteristic of that period. *"Instead of tyrannizing over them and holding them in subjection by brute force, he treated his subjects with consideration and won them as his friends. He was particularly considerate of the religions of conquered peoples."*[1]

Cyrus decreed that any captive Jews throughout Babylonia would be permitted to return to their homeland and rebuild their temple in Jerusalem which the Babylonians destroyed. His immediate successors honored that edict and this ushered in the period during which many of the Jews returned to Jerusalem. Hence, we come to our story of Nehemiah, a Jew who was born while the Jews were in exile.

Nehemiah was a cupbearer to the Persian king Artaxerxes (Cyrus' grandson). This position, obviously, held great trust and responsibility, as assassination was a constant threat to a king. When the King learned of Nehemiah's concern for the plight of his fellow Jews and the ruined state of Jerusalem, he was granted permission to return to Jerusalem to help rebuild it. He was provided with an escort of guards for his journey and permission to use timbers from the king's forest.

The story of Nehemiah is not grandiose like Moses parting the Red Sea, or valiant like David slaying Goliath, but nonetheless, shows a courageous fortitude to do what he knew was right. Nehemiah had joined others in rebuilding the walls around Jerusalem, but there were enemies in the region who did not want to see the Jews succeed. Nehemiah became a great leader under the circumstances. His faith in God gave him the strength and courage to inspire his fellow Jews to remain armed and vigilant while continuing the work of rebuilding the city walls.

At one point, some of those enemies tried subterfuge, not once, but five times to delay the work by trying to persuade Nehemiah to come down from his work so that they might "counsel together." Nehemiah's response was identical each time: "I am doing a great work, so that I cannot come down: why should the work cease, whilst I leave it, and come down to you?"

When I learned of this story, I was inspired by those words, "I am doing a great work, so that I cannot come down." As you will discover in this book, I have a unique story to tell, and I believe "a great work" must be accomplished.

I love this country; she has been good to me. I love the principles upon which it was built. I love the founding documents and those who were inspired to create them. The Declaration of Independence is timeless. The Constitution is no less important as it created a nation out of thirteen loosely connected colonies that would become the envy of citizens around the world. People from many parts of the world flocked to the United States of America to enjoy the privileges she espoused in those founding documents. The United States was a success story and other nations replicated our story by creating their own constitutions in hopes of achieving the same success.

The United States no longer shines as a "beacon on a hill." We've been struggling for decades with social and economic problems that I believe have been exasperated by an out-of-control federal government. We've even exported some of our problems. The solutions are not complicated. I will articulate those solutions in this book.

This isn't just my story though. My story includes you. We are bound together by geographic boundaries and other forces that will require us to work shoulder to shoulder. My story is really our story, and we have "a great work" to accomplish. As for me, "I cannot come down."

Chapter 1

A NATION IN STRUGGLE

When I was growing up in the nineteen sixties and seventies, there were three main television channels that broadcast over the VHF airwaves. Few people watched anything else. Each of those big three networks got their start in radio and converted to television as that medium gained popularity. Today, streaming services have added to our viewing choices and content and the big three networks have been joined by over 100 lesser known "over the air networks" and well over 100 cable network stations. I remember as a youth when my father complained one evening about a nightly news anchorman. He was expressing his disappointment that the anchorman was no longer objective. My father was concerned that he was receiving the news through the subjective lens of the anchorman and not receiving an unbiased view of the news. In other words, the anchorman was sharing his opinion.

It's hard not to see the world through our own lens but I surmise that my father once believed the news was broadcast objectively, or at least he thought it ought to be. How far we've come. Today, I cannot turn on the television, no matter what channel, and not get biased news. There are a few news anchors that do a fairly good job of not opining, but they are diamonds in the rough.

During my youth, I remember sitting with my father in the living room watching the nightly news that heavily focused on the Vietnam

War. The war images were constantly broadcasted on television. Presently, as I write this, the world is facing the invasion of Ukraine by Russia. It is hard to know the truth because there are always biases that come with an opinion about what the US, NATO, Russia, President Biden, Putin and/or others should or could be doing to end the conflict. In the meantime, the Ukrainian citizens are suffering and dying. It's always the innocent who suffer at the hands of national leaders.

Prior to the Ukrainian war, the world was slammed shut by the Covid-19 pandemic, or particularly, our response to it. Biases drove national responses, namely fear of contracting the disease caused by the virus. Being someone who favors natural remedies, it was disheartening for me to observe a deliberate attempt to suppress views that presented alternative solutions to widespread vaccination.

The barrage of daily news, whether it be worldly events, or national events such as the January 6, 2021, Capitol riots, or the Seattle riots in the summer of 2020, (both of which began peacefully) are indicative of a world that is becoming increasingly uncivilized, or at least has the appearance of becoming more uncivilized. In my little corner of the world, I see few disputes, if any at all, and nowhere near the amount that we see reported daily in the media. Conflict is common to human nature, but in a civilized community, we ought to seek resolutions to our differences. Conflict is bound to intensify when two parties become adamant and assert that their viewpoint is correct.

Resolving conflict requires a dose of empathy—the ability to place yourself in the other person's shoes. There is an adage, (author unknown), that "we have two ears and one mouth so we can listen twice as much as we speak." Another saying attributed to Eugene O'Neill states, "God gave us mouths that close and ears that don't... that should tell us something."

Another conflict that has taken the national stage is the Supreme Court ruling in June 2022 that overturned Roe v. Wade. It is an issue with extraordinarily strong opinions on both sides of the issue, and as with many issues in our day, some of those expressing their views have little tolerance or empathy for people with the opposing view. We each are influenced by our life's experiences, and we come to any issue with our biases that have been sculpted by those experiences. I am a man and cannot become pregnant; therefore, I cannot fully comprehend the difficult decision a woman may be faced with during an unplanned or unwanted pregnancy.

I often defer to my wife when trying to understand issues from a woman's point of view. Because I am a man, I come to this issue with my own biases.

I watched a documentary recently from one of my "streaming" services that alarmingly showed how our biases are reinforced by the social media accounts we subscribe to. To put it plainly, if you have political leanings in one direction, the social platform is designed to continue to provide like-minded material. The social platform makes its money from advertisers and advertisers make their money by presenting material to targeted audiences in hopes that viewers will succumb to the wiles of their advertising gimmicks.

If your social media account can keep you scrolling through your feed by reinforcing your beliefs and biases, then you will encounter more advertisers competing to get your hard-earned dollars in hopes of purchasing whatever it is they are peddling. The social media platform wins whether we make a purchase from an advertiser or not, as long as they can keep us scrolling, reading, or viewing the content they continue to feed us. This documentary showed that our biases grow even stronger because of this content targeting. Is it any wonder that since the advent of social media, our country has become increasingly more polarized along political party lines?

Political biases are not new. The extreme partisanship we see today was something that the Framers of the Constitution attempted to mitigate. They took every precaution when they crafted the Constitution to do so. Even the very proceedings at the Constitutional Convention in Philadelphia during the summer of 1787 were rife with political biases, but they managed to work through their differences to create *"the best [Constitution] that could be obtained."*[2] The biases they had were shaped more by geography than any other factor.

The Virginian was shaped more by his agrarian pursuits (including the issue of slave labor) as opposed to the mercantile pursuits of a Bostonian, or New Yorker. In general, the northern states had more industry and mercantilism, and the southern states had more agriculture, and they brought these and other biases to the Convention. They recognized the importance of dividing powers in the newly formed government so that no singular region, (or state, such as the very populous Virginia) would run roughshod over the other states. We won't go into a study of the genius of the well laid out structure of the Constitution at this time, but we need to recognize that the Framers understood political biases and made every attempt to mitigate their negative effects.

George Washington experienced political biases during his presidency. His own cabinet members disagreed about the merits of a national bank. Not surprisingly, the biases were in lock step with the same geographical differences previously mentioned. The cabinet members were Thomas Jefferson, a Virginian and Alexander Hamilton, a New Yorker. While Hamilton had been present at the Constitutional Convention, and even wrote several of the Federalist Papers in support of ratifying the Constitution, Jefferson had been absent (serving as the American minister to France) but had a greater understanding of the federal limitations of the Constitution. Hamilton argued for the merits of a National Bank whereas Jefferson understood the Constitution gave no such authority.

Washington was loyal to Hamilton, most likely because of their service together in the Revolutionary War. He often sided with Hamilton's economic policies instead of accepting Jefferson's "strict interpretation" of the Constitution. The divisions grew into what became the first political parties of this nation. Hamilton "stretched" the meaning of the Constitution to fit his ambitions, which meant a stronger Federal government, whereas Jefferson and those of the party to which he was aligned, the "Democratic-Republicans," favored the "limited" role of the Federal government. Today, the battle rages on, where the ideological views of the two major parties often oppose each other. Washington presciently understood the dangers of parties and warned of them in his Farewell Address. He saw them as a stumbling block which undermines the "United" in the United States.

A review of Washington's warning about parties in his Farewell Address not only suggests that he could look into his future and see our day, but also serves as a bulwark for the clarion call to aggressively move away from the destructive influence of political parties if we are going to save our nation. His first intimation about parties came from his personal observations of the ugly side of human nature. I quote,

> "*One of the expedients of party to acquire influence within particular districts is to misrepresent the opinions and aims of other districts.*"

We must remember that the biases of Washington's day were usually geographical, and the citizens of a "district" shared the same views, or biases. How often do we see political pundits or other talking heads lambast their political opponents and infer, or perhaps misrepresent their opponent's "*opinion*" and/or "*aim*" (intention)?

Let's take, for example, another very heated debate over an issue that our nation experienced recently (as of this writing), Disney and Florida. I won't suggest there is a right or wrong, only that people are aligning themselves with either Disney or Governor DeSantis because of words like "woke" or "Don't Say Gay." These expressions are intended to misrepresent or perhaps obfuscate the truth. We can't truly know what a person is thinking or what's in their heart, and any attempts to do so by labeling or name calling an opponent "*is to misrepresent the opinions and aims*" of their opponent. Washington continued his warnings.

> "*Let me now take a more comprehensive view and warn you in the most solemn manner against the baneful effects of the spirit of party, generally. This spirit, unfortunately, is inseparable from our nature, having its root in the strongest passions of the human mind. It exists under different shapes in all governments, more or less stifled, controlled, or repressed; but in those of the popular form it is seen in its greatest rankness and is truly their worst enemy.*"

Washington continued, "*The alternate domination of one faction over another, sharpened by the spirit of revenge natural to party dissension, which in different ages and countries has perpetrated the most horrid enormities, is itself a frightful despotism. But this leads at length to a more formal and permanent despotism. The disorders and miseries which result gradually incline the minds of men to seek security and repose in the absolute power of an individual; and sooner or later the chief of some prevailing faction, more able or more fortunate than his competitors, turns this disposition to the purposes of his own elevation on the ruins of public liberty.*"

As a student of human nature, I believe we have long arrived at the day when the "*minds of men*" choose our president with that very purpose in mind, "*to seek security and repose*" from our government and the public spectacle we call presidential elections is filled with candidates willing to make such promises for their own political gain.

Washington continued his admonitions. *"Without looking forward to an extremity of this kind (which nevertheless ought not to be entirely out of sight) the common and continual mischiefs of the spirit of party are sufficient to make it the interest and the duty of a wise people to discourage and restrain it. It serves always to distract the public councils and enfeeble the public administration. It agitates the community with ill-founded jealousies and false alarms, kindles the animosity of one part against another, foments occasionally riot and insurrection. It opens the door to foreign influence and corruption, which finds a facilitated access to the government itself through the channels of party passions. Thus the policy and the will of one country are subjected to the policy and will of another."*

Need I say more? Washington's warnings in the late 18ᵗʰ century are so intimate to our 21ˢᵗ century political landscape, it's as if he had been watching the daily news of our day. Human nature hasn't changed in all recorded history. There will always be tyrants who seek political power, and if we are not *"wise"* enough to *"discourage and restrain"* parties, we will suffer the fate many historians see in our future, the utter collapse of our nation. In the words of another 18ᵗʰ century statesmen (and economist and philosopher), Irish-born Edmund Burke, "Those who don't know history are destined to repeat it."

While historians might agree that our nation will suffer the fate of all empires that were destroyed from within, I don't think God has given up on us just yet. We are not entirely ripe for destruction. Not surprisingly, our electorate intuitively recognizes the problems associated with political parties and has been disassociating from them for decades. 42% of respondents in 2021 identified as independent voters according to this Gallup poll (See Figure 1).[3] That is nearly half of respondents and significantly more than those who identify as a Democrat or Republican.

Party Identification, Annual Averages, 1988-2021

In politics, as of today, do you consider yourself -- [a Republican, a Democrat]] -- or an independent?

— % Democrat   — % Independent   ···· % Republican

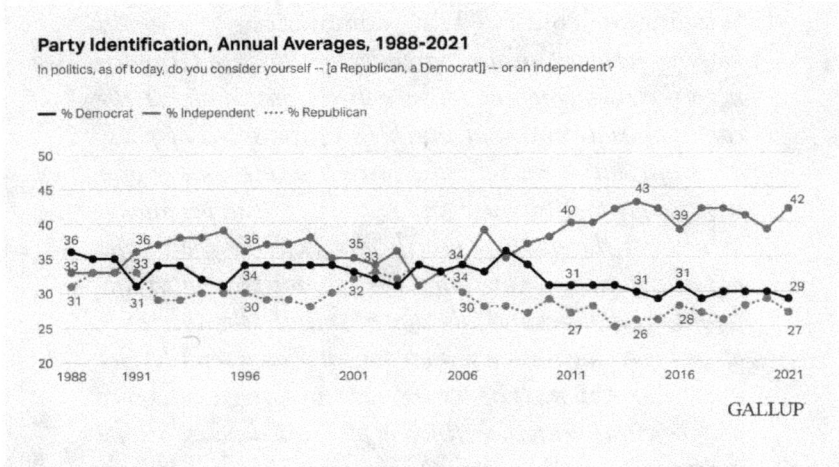

Figure 1: Used with permission;
https://news.gallup.com/poll/388781/political-party-
preferences-shifted-greatly-during-2021.aspx

I think most people will agree, we are a nation in struggle. Part of that problem lies in the political divisions with which we so willingly align ourselves, along with the inherent problems that social media, political pundits and talking heads exacerbate and Washington so eloquently warned us about.

Chapter 2

THE LAYOVER

Ronald Reagan National Airport lies at a bend in the Potomac River named Gravelly Point just across the river from the District of Columbia. While Reagan airport was not the first airport to serve the nation's capital, it has been providing air travel for our representatives in Congress since WWII.

During a press conference in the fall of 1938, President Franklin D. Roosevelt, having grown weary of inaction in Congress to determine a location for a much-needed newer airport than what then existed, declared the mudflats of Gravelly Point to be the site of the new airport. The ceremonial shoveling of dirt officially kicked off construction on November 21st, 1938. On June 16, 1941, Captain Bennett H. Griffin was the first pilot to land at National Airport after his employer, American Airlines, had won the honor by drawing straws.[4]

Today, a dozen airlines provide service in and out of Reagan Airport averaging 800 flights a day. It is a busy airport that reflects the pulse of the city for which it serves. I have flown to Reagan Airport many times for my work. It is always exciting to see the majestic beauty of Washington DC out the left side of our aircraft as we fly down the corridor of the Potomac River on our final approach to landing on Runway 19.

Runway 19 is the major and longest runway at Reagan Airport and is oriented north and south. Runways are named by starting with the magnetic compass direction they are oriented, in this case 187 degrees, then rounding to the nearest 10th or 190 degrees, and then dropping the zero giving "19." The same slab of concrete is named Runway 1 when taking off and landing in the opposite direction, to the north.

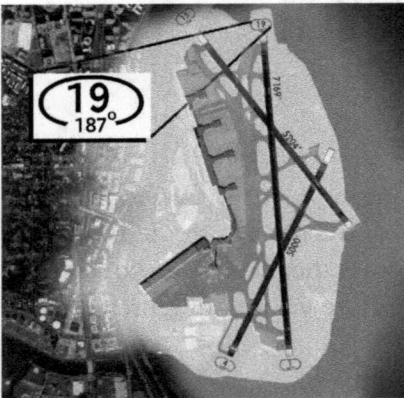

Figure 2: Reagan Airport

Runway 19 lies 14 feet above sea level and is officially 7,169 feet long. While it is the longest of Reagan Airport's three runways, it is short by today's standards for modern airports. Being built on a landfill at Gravelly Point, Reagan Airport cannot extend the length of her longest runway without dredging up more landfill on the banks of the Potomac and shutting down operations for an extended period. So, as demand grew for more airport capacity and larger transport aircraft were coming off the assembly line, a newer airport was needed and Congress approved plans for Dulles Airport, some 26 miles west of Washington DC. Dulles Airport was named after the late Secretary of State John Foster Dulles and was formally dedicated by President John F Kennedy in November 1962.

Large international jets do not have sufficient runway length to takeoff from Reagan National Airport, thus Reagan Airport provides service for narrow body aircraft only. When domestic travelers arrive on approach to runway 19, most are familiar with the sites of Washington DC including the Washington Monument. Without warning and just moments before landing, the plane suddenly banks its wings hard to the right obscuring the view of downtown DC. Alert passengers on the right side can observe the commuters heading across the George Mason Memorial Bridge barely 200 feet below the right-wing tip. The pilot will roll out of this final turn and align the aircraft with runway 19 just moments before landing.

Seasoned business travelers scarcely give this unusually hard turn prior to landing a second thought, but to the vacation traveler who has never flown this approach into DC, it can be alarming. Then, if the turn was not startling enough, the plane firmly lands on Runway 19 and comes to a screeching halt. If the pilot is having a good day, he may have gently rolled the plane onto the runway, but the average landing at Reagan is firm and noticeably harder than most landings experienced elsewhere by the frequent flyer.

The approach to Runway 19 at Reagan Airport has an official name, the "River Visual Rwy 19," according to the aviation community. It is so named because the pilot is required to fly visually down the Potomac River while being able to keep the airport in view. If the pilots of arriving aircraft can see the airport some 10 to 15 miles away, the air traffic controller will give commands or directions (which are officially called "clearances") to steer each aircraft to a point over the river about 10 miles northwest of the airport.

The controller is required to keep each aircraft separated by distances that will provide a safe margin between arriving aircraft. The airport is so busy that as one plane touches down for landing, the tower controller will "clear" a departing aircraft onto the runway to "line up and wait" for their turn for takeoff. When the preceding landing aircraft taxis clear of the runway, the tower controller will clear the departing aircraft to takeoff. Just seconds after the plane lifts off the runway, another arriving aircraft, having completed his hard bank to the right, lands on runway 19. This procedure happens repeatedly, hundreds of times a day at Ronald Reagan National Airport.

You might be asking yourself, why must the River Approach into Reagan Airport require a hard bank to the right just before landing on runway 19? Why can't arriving aircraft line up straight with the runway like other airports? With modern computer technology, the reader can find the answer to their own question. To answer that question, one needs only to access Google Maps, search for Ronald Reagan National Airport and look at the geography surrounding the airport. Lying just north of runway 19 is downtown Washington DC. A final approach into runway 19, aligned with the runway, would bring hundreds of flights a day within 400 yards offset from directly overhead the White House, not to mention over or near the Washington Monument, the Jefferson Memorial, the Washington Mall, and other visitor sites. Flying down the Potomac River affords our President and all of DC's daily visitors the luxury and safety of not having (and hearing) commercial jet aircraft flying overhead every few minutes of every day.

Figure 3 : Copyright: Bill Lang and used with permission.

Before continuing, I must explain a few fundamentals of aviation. Not every approach into Reagan Airport is flown according to the "River Visual Rwy 19." Sometimes aircraft land in the opposite direction, or runway 1. The runway in use is predicated upon the general direction of the wind. Flying into the wind means an aircraft is flying across the ground at a slower "groundspeed." Even though a pilot can adjust an airplane's airspeed, there is a minimum airspeed at which an aircraft can safely fly without stalling and crashing. Pilots intentionally fly as close to that minimum airspeed as possible when landing, with a buffer margin of safety. Higher airspeed requires a longer runway length to stop after touchdown. While in the air, "speed is life," meaning it is safer to be at a higher airspeed so as not to stall. But when landing, any excess speed could mean trouble.

If a plane lands too fast or too far down the runway (or both), particularly if the runway is slippery, the pilot runs the risk of running off the end of the runway. The amount of runway needed to stop the aircraft is related to the airspeed at touchdown. If there is no wind blowing down the runway, the plane's ground speed at touchdown will be the same as the airspeed. The higher the groundspeed, the longer the runway needed to stop. If there is wind blowing, preferably from ahead of the aircraft, or "headwind," the groundspeed will be less than the airspeed; therefore, the greater the headwind, the slower the groundspeed at touchdown and subsequently the shorter the distance required to stop.

Given that pilots and controllers cannot control Mother Nature, airport operations in the aviation industry are constrained by the direction of the prevailing winds and will almost always be towards the direction from which the wind is blowing for the reason described above. If operations at Reagan National Airport are not utilizing the River Visual Runway 19 approach, they are utilizing the same slab of asphalt and taking off and landing to the north. That same area over downtown DC would be abound with departing aircraft with their noisy jet engines running at nearly full throttle for takeoff if it were not for a takeoff departure procedure which requires a hard left turn after takeoff to remain over the Potomac River. No doubt, the First Family and all visitors to DC would be grateful if they understood the noise level they are spared every day.

We had just landed in DC, having arrived on the "River Visual Rwy 19" approach. From a passenger's point of view, the arrival coming down the Potomac River provides a splendid view of our nation's capital. From the cockpit, the view is even more impressive. It was the winter of 1995, January to be exact, when I had just completed the approach into DC, winding down the Potomac River flying one of our company's MD-88 aircraft from the copilot's seat on the right side of the cockpit. If the weather outside was not cloudy or misty, it meant that a cold front had pushed through, and the air was crisp and clear.

That is one thing I have always loved about the winter, the clean air that always follows a cold front. It is rare to have days in the summer when one can see for hundreds of miles. Summer days are often hazy days when visibility is usually limited to ten miles or less. Winter days, on the other hand, often provide pristine blue skies which are so clear that you can easily see both the east and west coasts of the Florida peninsula when flying to or from south Florida. As an airline pilot, the spectacular views I enjoyed from the cockpit were something I never tired of.

Less than a five-minute drive and within walking distance of Reagan National Airport is an area in Arlington, Virginia named Crystal City. Our layover hotel was in the heart of this business district. Business travelers and military personnel in uniform frequented the shops and offices found within walking distance. Only blocks away from our hotel was one of Washington DC's Metro Stations. I had predetermined I was going to make use of the Metro system during this layover to visit an obscure site—but one that is well known among DC's residents.

The average layover for an airline crew is between 12 and 16 hours, but some are shorter and some longer. The FAA (Federal Aviation Administration) has many rules that regulate the aviation industry, including the required rest period between duty days. The rest rules have been modified since 1995, but aircrew required a minimum rest period of 8 hours back then. Occasionally, due to shifting duty times, a trip may have a layover of 24 hours or more. It is during longer layovers when airline crews often explore the local sites. Washington DC is rich in history and there are many interesting sites to visit. DC was one of my favorite layover cities for that reason. However, this time I had made plans to visit an edifice on the city outskirts that could scarcely be labeled historical.

Approximately 11 miles north of Reagan National Airport as a crow flies, nearly in line with runway 19's centerline, just outward of Beltway 495 that circumnavigates the greater Washington metropolis lies an edifice unbeknownst to most US citizens. But to the daily Washington commuter who traverses Highway 495 on the north side of town, it is a well-known site. On every fair-weather day, the scene unfolds for each westbound commuter on Highway 495 just after the Silver Springs/Wheaton exit. The commuter proceeds up a gently rising slope that crests after a 50-foot rise.

Figure 4: Image courtesy of The Church of Jesus Christ of Latter-day Saints

At 360 feet above sea level, the highway peaks and lends itself to the first viewing of a regal, six-spired temple in full view. If the highway did not bend southwest just prior to the temple grounds, it would run directly through it. For one mile, and approximately one minute, each westbound commuter has a splendid view of the beautiful temple with its white marble exterior which rises to 288 feet, clearly above the treetops that frame the busy highway. My first experience of viewing this temple took my breath away. That was more than 25 years ago, when the trees were not nearly as tall. Today, the temple is still visible above the treetops on that one-mile stretch of highway.

As spectacular as the view of this temple is while driving westbound on highway 495, it is far more glorious when viewed from on foot around its well-manicured grounds. This temple, in all its majesty, is one of more than 167 operating temples found around the world (with more than 100 in construction, renovation, or planned), owned by the Church of Jesus Christ of Latter-Day Saints. Built in the early 1970's the Washington DC Temple was dedicated over a four-day ceremony from November 19 through 22, 1974 by then President of the Church, Spencer W. Kimball. It was renovated and rededicated in the summer of 2022. While it was not the first temple built outside of Utah by The Church, it was the first temple in the Eastern United States and still stands as the tallest—even taller than the renowned Salt Lake City Temple.

It was to this glorious edifice I had decided to visit during my layover in Washington DC. Faithful members of the Church of Jesus Christ of Latter-Day Saints are encouraged to visit and often attend their temples which dot the earth. The temples of the Church offer a special chance for spiritual growth, providing patrons with a unique and closer connection to God. Indeed, each temple has inscribed on its exterior walls, "Holiness to the Lord-The House of the Lord" which speaks towards its purpose. Dedicated to the Lord, each temple serves as a symbolic reminder of one's commitment towards God and His laws. Patronage at a Latter-Day Saint temple increases one's desire to keep God's commandments. Each patron takes his commitment seriously as he or she endeavors to make and keep sacred covenants found only within the walls of these temples.

While only faithful members of the Church of Jesus Christ of Latter-Day Saints are permitted entrance into their temples, the Church does provide a once in a lifetime opportunity for others to visit. Each temple is open to the public during an official Open House period which may last from two weeks to two months. Every newly built temple, or one that has undergone extensive remodeling, will have an Open House.

Figure 5: Image courtesy of The Church of Jesus Christ of Latter-day Saints

The Washington DC temple received well over 750 thousand visitors during its open house period from 17 September to 2 November 1974 including, then First Lady, Betty Ford.

It is during this period that visitors often feel the peace that can be found within the walls of these sacred buildings which, in the case of the Washington DC temple, resulted in 75,000 missionary referrals, or approximately 1 in 10 persons who felt inspired to learn more about the precious feelings they experienced which faithful Latter-Day Saints are privileged to experience every time they sojourn to spend time within the walls of a temple. It was for the purpose of enjoying a spiritually uplifting and renewing experience in the Washington DC temple that I made a commitment to attend. I had decided several days before my layover that during my off-duty hours as an airline pilot, I would make the effort to travel via the Washington DC Metro system from Crystal City and attend.

Utilizing the DC Metro system is straightforward. It was one of those rare subway systems not proliferated with graffiti. After making my way to the last subway stop, I transferred to a bus route which got me within a mile's walk of the temple. It took over an hour to make my way to the temple that day from my company provided hotel room in Crystal City. I had carefully planned my visit to return to Crystal City in plenty of time to make my evening departure for the airport from the layover hotel. I had allotted enough time to spend worshipping within the temple for about 2 to 3 hours without the need to rush back.

As I strolled onto the temple grounds, I was mesmerized by the beauty of its grounds, the sacred building itself and an inviting Visitors' Center. I had toured the Visitors' Center the year before with my wife, but this would be my first opportunity to enter the Washington DC Temple itself and I was filled with anticipation. My wife and I had joined the Church of Jesus Christ of Latter-Day Saints in November 1992, in our 10th year of marriage. We were the parents of two small boys at that time and part of our growing maturity as parents was to find a suitable church to help us teach our young family about the Christian faith, which we both were born into: my wife as a Southern Baptist, myself as a Catholic. We were relatively new to the Latter-Day Saints faith but were strongly committed to living the tenets, which we found quite agreeable. Our temple worship began about a year after we were baptized, and this particular layover took place 2 years and 2 months after we were baptized and confirmed as members of the Church.

Faithful Latter-Day Saints must undergo two separate interviews from their ecclesiastical leaders to receive what is referred to as a "Temple Recommend." During these interviews, members must honestly answer questions which provide the member an opportunity to do a self-assessment of their own moral standing with God. If it is determined that the member is in good standing with the Church, he or she is endorsed by each of the leaders who sign a valid "Temple Recommend." The third, and last signature on the "recommend" is that of the member, who testifies in writing that they too believe they are in good standing with God and the Church.

Without a "Temple Recommend," members will not be permitted entrance. Consequently, it is prudent for members to check their wallet or wherever they may safely store their personal Temple Recommend before venturing to a temple. I always keep mine in my wallet, along with my driver's license and my pilot's license. They are the three most important forms of identification to me: one recognizing my citizenship in the state where I live and the authority to operate a motor vehicle, one recognizing my authority from the US government to operate a commercial aircraft, and the last recognizing my authority as a "citizen" of God's kingdom on earth to enter His Holy House. I consider each document of considerable worth, the latter being the most important to me.

I entered the main doorway to the temple and was pleasantly greeted with a smile by the gentleman who sits near the entrance responsible for checking the validity of each member's Temple Recommend. Members routinely visit temples, and each temple is safely monitored during their operating hours by one or two individuals who are assigned this simple duty. Faithful Latter-Day Saint members staff the temples throughout the world to ensure their orderly and efficient operation. Among the many duties they perform, the "Recommend" checker is one. He or she will cycle through many duties during the standard six-hour shift for which there is no monetary recompense. Service as a staff member in the temples also requires the necessary "Temple Recommend" and although no monetary compensation is received by most of the staff, there is a small fraction of members who are employed by the Church full time to assist with the daily operations.

Volunteers who serve as part-time staff will usually serve one or two days a week for six-hour shifts. Due to the nature of the time required, seldom does one find the parents of young children serving as temple staff. Most often, temple staff volunteers are adults who have reached retirement age. Their cheerful countenance, such as the man who checked my Temple Recommend that day, is usually what adorns the faces of the many elderly volunteers. In their eyes, it is easy to see the maturity and wisdom of years peppered with many of life's experiences. It imparts a safe and comforting feeling, the sort of reassuring feeling that my passengers experience when they peek into the cockpit to discover my salt and pepper hair affirming my many years of experience as a pilot.

Each Church temple operates the same, although they have a variety of architectural designs and differing floor layouts. On the lowest floor level can be found a baptismal font, often perched atop the backs of twelve intricately stone carved oxen. Temples are rich in symbology, both in design and activities. The twelve oxen represent the twelve tribes of Israel, who received the covenant their fathers, even Abraham, Isaac and Jacob received from God. When members are baptized, they are adopted into the family of Abraham, Isaac and Jacob (Jacob's name was changed to Israel) and enjoy the privileges of that same covenant.

Moving up to the main level, one will find dressing rooms for women on one side and men on the opposite side. It is here where we will change from our street clothes into attire that is entirely white. Women will change into modest white dresses and men will change into modest white suits and ties. Even the footwear is white. The white attire is symbolic, representing purity, and all members inside, both workers and patrons, are dressed in white. Even maintenance workers are under the same obligation to be dressed in white, so they are not a distraction to patrons.

In all temples visitors will discover a larger room, rich in symbolic décor named the "Celestial Room." The doctrine of the Latter-Day Saints faith delineates different degrees of Heaven, the highest degree being that of the Celestial Kingdom wherein God dwells. It is to this Kingdom that faithful Latter-Day Saints hope to live after this life on earth. The promises are that dwelling with God in the Celestial Kingdom affords the recipient a fullness of joy, happiness, and peace.

The Celestial Room not only symbolizes the Heavenly Kingdom of God in its beautiful décor, but individuals will experience feelings of peace that is to be expected in God's Heavenly Kingdom as well. Visitors to the Celestial Room will often find church members sitting on one of the several sofas or chairs, in scripture reading, thoughtful contemplation or solemn and silent prayer. It is in the Celestial Room where members go to find solace and to receive answers to prayers concerning difficult questions or life's more perplexing problems.

After having provided some meaningful service in one of the other rooms in the temple, I eventually made my way to the Celestial Room. This day was during the middle of the week and there was only a handful of people in attendance at the Temple. Before long, I discovered that I was the sole remaining patron in the Celestial Room and across the room was one of the women serving on duty that day. I later discovered that her post there in the Celestial Room had a nickname, the "angel," and I have always assumed her duty was to help maintain a spirit of quiet reverence, which in my many years of attendance since then, has never been an issue of concern.

While sitting reverently on one of the sofas in the middle of the room, having had enjoyed a breather from the distractions of the outside world for the previous two hours, I began to ponder the beauty of the room. Not overly crowded with furniture, but

For the 2022 Open House, The Church posted images of the interior, including these two high resolution images that are best viewed on a desktop. https://1sh.me/CelestialRm1 https://1sh.me/CelestialRm2

always tastefully decorated with a large chandelier hanging from the center of the room, white or light-colored carpeting and upholstered furniture, exquisitely crafted wood-trimmed sofas and chairs, finely crafted wood tables, textured wallpaper also lightly colored, and floral arrangements scattered about, this and all Celestial Rooms appropriately match in appearance the Kingdom they symbolize.

Suddenly, as if someone approached me in surprise, I heard a voice. Looking around, I realized I was still alone apart from the "angel" who stood halfway across the room. The voice came into my mind as distinctly as if someone had been standing beside me, whispering in my ear.

The words were clearly discernable, but brief and directive. The gentle but firm command pierced my mind, "Run for President." I immediately thought, realizing that I was alone, "Is that you Lord?" He continued in His conversation to my mind, "If you do not believe it is me, go ask her," as my thought and eyes now turned to the woman across the room.

I took the counsel I received and proceeded across the room to speak with the sister. In the Church of Jesus Christ of Latter-Day Saints, we often affectionately refer to each other as sister or brother, respecting the nature of our spiritual heritage as sons and daughters of a Divine Being. The woman that served as the "angel" in the Celestial Room was mature in age and like most other workers in the temples, had that twinkle in her eyes that bespoke "wisdom and kindness."

Still somewhat new as a member and having gone to other temples only a handful of times during the previous year, I was unsure of what just happened to me. "If you have a thought in the Celestial Room, can you be certain it is from God?" Her response was that she believed it to be so; however, she recommended that I ask the temple president to be sure. I left it at that, satisfied with the affirmative words in her response. "Truly indeed," I thought, "God had just spoken to me!"

Chapter 3

A YEAR TO REFLECT

After changing back into my street clothes, I began my trek back to my layover hotel in Crystal City. As I walked through the wooded area between the Temple and the bus station, my mind was reeling. "Wow, I can't believe that happened to ME!" "I can't wait to tell my wife." "I can't believe God asked me." "I guess with His help, anything is possible." I kept thinking of all the biblical accounts of how ordinary men and women accomplished extraordinary feats under the direction of God. David slew Goliath. Moses was able to lead an entire nation from a life of bondage to migrate to the Promised Land.

I even remembered some of the accounts of unusual feats written about in the Book of Mormon. But why me? I had never had any interest in politics, I had zero experience in civic affairs, and I did not know who my congressperson was. "Why me?" That is a question I have often asked myself for many years. I think I know the answer, but as in all things in life, including revelations from God, I've discovered we don't know all the answers until everything is "said an' done."

1995 was a financially challenging year for us. We had purchased a home a few years prior that we could barely afford. The airline industry had been suffering losses for several years and my company was no exception. Management had been seeking concessions from our Pilot's Union (ALPA) for quite some time and the union leadership had been digging in their heels. As was often the case during that era, the battle was fought in public and public opinion was not in favor of pilots. Captains who had been with the company for years flying international flights on our wide-body aircraft were making particularly good money, well into six figures, and ALPA could hardly garner support in the court of public opinion. Knowing this fact, the company pressed hard.

Seeing the writing on the wall—a probable pay cut—we chose to sell our newly built home in Georgia, and we moved back to our more modest home in Florida that we had been renting out the past several years. The move would provide an opportunity to increase our monthly cash flow, save some money, and make an investment (both financially and emotionally) with extended family living in the Pensacola area. It was time, once again, to commute from Pensacola to Atlanta for my weekly work schedule. We sold our home in Georgia, packed up a truck and moved back to Florida during the summer of '95.

Prior to moving to Florida, we had made many good friends in the town where we lived. One of our friends was an elderly gentleman, who had become my mentor in our newfound religion. He was well into his 60's, treated his body like a temple and was the picture of good health, fit and lean. I will never forget the time when he and I were helping a family load furniture into a moving van and this good man was running circles around people half his age. He was as strong as an ox. In my mind, he was a spiritual giant as well. He treated everyone with kindness, was well versed in the scriptures and had that characteristic twinkle in his eyes that was common among the temple workers. He was a man I could trust, and I looked up to him like a father. As we worked on church assignments together, I studied his every behavior, taking in everything I could, like a newborn baby exploring his surroundings. This giant of a man was the first person, after my wife, with whom I shared my epiphany. Without batting an eye, he looked carefully at me and without hesitation said, "Chris, the first thing you need to do is study the Constitution." He suggested I read two other documents as well: The Federalist Papers and a well-researched book about the Federal Reserve. I was quite surprised that he never doubted me nor the authenticity of my experience. I would soon discover that others treated the telling of my experience with far more skepticism.

My wife was not one of those who treated my narrative with suspicion. We discussed the events of my temple visit with candor. Like me, she wondered aloud why I would be chosen to perform such a monumental undertaking. While we laughed at the irrationality of someone such as myself running for President, she had confidence in my abilities to succeed at whatever I set my mind to do, and she had greater confidence in the scriptural accounts of God working through men to accomplish great feats. She looked me squarely in the eyes and said, "Chris, you can do this!"

Not quite sure where to begin, I proceeded to tell other people in my circle of friends about my experience. I discovered that not everybody had as much confidence as my wife, nor as much trust as my church mentor. Their communication taught me a lot, though. Advice ran the gamut of sincere counsel. Some suggested I begin by running for city council while others offered historical facts regarding Presidential winners. I was given a plethora of ideas, but the unmistakable common denominator was that I needed political experience. While many people were genuine in giving advice, it was clear that others regarded my experience with a great deal of skepticism. I soon decided that sharing my experience was not helpful and I retreated to the safety of my own thoughts.

Our move to Florida was uneventful as we had become proficient at the art of packing our belongings and relocating the family. My wife enrolled our two sons in their new elementary school, we quickly assimilated with our new church family, reconnected with our real family and I resumed my weekly commute to Atlanta. One thought, however, kept resurfacing in my mind, flamed by my skeptical friends regarding my epiphany. "Was my experience truly from God?"

My wife and I joined the Church of Jesus Christ of Latter-day Saints in November 1992. We had been members less than three years and I had been to LDS temples only a handful of times before my experience in the Washington DC Temple. We were still babes in the Gospel, learning was a constant, and nearly every experience taught me something about our newfound faith.

To best describe how I felt then, it would be like comparing it to my early days as a Naval Aviator at Whiting Field near Pensacola. My father, a retired Naval Aviator, could fully appreciate my experiences as a student pilot, while on the other hand, I could not comprehend the things he knew about the career that lay ahead of me in aviation. Today, after more than 30+ years as a member of our Church, I can look back and without hesitation say that my experience was truly from God. But in the months following my epiphany, the seeds of doubt circled in my mind.

As a commuter in the airline industry, we are privileged to jump on any aircraft within our company's route structure and ride as a passenger, provided there are unsold seats available. In addition, nearly every commercial jet aircraft has one or two "jump seats" in the cockpit, primarily designed for providing access to trainees or check airmen, which may be used on a first come first serve basis for commuting pilots. This no cost privilege affords aircrew the luxury of living in one town and commuting to their crew base—the city where their trips originate and end. Some aircrew commuted as far as half-way around the world, but for me it was only an hour-long flight. Commuting adds additional stress, particularly when the list of commuters is longer than available seats, an all-too-common occurrence between Pensacola and Atlanta.

While many aircrews willingly trade-off the added time requisite of commuting for the benefit of living in their favorite town, commuting was a sacrifice I did not entirely enjoy. Yet, the next 16 months would become the second of three time periods where we lived in Pensacola, and I commuted to Atlanta.

People familiar with the Atlanta Airport know that it lies at the southern perimeter of the highway 285 beltway, just 15 minutes from downtown. On the opposite side of town, approximately a mile outside of the northern perimeter of the Atlanta beltway lies another Church temple which rests upon a little hill in the suburban town of Sandy Springs, Georgia. Perched atop the building's spire is a gold-leaf statue familiar to every Latter-day Saint, the angel Moroni. The statue of Moroni (an ancient prophet historian whose writings are found in the Book of Mormon), rests on top of most of the Church's temples, including the Washington DC Temple. Along with the baptismal font, the Celestial room and the Moroni statue, there are many similarities among the Church's temples.

The main similarity is the purpose of each temple: to make sacred promises with God. In addition, every temple is staffed by several members. The senior personnel consist of three married couples, a temple President, and his wife the Matron, and two counselors for each of them. They oversee the operation of their respective temple for a typical period of three years, a duty and privilege for more mature couples.

Because the Church's temples are considered sacred and are used for higher purposes than the meetinghouses which are used for weekly Sunday worship, there are far fewer needed. The Church currently has approximately 170 temples (in 1995 there were only 47) and more than 30 thousand congregations worldwide. New buildings are completed virtually every day of the year to house growing membership. The Atlanta Georgia Temple was the first to be built in the southeastern US and in 1995 it served the needs of Church members in that region. I would soon determine that a trip to the Atlanta Temple was needed, to meditate and sort out the nagging thought of whether my experience was from God.

As the anniversary of my epiphany in the Washington DC Temple approached, I remembered the counsel I received from the woman in the Celestial room: "ask the temple president" to be certain about the source of my epiphany. I decided to make a trip to the Atlanta Temple at the conclusion of my airline trip for that week. I left the Atlanta Airport, drove the half hour to the temple and proceeded to spend some time within those sacred walls. Before leaving the temple, I sought out the temple president. He invited me into his office, and we commenced to have a curious conversation.

While I never shared exactly what I heard in my mind, I asked, "If you receive a thought in the Celestial room, can you be assured it is from the Lord?" I was astonished at what he said next. He told me that it was "interesting" that I should be asking him that question. What made my question interesting was that he had been preparing to give a discourse on that very subject the coming weekend at a church conference of about 2500 members to be held in a nearby town in Alabama. Whether a person believes in coincidences or not, the fact that his subject matter was exactly in response to my question was remarkable. I did not believe it was a coincidence. I was certain that I had been inspired from Heaven to seek his counsel at that time. My year of creeping doubt was swept away in an instant and I no longer questioned what would become my life's mission: Run for President.

Chapter 4

IT REALLY BEGAN IN THE YEAR OF OUR LORD, 1992

There will be many people, even those of my faith, who will doubt that my experience was an epiphany from God. That is understandable. Prior to 1992, I too, would have doubted that it was possible. 1992 was the beginning of a new chapter in the lives of our little family. My wife and I had been married for only nine years and we had two small boys, ages 5 and 2. Most of our married life had been spent in the Navy, and some of it was spent apart while my P-3 squadron was on two separate 6-month-long deployments. Those deployments away from my young family spurred my desire to leave the Navy. The military expects you to put them first, over family or any other priority. It felt like it was time to put my family first. In December 1988, I left the Navy for a flying career with the airlines.

Family separation during deployments can cause havoc on families. It was not uncommon to hear of husbands or wives being lured into the arms of another during the loneliness of the long separation, and divorce became all too common after deployments. Some dealt with the stress of loneliness in other ways. For my wife and her friends, they attended church. For myself and my friends, we drank copious amounts of alcohol during our off-duty hours. We each found solace in our own ways. When we returned from deployment, my wife, who had found the better way for dealing with stress, pressed me to attend church as a family. I had abandoned religion long before.

My drinking habit was something I started when I was a young man in college. In the household where I grew up, drinking alcohol was the norm by my father and something I did not give much thought to. He too, was a Naval Aviator, and in my days working as a teenager in the Officer's Club, I would see him and his buddies drinking extensively during Friday night happy hours. I was keenly aware that my mother did not condone this habit. Nonetheless, I followed in my father's footsteps in every way, subconsciously seeking his approval by mimicking everything he did from choosing a flying career in the Navy to drinking hard during my time off. Drinking binges had become a way of life for me too.

I easily recollect my wife's expression of the joy she felt while attending church during my Navy deployments. I, on the other hand, had turned my back on God in my youth and no longer had any desire to attend church. As she persisted, I found myself attending church occasionally with her and our first-born son. My wife grew up near Pensacola, Florida and as a youth had joined a Southern Baptist Church. She fondly recalls the day she was "saved" at the age of nine and her many happy experiences attending church.

The seed of her faith had been planted long before by her loving grandmother when they attended church regularly during my wife's formative years. For myself, our family had been raised in the Catholic Church. We attended regularly until I was about eight years of age. After that, we only set foot in church when my father's parents came to visit. My grandparents were devout Catholics throughout their lives. The seed of faith had been planted and nourished in my youth and my teenage and adult indiscretions had all but extinguished it.

Between leaving the Navy in '88 until the summer of '92, my wife would occasionally convince me to attend church with her. My antipathy towards religion had not changed much, although there were subtle changes in my behavior. I had only been working for the airline for almost four years when our pilots' union negotiated a contract which ended the "B" scale pay-rates for those in their first 5 years. Financially, life was looking up. We decided to move to Atlanta in the autumn of '91, ending my first stint as a commuter from Pensacola. We tightened our budget while living in a two-bedroom apartment in Peachtree City, Georgia, saving for the down payment on our dream home, the first and only home we had built from the ground up. That home cost us $190,000 in 1991. In today's dollars, it would fetch over $600,000. We'll talk more about inflation later.

Not too long after moving to Peachtree City, I ran into a young woman I had previously met in Florida. She worked as a salesperson for a major jewelry chain store where my brother was her manager. My brother understood the importance of strengthening employees by highlighting their abilities. He introduced me to her when I came to visit him at his place of work in Florida, emphasizing her talents. She had curly long auburn hair and a vivacious personality to match. Surprised to see her working in Georgia a year later, I inquired about her situation. Her husband had recently landed a job with the FAA as an air traffic controller at the Atlanta Air Route Traffic Control Center in Hampton, Georgia. Having never met him, we made plans to get together soon as she reassured me that "you will like Jason, he's a great guy."

Jason and his wife were members of the Church of Jesus Christ of Latter-Day Saints. They were the second couple that we had ever become familiar with who were Latter-Day Saints. The first was a couple we met in our Navy days while living in Brunswick, Maine some 5 years earlier. What little we knew about the other couple was that they did not drink alcohol. Alcohol was served at every Navy social gathering where everyone, except the Latter-Day Saint couple, would drink. Many times, she would not even attend. Consequently, they stuck out like a sore thumb. Other than that, I remembered that he was a likeable fellow.

Upon meeting Jason, I liked him from the very first moment. He was levelheaded, not prone to boasting, and had a good sense of humor. Both he and his wife were friendly, and we quickly became good friends. The thing that I liked most about them is that they were genuinely good people and we felt like they were longtime old friends. We made a habit of getting together every Friday night to play cards and socialize. It did not take long before the subject of religion came up.

It has been said that there are two subjects that are taboo in social circles, religion and politics. I believe they are closely related which is why they both can easily cause division among people. Yet, with Jason, I could freely speak about religion without feeling judged. He had a way of communicating his beliefs without criticizing mine. I became more curious and for several weeks, religion became the topic of discussion at our weekly gatherings. The more he shared, the more I wanted to know his beliefs, or more particularly, the beliefs held by the members of his church.

Jason's church, The Church of Jesus Christ of Latter-day Saints, was a church that I was not familiar with. As the name implies, members believe in Jesus Christ. Teachings from the church are found in several sources including the Bible and another book called The Book of Mormon. Because the long history of the Church is replete with outsiders labeling members as Mormons, the term has stuck.

Because members would prefer others to understand that the Church is founded upon the teachings of Jesus Christ, there was a period in recent history during which an emphasis was made on the true title of the name of the Church, yet the label Mormon Church has remained, and members will forever be known as Mormons. Therefore, for brevity's sake, I will sometimes refer to the Church of Jesus Christ of Latter-day Saints as simply The Church, Latter-day Saints Church, or LDS Church and will refer to members as Latter-day Saints, or LDS or I might occasionally say Mormon Church or Mormons.

There were fundamental differences between Latter-day Saint theology and other Christian denominations and some of those differences made a lot of sense to me, as Jason taught me each week. My purpose is not to convert anyone, nor stir strong emotional discord towards anyone not of the LDS faith, but to share what I had been personally feeling and learning at that time. It is my hope that you will come to understand my experiences so you will better understand who I am, as well as my motives. The teachings of the Church made sense to me, and I could reason in my mind that they were true. As my understanding grew and our friendship continued, Jason and his wife invited us to some social gatherings with other Church members in addition to the Sunday services.

Sunday service was interesting to say the least. The Church of Jesus Christ of Latter-day Saints is particularly good at managing the size of congregations. When a congregation becomes too large, boundaries are realigned, and new congregations are formed. Sometimes membership in an area is so small that the congregation will meet in a member's home. When membership grows to a sustainable level in each area, the Church will build a nice new chapel. When we went to church for the first time with our friends, there was no chapel. The congregation was small, about 50 in attendance and the Church had rented out a few office spaces in a local business park, tucked quietly behind an old strip mall and a McDonald's restaurant. My wife chuckled in her mind as we entered that first Sunday service in that rented office building.

The service was unique and informal, far different from what I grew up experiencing in the Catholic Church. The sermon was not fiery or exciting, like I had experienced in Baptist meetings with my wife. There was one thing that was noticeably different, I felt extremely comfortable being there, in part due to the friendly nature of the members. There was a feeling of peace that I had never experienced before. This was a unique experience and it felt good. I soon discovered that no matter where we were, when I was among their members, I felt peace. We were invited to several events over the course of several weeks, all with the same comfortable feeling of peace.

It was in the fall of 1992 that our friendship with Jason and his wife blossomed and our interest in the Church was piqued. Then the letter came. A family member sent us a letter, warning us about the Mormon Church. To put it succinctly, the Church was "a cult" and we should not join. The news frightened my wife, and our defenses were up. By this time, we had grown to love our Mormon friends, yet we were concerned about the material we had received. At the following weekly gathering with Jason and his wife, we expressed our concern and asked that they no longer speak about their religion. They honored our request, and we remained friends. Church was no longer spoken of for several weeks.

In October, the Church has a unique Sunday Service, held once a year in almost every congregation throughout the world. The typical Sunday service, termed the Sacrament Meeting, was a 70-minute meeting which centered on the sacrament (the blessing and partaking of bread and water, symbols of Christ's body and blood and His sacrifice), and also included worship hymns, prayers, and talks given by adult and teenage members about various doctrinal subjects. This Sunday in October was different.

Apart from the sacrament, hymns and prayers, the remainder of the service was devoted to a well scripted presentation and songs given by children ages 3 to 11. It is referred to as the "Primary Sacrament Program" because "primary" is the term used for the Sunday school program for children ages 3 to 11. I was travelling that weekend, but Jason's wife felt inspired to invite my wife to this special Sunday service. It must have been a difficult decision for our friend because of our aforementioned request that they no longer speak of church. Nevertheless, our friend followed her heart and the spiritual prompting she received and invited my wife to attend church that day.

That same evening, the local congregation hosted an Open House event which my wife and friend also attended. The Open House had several static displays attended to by members for the purpose of sharing with the community the beliefs of the Church. It was at this Open House that my wife first met a pair of missionaries. It is hard to miss these emissaries of the Latter-day Saints Church. These missionaries can often be seen pedaling through town on their bicycles or on foot. They always travel in pairs, are either young men dressed in suits or young women clothed in modestly tasteful dresses, ("Sunday best clothes" is the vernacular used in the South) and they each wear the recognizable nametag labeled with "Elder [Last Name]" or "Sister [Last Name]" and "The Church of Jesus Christ of Latter-day Saints" engraved on it.

Each set of missionaries is assigned to a specific area or local congregation, tasked to serve their community as well as proselyte, find, teach and baptize individuals that accept the teachings and doctrine of the Church. My wife was impressed by the demeanor of the two young missionaries she met at this Open House.

It was the following Friday, at our weekly social gathering with Jason and his wife that I learned more about the previous Sunday service and Open House. As our discussion moved to the topic of the previous Sunday, my wife related all she experienced, with her attendant feelings. She had always sought a church to raise our family in, this being her primary motivation to seek out different denominations, and the Children's Sacrament Program had duly impressed her. The members were pleasant and friendly, but the evening's Open House had introduced her to something more. The young missionaries she met had left an impression on her that seared her very soul. Deep inside, she realized that the two missionaries she met were more than just young men, but had a noble, regal presence about them, a feeling that she felt when she first came to appreciate religion as a young girl, twenty years prior.

The recounting of her previous Sunday experiences was a deeply moving narrative from my wife. In our previous nine years of marriage, I rarely saw her emotionally moved, and this story was stirring. As my wife continued to share her experience, she was brought to tears as she reflected on the very personal heart-rending feelings that she had realized the previous Sunday. As her joyful tears began to flow, I was deeply touched, and I could no longer restrain my feelings. My eyes began to water, and I fought back the tears that welled up. As I tried to wipe away the embarrassment and my tear-stained face, I pondered about what I was experiencing. I realized that for my entire life, I had been able to restrain my deep emotional experiences and had never cried in front of any living soul.

My father was a hard man and when I disobeyed as a youth, we were severely punished. Along with our punishment, usually accompanied by the "spanking shoe," came the verbal threat, "If you cry, I will spank you more." My older sister and I experienced our fair share of spankings and we learned to suppress our dreaded fear and pain and learned how to hold back our tears. For the first time in my recollection, as my wife shared her moving testimony, I could not hold back my tears. As I continued to ponder, I realized that something that could move me to overcome years of suppressed feelings and bring me to tears, had to be something powerful. God has a marvelous and infinite capacity to heal wounded souls.

As Jason witnessed our deeply poignant feelings, he invited us to meet with the missionaries to learn more about the LDS faith, to be taught, and as I am sure he hoped, to be baptized as new converts to the faith. We accepted his invitation and within weeks, we met with the missionaries to be taught the basic tenets of the Church of Jesus Christ of Latter-day Saints.

Church missionaries are tasked and set apart for one purpose, to teach people about the Church of Jesus Christ of Latter-Day Saints, and to invite them to be baptized. Our new missionary friends did the same. As they taught my wife and myself about the origins of the

Church and its priesthood authority and doctrines, I felt completely at peace, and gladly accepted their invitation to be baptized. My wife and I were baptized on November 20, 1992, beginning our life as members of the Church of Jesus Christ of Latter-day Saints.

My journey was just beginning as a Latter-day Saint. The first two principles I learned were to pray and to read the scriptures. I was anxiously engaged in both. I found that reading the scriptures was both enlightening and comforting. There was a profound sense of peace derived from reading the scriptures, something I discovered as we were being taught by the missionaries. Prayer was becoming a habit as well.

My conversion became sealed when I was pondering one evening about mistakes in my past. My thought caught ahold of past sins that I realized I would have to stand before God one day and be held accountable for. I ventured out onto our backyard deck one evening with the desire to pour out my heart and soul to God. As I looked up into the starry heavens, I began to pray. Feeling a deep sense of remorse for the sins, I began to cry, sensing a foreboding eternal judgment awaiting me. I asked God, "Can you possibly forgive me?" No sooner had I uttered those words than a miracle happened to me.

The words barely came out when I felt a sensation that came through me that is exceedingly difficult to describe, and for which words cannot adequately convey. A feeling descended into my body very gradually, beginning at my head and moving down to my toes, fully enveloping me. The feeling was divine in nature and not something I have ever experienced in my life, before or since. It was the most sublime feeling of love. My feelings of remorse and sorrow had been replaced with this beautiful feeling of love and peace. It left a lasting impression on my mind and spirit, one that cannot be erased with time. I learned several things from that experience.

The first thing I learned is that God hears our prayers. The second thing I learned is how he often communicates to us, providing peace, comfort and love. The third thing I learned is that the sacrifice Jesus Christ made for our sins was very real. My feelings of remorse and guilt were swept away. To this day, I feel no sorrow, shame or guilt for those past sins, although there was some reparation required at my hands for those I had injured emotionally. This spiritual experience, along with other less powerful ones, has convinced me that I am on the right path, one that God has set me on, and one that leads to eternal happiness.

One of the teachings of the Church is that after baptism, a person is given the gift of the Holy Ghost. The giving of the gift of the Holy Ghost is performed by someone with priesthood authority who will lay (place) their hands upon your head while you are seated and pronounce a declaration of promised blessings as dictated by inspiration. This procedure is referred to as an ordinance.

An ordinance is something physically required to be performed in the Church by someone with priesthood authority, such as the ordinance of baptism requiring immersion of the individual fully under water and lifting them out of the water. The ordinance of the gift of the Holy Ghost was performed by an individual whom I did not know. What astonished me was that while he was bestowing the gift of the Holy Ghost to me, he declared things about me that I thought only I knew. I realized that there was more to this Church than meets the eye.

In the Bible, there is a story of a man of great standing in the Jewish community named Nicodemus who, because he feared losing his position of standing in the community, sought council with Jesus in the dark of the night. Their conversation follows.

> *Jesus answered and said unto him, "Verily, verily, I say unto thee; Except a man be born again, he cannot see the kingdom of God.*

Nicodemus saith unto him, "How can a man be born when he is old? Can he enter the second time into his mother's womb, and be born?"

Jesus answered, "Verily, verily, I say unto thee, except a man be born of water and of the Spirit, he cannot enter into the kingdom of God.

That which is born of the flesh is flesh; and that which is born of the Spirit is spirit.

Marvel not that I said unto thee, Ye must be born again.

The wind bloweth where it listeth, and thou hearest the sound thereof, but canst not tell whence it cometh, and whither it goeth: so is every one that is born of the Spirit."

Nicodemus answered and said unto him, "How can these things be?"

Jesus answered and said unto him, "Art thou a master of Israel, and knowest not these things?" (King James Version, John 3:2-10).

These verses from the Bible refer to being born again as being first baptized with water and then being baptized by the Spirit. The ordinance of water baptism and the ordinance of the gift of the Holy Ghost (or Spirit) fulfill these two requirements as expounded upon by Jesus to Nicodemus. I do not mention this biblical verse to make a point about being born again, but to point out the uniqueness of the Spirit as pronounced by Jesus to Nicodemus. He proclaimed that the Spirit is like the wind in that you cannot see it, nor tell from where it comes, but you can feel the effects of it and see the influence it has on people. I mention this scripture because of the implications it has for myself, and every individual who experiences the Spirit, or Holy Ghost as it is otherwise referred to.

What is the Spirit, or Holy Ghost? What is the "gift of the Holy Ghost" as received by Latter-day Saints? The Holy Ghost is like your conscience. When you might be tempted to do something wrong such as lie, steal, or cheat, the voice in your head that tells you it is wrong and tries to persuade you to do otherwise is the Holy Ghost. The Holy Ghost will abide with you permanently, provided you remain worthy to have him as your companion. Latter-day Saints believe that the Holy Ghost is a personage of spirit, i.e., he lacks a body, but is like God in every other way. He is, what we call, the third member of the Godhead. Heavenly Father, Jesus Christ and the Holy Ghost constitute the Godhead.

We believe they are three distinctly different individuals with one common purpose and are of like mind, heart and personality. When a member of the Church is given the "gift" of the Holy Ghost, they are promised that if they continue to make every effort to "walk the walk" and follow the teachings of Jesus Christ, they will have the "conscience" of the Holy Ghost as a guide throughout their lives. This gift has been invaluable to me since given to me in 1992. Let me share a few experiences.

Once, while driving home from the airport after a 4-day trip, I was in a hurry, as I often am, to be with my family again after the days of separation. On my usual route home, I was stopped at a traffic light at the intersection of highway 279 and the crossroad of highway 138. I was the first vehicle in the right lane and there was another vehicle beside me in the left lane. I was anxious to get home and I wanted to pass the other vehicle as quickly as possible the moment our light turned green because 100 yards beyond the intersection, my lane would merge into his lane.

This was a common practice of mine, looking for any possible way to shave a few minutes off my drive home. I would observe the intersecting traffic signal, watching for it to turn yellow, followed by red, my cue to my green light. At the moment I looked at the intersecting traffic signal waiting for my cue, a voice spoke clearly and distinctly, as though he read my mind, yet there was no one else in my car. "You don't want to do that!" It was a firm voice, and my inclination was to obey and not blast off the moment my light turned green. No sooner had I decided to obey the voice, when the traffic signals began their sequence of switching colors and I received my green light. I hesitated, as I thought I should, when a vehicle raced through the intersection from the left, running his red light.

Had I not hesitated; I would have been careened on my side of the car by the speeding vehicle racing through the intersection. I would have been seriously injured, if not killed. I am glad to be alive to tell this story. This was one of those moments when the Holy Ghost helped me, but it has more often been there to direct me in helping others.

In this following story, I was directed by the Holy Ghost to aid a stranger. While driving on a state highway in Florida, several miles from my home, I passed a hitchhiker. In my parent's day, giving hitchhikers a ride was common; in our day, we are cautioned of the dangers. As I passed this man at about 65 mph, I got no further than 100 yards when the voice spoke to my mind, "Turn around and give him a ride." I felt peace and a calming assurance that all would be well, so I circled back and picked up the hitchhiker. After graciously thanking me for stopping to pick him up, he stated, "I was praying for someone to pick me up."

I will share one more instance of divine help so that the reader may fully appreciate the simplicity with which I, and many others, are helped by the Holy Ghost once we have received that "gift" after baptism. This third story is one of many experiences I could share, but for the sake of brevity, it will be my concluding example.

It was a rainy day, a Monday or Tuesday, I cannot remember, but I was in town, running some errands. I was not far from my friends' house, a young couple we had become acquainted with through the church. I remembered that they were not in attendance at church the previous Sunday and I felt the prompting in my mind to "check on them, see if everything is all right."

When I knocked on their door, the husband answered, and I inquired if everything was all right and that I noticed they had not come to church. He replied that everything was okay, that his wife suffered from depression and was not feeling up to going to church Sunday, but they were better now. After he assured me there was nothing I could do for them, I left. Several weeks later, the man's wife shared with me the following account. She told me that because of the depression she suffers, they did not attend church that Sunday. Due to the depression, she was feeling very alone and had prayed earlier the very day I had come by their house, asking specifically in her prayer that God send someone by the house to check on her, to affirm in her mind that she was loved. I was the answer to her prayer.

The gift of the Holy Ghost has been a blessing in my life and has been a blessing to others. When I willingly obey the promptings, life goes well and someone, be it myself or others, is helped in some way or another. People throughout the world have similar experiences and may call it a hunch, or "women's intuition." As for myself, I know my experiences are a gift from God. In 1992, my life changed for the better and the gift of the Holy Ghost has been a guiding influence ever since.

Chapter 5

THE LORD'S PATTERN FOR CALLING SERVANTS'

The purpose of this chapter is to help the reader recognize the pattern that God uses when He calls servants for a greater purpose. In doing so, it is my hope to draw parallels between my experiences and that of biblical characters. I hope to draw faithful believers to this cause, helping them recognize that the mission God has tasked me with, is greater than any one person can accomplish, and it fulfills a greater purpose.

Let us examine a few biblical characters. I will share the experiences of three characters from The Bible for the Jewish and Christian reader, so that they may better understand my purpose, and I will share the example of three Book of Mormon characters for Latter-day Saint readers as well.

Let us examine the life of Moses. Moses was saved as an infant from a sure death. The edict of the Pharaoh of Egypt demanded that all males born of Israelite slaves be put to death because Pharaoh was concerned that the Israelite population would soon outnumber the Egyptians. Through the clever machinations of Moses' family, Moses was preserved and raised by the daughter of Pharaoh until his years as a prince. He was tutored in all things about the Egyptian way of life, lived as a prince, and yet he knew his heritage was of the Hebrew slaves. Many years passed and his conscience could not bury the empathy he felt for the plight of his Hebrew brethren. Moses slew an Egyptian taskmaster that had been beating an Israelite slave. Pharaoh demanded his arrest and execution. In fear of his life, Moses fled to the land of Midian where he met and married Ziporah, a daughter of a local priest named Jethro, and lived an ordinary life for about 40 years before his revelatory experience at Mount Sinai.

When Moses went to Mount Sinai and saw the burning bush, he was commanded to take off his shoes for he stood on "holy ground." This commenced his conversation with the Lord. Moses was instructed to go back to the Land of Egypt for God had heard the cries of the Israelites and would vanquish their Egyptian taskmasters by freeing them from their bondage under the Egyptians. Moses had some serious doubts. The first doubt was that nobody would believe him that God had sent him. The second concern was that he was not eloquent of speech and felt unqualified for the task. The Lord boosted his confidence and Moses set out to accomplish what was asked of him.

Here are some parallel experiences that have helped affirm to me that my experience was divine in nature.

First, Moses was well educated, enabling him to understand the ways of the Egyptian world. His years as a sheepherder would prepare him as a leader of the Israelites while they would wander the deserts. I too, have had formal education, as well as training in responsibilities of leadership and trust.

Secondly, Moses' calling came while standing on "holy ground." My calling came while in the holy temple of our Church.

Third, Moses had lived a humble life in Midian for 40 years. There was nothing extraordinary about his life and position in the community. My life, too, can be characterized as very ordinary by worldly standards.

Moses had doubts. First, that nobody would believe his experience was from God. Second, he lacked a necessary skill, that of eloquent speech. I too experienced doubts, which led me to question my experience, as well as continuous doubts of possessing the necessary skills.

While Moses was able to accomplish the great task of liberating his people from the Egyptians, my task has yet to be accomplished. I realize that it can only be accomplished if I trust in God, as did Moses. This requires me to stay firm in the faith, trust in God and to surround myself with others who also see the need to be firm in the faith, much like the moral support given to Moses by his brother, Aaron, and his sister, Miriam.

The second biblical character I would like to examine is David, who slew Goliath. We are introduced to David in the Bible from the first book of Samuel, a prophet. The King of Israel, Saul, had lost favor with the Lord and was to be replaced. The Lord commanded the prophet Samuel to go to the house of Jesse (David's father), where he would find, from among the sons of Jesse, the Lord's choice for the next king.

When Samuel met the first son, Eliab, he was certain Eliab was to be the chosen king. The Lord told Samuel, "Look not on his countenance, or on the height of his stature… the Lord seeth not as man seeth; for man looketh on the outward appearance, but the Lord looketh on the heart." (1 Samuel 16:7 KJV). Jesse paraded the remainder of his sons before Samuel. The last and youngest son, David, was brought in from the fields to be examined. The Lord told Samuel to anoint David because David would be the next king. Before becoming king, David would soon prove himself worthy.

Three of David's brothers were enlisted in the battle between the Israelites and the Philistines. At one point, the Israelites and the Philistines were at a stalemate and one Philistine named Goliath had been taunting the Israelites to a one-on-one fight. Goliath was their largest and most fearsome soldier. None of the Israelites had the courage to face him, not David's brothers, not even their king, Saul.

For 40 days, Goliath taunted the Israelite army and mocked their God. When David came to the army's camp with provisions for his brothers, he heard the ranting of Goliath. Offended by Goliath's mockery and in defense of his God, David convinced King Saul to allow him to fight the mighty Philistine. Armed with only a sling and some stones, David faced the giant. Goliath was not amused by the appearance of "little more than a boy," someone not worthy of this challenge and cursed him.

After words were exchanged, David prevailed with one well aimed stone from his sling which sank deep into Goliath's forehead, causing him to fall to the ground dead. David concluded his triumphant battle by running to the vanquished foe, drawing Goliath's sword from its sheath, and cutting Goliath's head off with his own sword. Upon witnessing the loss of their champion, the Philistines abandoned their conquest and fled from the Israelites.

Here are some parallels between David and me.

The Lord told Samuel that when the Lord chooses a servant for his purposes, he looks on the heart and not on the outward appearance as men do. As I endeavor upon the task at hand, many will say that I am unqualified. They will judge me in many ways, but they will judge me outwardly. It will be my heart that will help me prevail.

The battle of David against the Philistines' best and formidable soldier was one that outwardly appeared impossible, even to those of David's family and associates. Goliath was a soldier's soldier. He was large, well-armed and undefeated. To everyone except David (and God), Goliath was expected to win the confrontation. The task of David defeating Goliath seemed impossible and yet through the one simple task of a well-aimed stone, Goliath was defeated, and the enemy withdrew. As I endeavor to fulfill God's direction and run for

President, it will appear and be said by many, including many of my friends and family, that the task is impossible, that I cannot win. If I trust in God and remain a faithful disciple in The Church and follow His directions, I know I can run a successful campaign. Whether or not I win depends on whether our citizens recognize good over our slippery slope of self-destruction, the path of destruction we've been on for over a century.

David fought Goliath in an unconventional form of battle, without sword or armor. He also had no battle experience. My campaign and fight against the establishment (often referred today as the deep state) will appear unconventional and unorthodox. I have had no "battle" experience.

As I have pondered over the years regarding the challenge of running for President and as I have been bolstered by the biblical accounts of seemingly ordinary men accomplishing extraordinary tasks, I often fear that my shortcomings will be apparent, as were the men whose lives I have highlighted. This fear has been something that has not only caused me great concern for the welfare of my soul but has caused me to hesitate to act and move in the direction I have been called. The direction our country and government has moved, and the immorality that our country blatantly reveres has inspired me to take action, regardless of the personal costs. While I would be honored to consider myself among the great men I have described so far, I esteem myself as far less worthy an individual. My confidence and hope in running a successful campaign is the understanding that God knows me better than I know myself.

The last biblical person whom I would like to draw parallel accounts with, is that of Paul, the apostle and missionary. Let us examine Paul. Jesus Christ had laid the foundation for his church by calling apostles and other leaders and He taught the way to eternal life. However, there were many religious scholars who did not believe Christ was the son of God, including Paul. Paul was formerly known as Saul. He was a world traveler, well educated, and his religious beliefs were rooted in Judaism. After Christ was crucified, his apostles continued the work of the Church. Many Jews persecuted the early Christians, Saul was one of them. Saul witnessed and condoned the stoning death of Stephen, a disciple of Christ. Saul worked tirelessly to persecute the early saints of the Church "beyond measure."

It was while he was on an errand to Damascus to arrest more Christians that he experienced a miraculous event. A brilliant light shone from above, blinding him, and from the light a voice was heard, "Saul, Saul, why persecutest thou me?" Saul inquired of the voice who it was. The reply came, "I am Jesus, whom thou persecutest." Saul, trembling and astonished said, "Lord, what wilt thou have me to do?" And the Lord said unto him, "Arise, and go into the city, and it shall be told thee what thou must do." This singular event taught Saul that Jesus Christ was indeed true, and that Saul's prior religious convictions regarding Christians were misguided. In due time, Saul became known as Paul, and was one of the greatest missionaries the Church had known in its early days.

What are some of the parallel experiences I share with Paul? First, let me be clear that I am not a great missionary. There are many others who are far better missionaries than me. My two oldest sons are among them. My two sons both served full time missions for our church, for two full years. Our oldest served in Uganda, Africa, and our second served in Mexico City. They, along with hundreds of thousands of Latter-Day Saint missionaries since the Church's inception, have served valiantly for up to two years, sharing the "Restoration" message of the Church of Jesus Christ of Latter-day Saints. I would love to dedicate my retirement years to serving as valiantly as they have. It is something I look forward to and perhaps could share with Paul, but there are some things I do have in common.

Paul persecuted the Christians before his conversion to Christianity. I too had contempt for Christians before my conversion.

Paul had a miraculous conversion, one that sinks deep into the soul and cannot be denied, the evidence of which is his laborious missionary efforts. I too had a miraculous conversion, one that sank deep into my soul, the memory of which cannot be erased by time.

Paul loved the Lord, as evidenced by his missionary work. I too love the Lord, as evidenced by my dedicated church service and as witnessed by those who know me personally.

There are some valiant Book of Mormon personalities, many of which demonstrate that through faith in God, all things are possible. I draw added strength from reading about these individuals as much as I do from biblical characters. Because I have read the Book of Mormon many times, I am familiar with its characters. Additionally, it has been said that the Book of Mormon has been written for our day. Much of the history of the Book of Mormon civilization parallels our current history. Because of the similarities to their society and our modern society, I can appreciate their trials and I understand more fully the challenges we are faced with today.

The first individual I would like to draw attention to was named Nephi (pronounced, 'Knee-figh'). The Book of Mormon spans from about 600 BC to 400 AD, and later generations named their children after the famous Nephi who lived about 600 BC. Nephi, with his father Lehi and Lehi's entire family, left Jerusalem prior to its destruction and Babylonian captivity. Nephi was an obedient son to his father. His father led the family as directed by inspiration from the Lord on a journey that lasted several years in search of a promised land. They were led away from Jerusalem, around the Arabian Peninsula, and then set out to sea across the "many waters" only to arrive in the Americas.

Their exact landing location is not known, but many Latter-Day Saint archaeologists and scholars continue their research for evidence of their civilization in the Americas. There are many skeptics that doubt the veracity of the Book of Mormon, and whether there is supporting archeological evidence, but I have never concerned myself with them as I have extreme confidence that God will validate the authenticity of that Book to all non-believers at some future event. He has, though, born witness to my soul in an undeniable way that the Book of Mormon is of divine origin, as it claims to be.

Nephi was not only an obedient son, but he became skilled at following the direction of the Lord for his own life as well as for those he later led when the family became fractured and divided into two separate civilizations. A significant event in his life happened when, after his father's family had settled near the shores of the Arabian Peninsula in a fruitful land, Nephi was commanded by the Lord to build a ship. This ship would take them across the "many waters," or from the shores of the Indian Ocean across the seas to settle in the Americas. There are several plausible routes which the ocean currents could have transported their party across the seas; however, the interesting part of the story I want to share is in the building of the ship. Let me quote from the Book of Mormon.

> "And it came to pass that the Lord spake unto me, saying: Thou shalt construct a ship, after the manner which I shall show thee, that I may carry thy people across these waters.
>
> "And when my brethren saw that I was about to build a ship, they began to murmur against me, saying: Our brother is a fool, for he thinketh that he can build a ship; yea, and he also thinketh that he can cross these great waters.
>
> "And thus my brethren did complain against me, and were desirous that they might not labor, for they did not believe that I could build a ship; neither would they believe that I was instructed of the Lord.
>
> "And now it came to pass that I, Nephi, was exceedingly sorrowful because of the hardness of their hearts."

After a lengthy dissertation to his brothers to convince them that the work of building the ship was of God, and that historically, with God, all things are possible, his brothers still did not believe him. Then, because of their unbelief, God told Nephi to stretch forth his hand that his brothers might know the real power of God.

And it came to pass that the Lord said unto me: Stretch forth thine hand again unto thy brethren, and they shall not wither before thee, but I will shock them, saith the Lord, and this will I do, that they may know that I am the Lord their God.

And it came to pass that I stretched forth my hand unto my brethren, and they did not wither before me; but the Lord did shake them, even according to the word which he had spoken.

And now, they said: We know of a surety that the Lord is with thee, for we know that it is the power of the Lord that has shaken us.

And it came to pass that they did worship the Lord and did go forth with me; and we did work timbers of curious workmanship.

And the Lord did show me from time to time after what manner I should work the timbers of the ship.

Now I, Nephi, did not work the timbers after the manner which was learned by men, neither did I build the ship after the manner of men; but I did build it after the manner which the Lord had shown unto me; wherefore, it was not after the manner of men.

And I, Nephi, did go into the mount oft, and I did pray oft unto the Lord; wherefore the Lord showed unto me great things.

> *And it came to pass that after I had finished the ship,*
> *according to the word of the Lord, my brethren beheld*
> *that it was good, and that the workmanship thereof was*
> *exceedingly fine. (1 Nephi 17-18).*

The story continues as they gathered provisions and set sail for their new home, a promised land. The attributes of Nephi, which I desire to draw parallels to are the following.

Nephi was an obedient son. He followed the counsel of his father and respected his father as the head of the family. This is in keeping with one of the Ten Commandments: honor thy father and mother. Like Nephi, I was an obedient son. I followed the council of my father as a young man, including his recommendation and insistence that I apply for and attend the Naval Academy.

Nephi trusted in the Lord and accomplished a task at the direction of the Lord, despite the fact he had no prior experience at ship building. I too, am embarking on a task, at the direction of the Lord, with no prior experience.

Nephi was tutored by the Lord in the manner of how to build the ship. As was mentioned, the ship was "good," and the workmanship was exceedingly fine. I too have been tutored by the Lord in the manner of how to run the campaign. I have a plan, and like Nephi, will require the help of others to "build the ship," and the blueprints for running a campaign I have received from the Lord, and it will not be like traditional campaigns.

Nephi's brothers did not believe he was commanded of God to build the ship and they murmured. He was not only given the blueprint of how to build the ship, but he was given the power from God for the convincing of others to help him with the undertaking. As I have shared my story with others, the power of the Holy Spirit has born to their hearts and minds the truth of which I speak, and it will continue to do so until God deems I have enough help to carry out the task.

The next Book of Mormon character I would like to examine was a nephew of Nephi and a custodian and author of the historical records that they were commanded to keep. His name was Enos. The following is his account.

Behold, it came to pass that I, Enos, knowing my father that he was a just man—for he taught me in his language, and also in the nurture and admonition of the Lord—and blessed be the name of my God for it—

And I will tell you of the wrestle which I had before God, before I received a remission of my sins.

Behold, I went to hunt beasts in the forests; and the words which I had often heard my father speak concerning eternal life, and the joy of the saints, sunk deep into my heart.

And my soul hungered; and I kneeled down before my Maker, and I cried unto him in mighty prayer and supplication for mine own soul; and all the day long did I cry unto him; yea, and when the night came I did still raise my voice high that it reached the heavens.

And there came a voice unto me, saying: Enos, thy sins are forgiven thee, and thou shalt be blessed.

And I, Enos, knew that God could not lie; wherefore, my guilt was swept away.

And I said: Lord, how is it done?

And he said unto me: Because of thy faith in Christ, whom thou hast never before heard nor seen. And many years pass away before he shall manifest himself in the flesh; wherefore, go to, thy faith hath made thee whole.

Now, it came to pass that when I had heard these words I began to feel a desire for the welfare of my brethren, the Nephites; wherefore, I did pour out my whole soul unto God for them.

And while I was thus struggling in the spirit, behold, the voice of the Lord came into my mind again, saying: I will visit thy brethren according to their diligence in keeping my commandments. I have given unto them this land, and it is a holy land; and I curse it not save it be for the cause of iniquity; wherefore, I will visit thy brethren according as I have said; and their transgressions will I bring down with sorrow upon their own heads.

And after I, Enos, had heard these words, my faith began to be unshaken in the Lord.

Enos, apparently, had some sins that had been troubling him causing feelings of guilt. When he prayed with all earnestness, his guilt was "swept away." I too experienced a similar cleansing process after praying in earnest and my guilt was swept away.

Enos' conversation with the Lord was not audible to the ears, but "came into" his mind. My experience in the Washington temple was also a conversation in my mind, as clear as any audible conversation I have experienced.

After Enos' conversion, he was concerned for the welfare of his brethren. After my conversion, I too became concerned for the welfare of my fellow beings, which has led to many conversations with others about the gospel of Jesus Christ.

One thing I would like to highlight from Enos' writings, is the purpose of the Americas. The Lord said unto Enos that this land is a holy land, and he would not curse it except it be "for the cause of iniquity." The settling of America was, in part, for religious freedom, and righteous people were led here so they could worship according to the dictates of their conscience.

Our country has strayed significantly from the moral compass which prevailed at the dawn of the United States' founding. In similar fashion as the Nephite civilization of the ancient Americas, the United States, in general, has become morally corrupt as evidenced by those we elect as our national leaders. If we continue this course, our fate will be that of the Nephite civilization of 400 AD and we can be assured of self-destruction. This, I believe, is one purpose that God has called me to this work, to give the United States one more chance before His righteous indignation is manifest. The test for this country will be in who we choose.

The last Book of Mormon character that I wish to spotlight is the person that had the final role among the Nephite civilization of ancient America. His name was Moroni (More-rhoan'-eye). Moroni was the last prophet, historian, and concluding author of the Book of Mormon. He, along with his father Mormon, were responsible for abridging the records found in the Book of Mormon. Mormon was charged with the duty of compiling and abridging the sacred records and adding to them the history which he witnessed. Mormon passed this duty to his son when he knew he would not survive the destruction of his people at the hands of their enemies. Moroni carried on the work and added other sacred writings to the abridgement that his father had nearly finished. It is Moroni who finished the abridged record and buried them around 421 A.D., later to be discovered by Joseph Smith, Jr. in 1823, and to be translated into English for the first 5000 copies of the Book of Mormon published in 1830.

Moroni concludes his writings in the Book of Mormon with the following passage.

> *Now I, Moroni, write somewhat as seemeth me good;*
> *and I write unto my brethren, the Lamanites; and I*
> *would that they should know that more than four*

hundred and twenty years have passed away since the sign was given of the coming of Christ.

And I seal up these records, after I have spoken a few words by way of exhortation unto you.

Behold, I would exhort you that when ye shall read these things, if it be wisdom in God that ye should read them, that ye would remember how merciful the Lord hath been unto the children of men, from the creation of Adam even down until the time that ye shall receive these things and ponder it in your hearts.

And when ye shall receive these things, I would exhort you that ye would ask God, the Eternal Father, in the name of Christ, if these things are not true; and if ye shall ask with a sincere heart, with real intent, having faith in Christ, he will manifest the truth of it unto you, by the power of the Holy Ghost.

And by the power of the Holy Ghost ye may know the truth of all things.

And whatsoever thing is good is just and true; wherefore, nothing that is good denieth the Christ, but acknowledgeth that he is.

And ye may know that he is, by the power of the Holy Ghost; wherefore I would exhort you that ye deny not the power of God; for he worketh by power, according to the faith of the children of men, the same today and tomorrow, and forever.

I would like to extract from these paragraphs certain key points, not points about Moroni's character, but points about his writings.

Moroni makes certain promises and assertions to the reader of the Book of Mormon.

In paragraph 7, Moroni asserts that God is the "same today and tomorrow, and forever." Simply stated, if God is unchanging, his dealings would be the same for myself as were his dealings with those biblical and Book of Mormon characters I previously mentioned.

Secondly, in paragraph 4, Moroni promises to the reader that they may know of a surety that the Book of Mormon is "true" by asking God with a "sincere heart" and with "real intent" and "with faith in Christ." He states that the answer will be manifest by the "power of the Holy Ghost." We ask God through prayer; He answers through the "power of the Holy Ghost." Moroni affirms, in paragraph 5, that *all truth* may be received through this process. To you, my readers, I testify that this process is real, and I invite you at this time to ask God if He did indeed ask me to "run for president." If you ask with "real intent," a "sincere heart" and have faith in Christ, God will affirm to you I speak the truth.

What now? The answer is simple, continue reading. As you read, you will learn more about my discovery and with God's omnipotent guidance, together, we can restore a sound, honest and righteous national government.

Chapter 6

YOU NEED TO STUDY THE CONSTITUTION

After my experience in the Washington D.C. Temple, the first person I shared the experience with, outside my family, was the gentleman I mentioned in Chapter 3. He was in his late 60's and had grown up in the Church of Jesus Christ of Latter-day Saints. He became my mentor in the Church. I learned a great deal from him because we had assignments where we worked together for several years. His name was Paul.

The first thing that Paul suggested I do was study the Constitution. It was a wise suggestion from a wise man! Should not the framework of the government be the first thing that should be studied? In addition to the Constitution, Paul suggested I study the Federalist Papers. For those of you who do not understand the Federalist Papers, they were a series of articles written to advocate the adoption of the Constitution.

Admittedly, I did not pour over the Federalist Papers as he suggested. The style of grammar from that era made digesting the two sets of documents tedious and boring. Nevertheless, I made the attempt to study both, and I concentrated on the Constitution.

Most US citizens today *know of* the Constitution, fewer have *read* it, and even fewer *understand* it. Our general ignorance of that document has led to many decades of problems in our national government. On the other hand, the Constitution was understood by the founding generation after its ratification in 1789. Why the difference? There are many reasons, but the single most important reason is that study of the Constitution in our education system is no longer required. Some institutions, including churches and universities, are recognizing the prevailing ignorance of the Constitution among our citizens and have been incorporating its study into their curriculum.

What makes the Constitution so important? As I mentioned earlier, the Constitution is the framework for our government, yet it is more than a framework; it is a well-crafted document born out of the need for the newly independent nation to strike a balance between a strong national government to fix the problems of the 18th century American experience, and weak enough to avoid the plague of problems that the patriots of the American Revolution fought to overcome.

Students of American history are well acquainted with the events that led up to the creation of the Constitution. The dilemma the Founders faced was to create a government strong enough to combat domestic issues and foreign invasion, and weak enough to avoid trampling on individual freedoms and state governments. For example, the colonies had defeated an overwhelmingly well-equipped and larger foreign military. The Constitution needed to ensure they could do so again, without running the risk of creating a well-equipped and strong military that could be used to enforce unrighteous laws of any future despotic rulers.

Part of their solution to solve this problem was to have safeguards in the Constitution designed to limit the national government's scope and powers of maintaining a standing army. In similar fashion, all the powers authorized in the Constitution for the national government were *few, limited and carefully constructed to prevent tyranny.* Thomas Jefferson best summed up this view, "*In questions of power, then, let no more be heard of confidence in man, but bind him down from mischief by the chains of the Constitution.*"

The human soul is an independent, thinking, corporeal being, capable of providing his or her own needs for survival. But human beings are more complex than that. To perpetuate the species, we must have a companion of the opposite sex. Until we mature beyond our childhood, we are dependent on the adults in our species. We are also social beings that have certain needs, spiritually and emotionally. Without exploring deeply who we are as a species, let us acknowledge that we are distinctly individual, having associations with other individuals.

Fundamental associations are friends, couples, families, neighborhoods, communities, cities, and larger geographical associations such as counties, states, and nations. We are simply social beings, and we make and keep associations, often with like-minded people. Our character, which defines who we are and the associations we keep, is formed in our childhood and molded by our life experiences. Every person is on a distinctly different path in life. If you doubt that, you are invited to have a conversation with two identical twins and see if they cannot persuade you that they are distinctly two different people with some differences.

When two people's paths cross, they can learn from one another. We can also learn indirectly from another person when we read about their life, accomplishments, or discoveries. Sometimes we will maintain that new association. (In my opinion, a rich life is one in which a person has a multitude of associations.) We are distinctly different individuals, navigating through our own lives, searching for meaning and happiness. It is evident that no individual's life is less or more valuable than another.

Thomas Jefferson aptly addresses this principle in The Declaration of Independence when he stated, *"We hold these truths to be self-evident, that all men are created equal..."* It is my duty as a person to not diminish my fellow human beings from the opportunity of enjoying the same privileges and fundamental rights to their lives as I have for mine. We call this principle, freedom.

If you have ever been married, it is obvious that the blending of two lives in a marriage is one of the greatest means to test and teach the principle of freedom. To coexist happily, the marriage partners must learn how to respect the freedom of their partner, if in turn they want the same privilege. The principle of freedom exists in many forms in a marriage. Allowing your partner to express their opinion during a discussion is one form of respecting freedom. Allowing your partner to choose the food they eat is another form of respecting freedom. A healthy marriage is one in which each partner respects the other partner's freedom. I have yet to meet a married couple in which both partners are identical in thought, deeds, behaviors, ideals, and actions.

Therefore, the blending of two lives in a marriage is a perpetual exercise in freedom whereupon each partner, in association with the other, is learning and growing as they discover their differences. There are many other principles important to the successful blending of two lives in a marriage. We will not delve into that topic here. We need only to fully understand freedom.

Freedom is something we intuitively understand, particularly when our own freedom is diminished. For example, if you were held at gunpoint and asked to do something you would not otherwise do, or to restrict you from doing something you would choose to do, your freedom becomes diminished. Who has the right to restrict your freedom? When would someone else have that right? Should others have the right to restrict your freedom? These are difficult questions when we give them serious reflection.

Let us reflect a moment on a hypothetical situation to dive further into this discussion on freedom. Imagine transporting through time to a period when the vast resources of our planet were shared by the tiniest fraction of our current population. Let us examine two families which share a geographical region abundant with resources, livestock, and rich soil for growing food. Our two hypothetical families could share all available resources, with hardly a care or concern for scarcity.

But what happens when those two families grew into two civilizations distinctly different from each other, but homogenous within each civilization? Imagine now that those two civilizations were competing for the use of the available resources, where the supply of resources could scarcely meet the demand. History reveals several examples of how two different civilizations compete for available resources.

The first example of civilizations competing for resources would be the utter disregard for human freedom through conquest. Conquest is not accomplished without much bloodshed and heartache. This is the ultimate expression of disregard for the freedom of others. Conquest evolves into subjugation or slavery, if the vanquished are even allowed to survive. Conquests are the antithesis of civilized societies and an absolute disregard for freedom.

Another example of civilizations exercising unrighteous dominion and disrespect for the freedom of others is through theft. The fruits of the labor of one society are entirely their own, without equivocation, provided it is done so without trampling upon the freedom of another society. When a group, society, or civilization steals from the fruits of the labor of another group, society, or civilization, it is categorically wrong. The fruit of one's labor is found in many forms, such as food or property and even income.

When governments tax income from one sector of society and give it to another, it is still theft, plain and simple. It may have the appearance of virtue, cloaked in law, but it is theft, nevertheless. The only means to justify this theft and make it morally acceptable is if that sector of society whose labors produced the fruits (the "haves") consent, without threat or force from their government, to give to the "have nots." We will discuss consent later.

The only civil and morally acceptable form by which civilizations should compete for diminishing resources while respecting freedom would be through the process I will label as compacts. Compacts are agreements, written or oral, which outline the conditions which are mutually beneficial and/or mutually agreeable to both societies. We witness compacts in all forms in modern societies. We have compacts between employers and employees, citizens and governments, husbands and wives, neighbors vs. neighbors, and nations vs. nations.

The Constitution is a compact. It was written by wise men who wanted to provide the colonies and future generations a solid government with all the possible safeguards to individual freedoms that those men could conceive. Many compromises were made at the Constitutional Convention in 1787, and in the eyes of many delegates, it was not perfect, as evidenced by only 39 signers of the final draft from the 55 delegates who initially attended. It was not perfect, but in the words of George Washington, "*the best that could be obtained at this time*" and the adoption of it "*desirable.*"[5]

When the 39 delegates finished the final draft of the Constitution and affixed their signatures to it, it may have ended an arduous 127-day process, but it was only the beginning of a long and challenging ratification process. As a compact, it was an agreement among the citizens of individual states and among their respective state governments.

The Constitution was designed to create a national government which would be endowed with powers that were previously held by the states. In other words, state governments would be relinquishing some of their powers. This transfer of power concerned many citizens who feared that the colonies were supplanting a powerful government seated an ocean away with one of their own choosing in their own backyard. This group's moniker was the "Anti-Federalists."

The Anti-Federalists were concerned that the Constitution, if adopted, would create a national government which would trample on the precious freedoms they had fought valiantly against Great Britain to regain. Many feared that the Constitution threatened personal liberties.

The premise the Framers adhered to in their construction of the Constitution was simple; **IF** the Constitution did not authorize the national government to have a clearly defined power, it was retained by the states or the people. The Anti-Federalists wanted assurances that this was indeed the case, that personal liberties and states' rights would be protected. Amendments were proposed and adopted to assuage the concerns of the Anti-Federalists ensuring the ratification of the Constitution. These first Amendments are aptly named, "The Bill of Rights."

I took the challenge of my friend Paul very seriously and I have studied the Constitution through and through. I have read many scholarly works regarding it and the Framers who created it. It is a powerful and well-crafted document for the purpose for which it was created, namely creating a national government designed to be strong enough when needed, but weak enough to prevent trampling upon the freedoms of its citizens. It is indeed a masterpiece! Can it be improved upon, yes; nevertheless, it is genius in its construct and would make an excellent starting point in correcting the many ills of our current federal government. I have concluded several more things from my study of the Constitution, which we shall examine later in this book.

Chapter 7

YOU NEED POLITICAL EXPERIENCE

While discussing freedom in the previous chapter, I elaborated on the fact that we are all individuals uniquely different in our thoughts, desires, passions, and path in life. Similarly, there are a multitude of opinions in our political environment today regarding what's best for our country and how best to achieve those goals. Not surprisingly, there are many opinions on how best to run for and become president, as I quickly found out from my friends.

To have an epiphany from God is also a uniquely personal experience, seldom shared with others. Naturally, when sharing an experience of such grand purpose, there will be mixed reactions, as I alluded to in Chapter 2. Why circle back to this topic? I want to share some of the advice I received about political experience and the conclusions I have drawn.

What is political experience? It is experience in politics. So, what is politics? Politics is derived from the Greek word, *politiká, or "affairs of the city."* In its rudimentary form, politics are activities associated with decisions in a group. We often think of politics as merely government activities, but politics are found in any organization that has a purpose or goal they hope to achieve.

The prevailing advice from my peers is that I needed political experience, or more specifically, I should have experience in government affairs. I should campaign for and gain experience in an elected office in a local or state jurisdiction before ever attempting to run for president. So, let us examine and reason together on the pros and cons of what appears to many, including many well-meaning friends, the importance of political experience in government.

The first question we need to ask is what can be gained by having political experience? The obvious answer is to understand the mechanics of government, or the process of lawmaking and enforcement. When a congressman (or woman) is elected for the first time to the US Congress, they are labelled "freshmen" and receive orientation meetings designed to help them understand the mechanics of their new job. How long does this orientation last? It can last up to several weeks, but no doubt is helpful in providing incoming representatives with a solid footing on procedures and other mechanics associated with their new job.

The office of president, however, has no such orientation, but does have a transition period. This transition period provides a newly elected president the opportunity to hit the ground running on inauguration day. The transition period includes the opportunity to receive security briefings, funding for office space, equipment and expenses, and a listing of appointees the Executive branch (the president included) will need to fill. No amount of political experience can prepare a newly elected president for the overwhelming amount of responsibility he or she will assume on their day of inauguration. However, there are career experiences that can help prepare an incoming president for those duties. We will discuss these in later chapters.

The second advantage of having political experience would be learning how to best navigate the differences of opinion and personalities to achieve a political goal. This would be helpful if trying to achieve compromise, but from my perspective, and what I hope to achieve, it is antithetical. Compromising political views in a broken system still leaves a broken system. Let me share a quick analogy.

You and your companion are traveling down a road and come upon a fork (this would be in the days before GPS navigation). You discuss your options and agree to take the left fork. As you travel down this path, daylight turns to night, you are getting more tired and hangry. There are no restaurants nor hotels in sight, and you are not any closer to your destination. No amount of compromise as your travel down this left fork will get you closer to your destination because you chose the wrong direction at the fork in the road. You could continue down this path, getting farther from your intended destination or humble yourselves by admitting you may have taken the wrong path and return to the fork and commence down the other path.

America has been traveling down the wrong fork for generations and no amount of compromise will help. I intend to show where we went wrong, and it is to that fork where we need to return. Both major political parties need to accept the fact we've been heading down the wrong path for about a century; otherwise, we will be no better off in four or eight or thirty years from now. My goal while running for president is to help Americans understand where that fork was and return to that point and travel the correct path. ***This correct path will lead to the future most Americans desire: peace and prosperity.***

I have concluded I do not want to be tutored by a system that has been broken for a century and become part of that system. If we look back at a few campaigns in my lifetime, we learn one invaluable truth: a presidential candidate does not need political experience to run a successful campaign. Let's examine our first two.

In 1992, a businessman by the name of Ross Perot threw his hat in the ring for president. He spent millions of his own money buying television airtime for infomercials and had several appearances on talk shows, in particular Larry King, a well-known late-night host.

While the campaign was fraught with challenges, Perot earned a spot in the three presidential debates. There is a lot of speculation as to why he lost, but he proved a point: a person with no political experience can have an impact.

There are lessons we can learn from his campaign, but he proved that an independent candidate has a voice and the potential to win a presidential election. Ross Perot paved the way for a second billionaire businessman to run for president in 2016, Donald J. Trump.

Donald J. Trump, unlike Ross Perot, chose to utilize the machinery of a political party to begin his campaign run. Due to his business experience and ideology, he threw his hat in the ring with 16 other republican primary candidates, the largest primary field of candidates in American history. To say his personality is bristly might be an understatement. Many republicans had to hold their nose to support him when it was becoming clear he would be the presumptive nominee, but the voice of the people had spoken.

Trump's rhetoric either endeared people to his campaign or polarized them. Rarely had an election in history become one about character, but in my humble opinion, character was the primary factor that most of the electorate used as their barometer to choose between candidates Donald Trump, democrat nominee, Hillary Clinton, and a slew of other little known third party and independent candidates. Trump proved what Perot couldn't, that someone who had never held an elected government position could win the presidency. His billionaire status didn't hurt either. He had already earned himself notoriety throughout his personal and professional life. His billions afforded him the ability to finance his campaign to the tune of $18.6 million of his own money.[6]

It's clearly obvious that money is key to launching a successful campaign and notoriety and/or fame plays an even larger role. However, an obscure senator from the state of Illinois with no significant personal achievements proved you can win the presidency without either fame or personal wealth. His name was Barrack Hussein Obama II.

Barrack Obama had what very few candidates have, that helped him win—charm. Even if you disagreed with his politics, it's impossible to dispute the fact that former president Obama could schmooze better than any politician I've seen in my lifetime. He knew it too and played that fiddle on every talk show imaginable. It didn't hurt that he was handsome too with a great smile.

His candidacy as the first Black nominee for a major political party in our nation's history provided a litmus test of how far we had come from the days of slavery a century and a half ago. Some of our African American friends were giddy when an intelligent and articulate and handsome man of color was winning the democratic primaries and appeared as if he would go toe-to-toe against the republican nominee in the general election.

While many people thought he lacked substance during his first campaign in 2008, he defeated Hillary Clinton for the democratic nomination and handily won the general election against republican nominee, John McCain, a Vietnam war veteran with a distinguished career. In my humble opinion, Obama proved that charisma was the defining principle upon which his campaigns were won, including his second victory against Mitt Romney (who was labeled as stiff or robotic) in 2012. The money and fame followed.

In conclusion, preceding presidents have paved the way for candidates with no money, fame, or political experience to win the presidency. I am grateful they proved what I've always known was possible. This election just might add one more element to a presidential election yet to be achieved in modern politics—a winning campaign by an independent presidential candidate. The voice of the people will, of course, decide.

Chapter 8

PRESIDENTIAL POWER

The office of President of the United States has often been coined as the most powerful position in the free world. Why do we label that position with such a venerable title? Let's examine the word "power" first and do a deep dive to see, perhaps, why the President of the United States is considered the most powerful person in the free world.

Power, as defined in the dictionary[7], follows:

> great or marked ability to do or act; strength; might; force.
> the possession of control or command over people; authority;
>
> influence: delegated authority; authority granted to a person or persons in a particular office or capacity: legal ability, capacity, or authority

An examination of these definitions provides a clear distinction between two types of power, positional and ability. Positional authority is power granted to the office holder, who has been elected, appointed, or delegated to a position that, by definition, has authority over other persons in that organization. One can hold a position of authority and lack the necessary skills to motivate, inspire, or lead the organizational unit to produce maximum results. In that case, an organization often suffers. We've all seen it. We have all had a boss at one time or another where we had to painstakingly learn to navigate through their terrible leadership. It's obvious when you encounter a terrible boss versus a good one.

Let me share an experience when I was a copilot for our airline. Copilots, or "First Officers" in our present-day vernacular, are second in command. The captain is first in command of the entire crew and is ultimately responsible for the safe operation of the aircraft and the safety of all onboard, along with other important duties. While both pilots alternate in the duty of flying, the captain has the final authority for all operational decisions.

I once found myself on a trip with a captain whose skills as a pilot were weak in my estimation. He was "behind the aircraft" constantly. Due to the nature of flying and the tempo of the operation, a pilot must always be thinking two or three steps (or more) ahead to manage the operation smoothly and safely. If not, then the pilot is "behind the aircraft." This particular captain was barely keeping up and it made me extremely nervous. To make matters worse, he didn't appreciate my help in staying ahead of the aircraft. It was a miserable trip for me. While he possessed positional authority, or positional "power," he lacked the fundamental skills commensurate with the position.

He was not confident, his airmanship was below average, and he lacked interpersonal skills too. To be fair, I was young, had a sharp mind, and had been flying that aircraft type for many years. I knew that aircraft intimately, backwards, and forwards. He did not, and in that situation, a good leader would and should rely on the strengths of his or her team. Even though he had the first type of power, positional authority, he lacked the second type of power, ability.

Revisiting the definition of power associated with ability, it reads: "great or marked ability to do or act; strength; might; force." If I were in a boxing ring, or wrestling match, we might think of power as strength, might or force. But there is another type of power associated with ability and that type of power is power to do or act. I would like to share another experience as an airline copilot to illustrate a point.

I flew many years as a copilot on the MD-88 in and out of Atlanta. Most of that flying was to and from cities within an hour's flight of Atlanta. Atlanta was and is still one of the busiest airports in the world. The region's air traffic controllers, from the Atlanta TRACON to Atlanta Center, were the sharpest I'd ever encountered in my years of flying.

The best controllers could move traffic well and with precision. Yet, as often was the case, weather or overscheduling flights into Atlanta would require delays to facilitate the flow of air traffic into and out of Atlanta. Shorter flights would absorb the delay on the ground before takeoff. All too often, we would pushback from the gate only to receive a ground hold. If it was a weather delay, it could turn into a real fiasco.

Atlanta was prone to afternoon thunderstorms that could cause delays exceeding two or more hours.

On occasion I would fly with a captain who just didn't seem to care about the experience passengers were having locked up in a metal tube, sitting at the end of the runway waiting for hours until we could take off. It infuriated me that the captain lacked empathy for the people who were paying his fat salary. Years later, when I became a captain, I handled the situation entirely differently. If I knew the delay would be longer than an hour, I would negotiate with the operations team to allow us to go back to the gate, deplane the people and allow them to absorb the delay in a more comfortable setting.

While it meant more work for the gate agents, I was more than willing to help them if needed, and I would often do so. As captain, I could make this decision, but it required effort and some coordination on my part. The aforementioned captains lacked empathy because, in part, all they saw were dollar signs.

Most pilots and flight attendants get paid when the aircraft pushes back from the gate, whether the plane is airborne or not. I can't be certain of their motives, but it was obvious to me they chose to handle the situation far differently than I wanted to, even when I voiced my opinion. In that situation, unlike the alternate experience which I chose as a captain, only one person was happy, and it wasn't any of the 142+ people sitting aft of the cockpit door.

How do you take a bad experience and make it worse? You do it by being a lousy leader with the positional authority to do what you want, regardless of how it affects others. True power, in my opinion, is having positional authority and exercising that power by "doing" or "acting" to benefit those in your stewardship. When a good leader exercises power, everybody wins. I'm reminded of a phrase coined by Stephen Covey, the author of *The Seven Habits of Highly Effective People:* "Think win-win."

I went to a seminar where I saw Stephen Covey present his material to a live audience. It was fun watching him try to illustrate the principle of win-win. If you are negotiating with someone, all too often in our machismo world, you aren't winning unless you force the other party to lose. (President Trump comes to mind.) It's obviously that way in sporting competitions, but it doesn't have to be that way everywhere else. Covey was trying to demonstrate this principle of win-win to an audience member who was invited on stage with him. I was embarrassed for the individual because no matter how many hints or how much help Mr. Covey gave the gentleman, the principle of win-win never registered in his mind.

The demonstration went something like this. Mr. Covey explained to the gentleman, whom we will call John, that members of the audience would give John a dollar every time John beat Mr. Covey at arm wrestling while they stood toe-to-toe. Mr. Covey would receive a dollar every time he won. (Do a YouTube search for "Covey demonstrates win-win" to see what I'm talking about.) Mr. Covey let John easily win. Then he let him win again, and again. The object lesson was for John to allow Mr. Covey to win because they would each receive a dollar for every win. But our world is poisoned by the idea that the other person has to lose for you to win.

In my opinion a true leader, one with real power, allows all who work for them to win. Something magical happens when a person with positional authority is anxiously engaged in helping those who are under their authority to succeed. The subordinate wins, the leader or manager wins, and the organization wins. It is truly "win-win." Real power inspires loyalty, discipline and the type of faith that lifts and motivates a person to win.

The world is rife with people with positional power, but far fewer examples exist of people with the ability to lead and inspire greatness. It is this kind of leadership that has been lacking in the office of President for far too long. In my lifetime, I have to look back decades to find someone who I believe possessed the type of leadership that America needs now. I will name but one, President Ronald Reagan. My college roommate, a political science student, was a huge fan of President Reagan. I wasn't interested in politics back then, but since 1995 when the Lord laid this heavy burden on me, I've observed the workings of government and real leaders with more scrutiny.

Why do we label the office of President of the United States the most powerful position in the free world? In addition to the title and power of "Commander in Chief" (the head of the world's greatest military force), the president wields tremendous influence, good or bad, on our nation (and the world) by virtue of that position. No other person in our country—or perhaps the world—has greater "celebrity" status than the president. The media coverage a president receives is breathtakingly overwhelming, and yet, undeserving in my opinion. Consider for a moment, the amount of television coverage leading up to and including the day of the general election every four years. The media practically deifies the office of president, and we soak it up like obedient lap dogs.

The positional authority the president of the United States has is far more limited in scope and responsibility than what we, the public, assumes. To fully comprehend how limited presidential power is, we need to carefully study and understand the Constitution. Certainly, the Framers never intended a president to have the unrestrained authority we see exercised all too often by presidents from both political parties.

The type of unrestrained authority I'm referring to is the power of the pen, or "Executive Order." We will discuss this in greater detail in a subsequent chapter, but understand this, if the Framers of the Constitution had intended our president to have the unrestrained power of the "Executive Order," they would never have fought the War for Independence from 1775 until the signing of the Treaty of Paris in 1783; but would have remained loyal subjects of the British crown. What we have done in our federal government is an affront to the genius of the Founding Fathers and all who died to lay the foundation of freedom in this country and the transformative effects on the entire world.

The "most powerful position in the free world" is a venerable title we've bestowed on the office of President of the United States, but it was never intended, nor designed to be. The United States grew in greatness, not because of the President or our federal government, but because we were a free nation. We were a free people, able to pursue our dreams and the federal government was responsible, in part, to ensure we could do so unimpeded. For example, prior to the Constitution, states restrained commerce by imposing tariffs and "petty regulations designed to promote local prosperity"[8] on interstate commerce.

The Framers took that impediment away and gave it to the federal government when they drafted The Constitution. *"The Congress shall have Power… To regulate Commerce with foreign Nations, and among the several States, and with the Indian Tribes" (US Constitution, Article I, Section 8).* Our founders understood that removing those state sponsored tariffs would allow more free trade and help unify the nation, and so it did. We were a free people and became the envy of the world. Individuals flocked to our country (See Figure 6), fleeing their oppressive governments to seek the opportunities that **only America provided**.

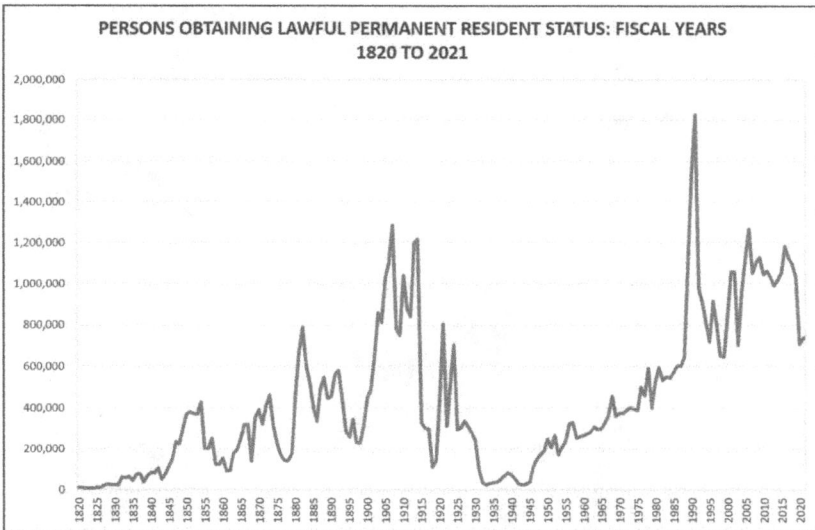

Figure 6: Data taken from Table 1 from--https://www.dhs.gov/sites/default/ files/2023-03/2022_1114_plcy_yearbook_immigration_statistics_fy2021_v2_1.pdf

The principle of freedom which invites innovative thinking and the opportunity to pursue one's dreams was protected for decades by the government designed by the Framers to preserve that freedom. Freedom is the single most important principle that allowed the United States to become the greatest nation in modern history. The president has the privilege of being the head of state, or chief executive, along with the coined yet grossly misunderstood title, the most powerful person in the free world. My goal as a president would be to help clarify that misunderstood title and restore the power that has been usurped by past administrations to those to whom it rightfully belongs: the people, their representatives, and their state governments.

Chapter 9

LEADERSHIP

Leadership is, by far, my favorite subject. I have this yearning desire to study every facet of it. I observe those in leadership positions with great seriousness, gleaning every aspect that I suppose gives them the power we discussed in the previous chapter to inspire and influence others. My library consists of a multitude of books on the subject and every ancillary topic remotely similar, ranging from self-help to management principles. It is my passion to practice the principles I learn, always attempting to hone them to the best of my ability. Leadership is "in my blood," so to speak. I know and understand leadership.

I've concluded that we all intuitively recognize and follow good leaders, but to quantify what that means and to define a good leader may be hard for some of us. I would like to share several stories that I think exemplify good leaders. I'll begin with a famous football player whose heyday began when I was just a toddler. He quarterbacked for the Crimson Tide under the famous Coach Paul "Bear" Bryant at Alabama, leading them to a National Championship in 1964. I'm referring to Joe Namath.

Joe Namath was drafted by the New York Jets in the AFL. The AFL, or American Football League, consisted of newer teams and was an entirely different league than the long-established NFL. The AFL ran from 1960 to 1970 and competed against the NFL for fans. The success of the AFL was helped by none other than Joe Namath. The 1966 season saw the first Championship game between the two leagues and the NFL champion Green Bay Packers (coached by the legendary Vince Lombardi) dominated against their AFL rivals. The third Championship game, officially dubbed the *Super Bowl* for the first time, saw the AFL champion New York Jets defeat the heavily favored Baltimore Colts. The game pitted quarterback Joe Namath against legendary quarterback Johnny Unitas and Earl Morrall of the Colts. What made the game even more exciting was Namath's boastful yet prescient prediction that they would win. He would "guarantee it." None of these facts matter regarding understanding leadership except for the fact that Namath's talent was coupled with a leadership quality I want to spotlight.

Namath respected his offensive linemen. He praised them in public and in private. Joe Namath understood that his success depended on the success of the men that protected him in the pocket, and he showed his gratitude often. The proof in the pudding is the mutual respect those men have of "Broadway Joe" (a moniker given to Namath by one of the offensive linemen) when they reminisce about those glory days. Namath respected those around him and what they contributed to the organization. Even to this day, Namath continues to hurl accolades to his teammates. Leadership quality number one is respect. Respect your supporting teammates. There are three more pillars I believe are critical to good leadership. Let's look at the next pillar.

Moving from the football field to the battlefield, let's examine a man whose name everybody knows, George Washington. George Washington's contributions are studied in elementary school history classes throughout this nation. Every native-born US citizen knows who George Washington is. What they don't study is his leadership skills. Washington was chosen to be the Commander in Chief of the Continental Army because of his military experience in the French and Indian War.

Like Namath of football fame, Washington knew that success on the battlefield depended greatly on troop morale. Funding the Revolutionary War was a major obstacle, and it would result in a lack of provisions and ammunition for the troops, particularly during the bitter winter of 1777-1778 at Valley Forge. A beleaguered band of soldiers was held together by the leadership of General Washington.

In addition to his ability to inspire loyalty to their cause, Washington knew his limitations and was humble enough to acknowledge and accept help from Baron Friedrich von Steuben, a distinguished Prussian soldier willing to help America's fight for independence. Baron von Steuben organized and trained a ragtag group of soldiers into a disciplined fighting army that would soon hold its own against the more powerful British army. Washington had a quality of leadership that all too often is overlooked—humility. To recognize and accept our own shortcomings and to look to others to fill those gaps is a sign of strength, not weakness. In a way, it's not too different from Broadway Joe, who recognized he needed the strength of his offensive linemen to do his job well. Washington freely acknowledged he needed the strength of another skilled soldier to fill the gap in his own armor.

Washington was a pious gentleman, too. He often sought divine help from the Creator of the Universe through humble prayer. God supports those who honor Him and throughout Washington's life, the Provident hand of the Almighty can be seen. One story warrants a closer look.

Two decades prior to the Revolutionary War, Washington fought in the French and Indian War. During the Battle of the Monongahela, Washington miraculously remained unscathed. Serving as British General Braddock's aide-de-camp, more than 900 were wounded or killed from among more than 1400 British and colonial soldiers.[9] Washington recorded the event,

> *"By the all-powerful dispensations of Providence, I have been protected beyond all human probability and expectation; for I had four bullets through my coat, and two horses shot under me yet although death was levelling my companions on every side of me."*[10]

An Indian chief from the opposing forces was so impressed by what he witnessed; he travelled a great distance to meet the man fifteen years later when he had learned Washington was surveying the area in the Ohio wilderness.

After showing great "reverential deference" towards Colonel Washington, this Indian chief told the tale he witnessed during that great battle to the two small parties that accompanied him and Washington. Prior to the Battle of the Monongahela, Washington had become well acquainted with Indian warfare tactics, but General Braddock was not, and the Indian chief recognized the difference and had ordered his fellow warriors to take aim, specifically on Washington. The chief recounted the events, as told through Joseph Nicholson, an interpreter during this encounter.

> *"I am a chief, and the ruler over many tribes. My influence extends to the waters of the great lakes, and to the far blue mountains. I have travelled a long and weary path, that I might see the young warrior of the great battle. It was on the day, when the white man's blood, mixed with the streams of our forest, that I first beheld this chief: I called to my young men and said, mark yon tall and daring warrior? He is not of the red-coat tribe—he hath an Indian's wisdom, and his warriors fight as we do—himself is alone exposed. Quick, let your aim be certain, and he dies. Our rifles were levelled, rifles which, but for him, knew not how to miss—'twas all in vain, a power mightier far than we, shielded him from harm. He cannot die in battle."*[11]

The Indians had been instructed to wipe out all soldiers riding on horses (the leaders), but of Washington, they could not. The Indian Chief concluded,

> *I am old, and soon shall be gathered to the great council-fire of my fathers, in the land of shades, but ere I go, there is a something, bids me speak, in the voice of prophecy. Listen! The Great Spirit protects that man and guides his destinies—he will become the chief of nations, and a people yet unborn, will hail him as the founder of a mighty empire!"*[12]

Washington was a man who possessed great humility. He sought not just help from those who possessed skills that he did not, **_but he also sought help from heaven._** Humility is a strength and good leaders possess it. Humility requires a person to look inward, to know oneself: the good, the bad and the ugly. The ugly and bad drives the humble leader to seek to become better, but also to look to others to complete and round out the leadership team. A good leader surrounds himself or herself with others with varying degrees of talent and will council together with them to seek an appropriate direction to move the work that they are engaged in forward. The second pillar of good leadership is humility.

Pillar three of good leadership is honesty. Honesty begets trust. Trust is necessary when a leader represents those who put their trust in him or her to do what is required to accomplish a particular goal or purpose. Let's examine a few scenarios.

This first example is one which we are all probably familiar with, whether it be from our own experience, or having heard it from others. I'm going to borrow this example from a person I'm well acquainted with. This person was a child of divorced parents. Their mother had full custody and the father had visitation rights. Children are impressionable with high hopes and expectations, until we, as parents, squash that idealism with an overabundance of practicality and rules, often referred to as "helicopter parenting." This person I'm describing was about 10 years old when her parents divorced. Her father would promise, from time to time, to come by and get the three siblings to take them out for dinner and some type of fun activity. On occasion, he would either simply forget, or other plans would get in the way.

Disappointment after disappointment led to an understandable and yet predictable lack of trust. Thus, any future promises of outings with dad were no longer met with hope and enthusiasm, but a healthy dose of skepticism. This man, in the eyes of his children, became untrustworthy.

Let me share another example, one closer to home, that I experienced in my flying career with my airline. The time frame was not long after 9-11. My youngest children were toddlers. They represent a good portion of the voting block today, but they have no recollection of the tragic events of that day and the decade that followed. We lived the horrors of that fateful day in September 2001. George W. Bush had been president for less than one year and he was caught on camera when his chief of staff whispered in his ear what was happening that morning as he sat in front of a class of second graders. The look of shock says it all when he heard "America is under attack."

Imagine the horror of seeing an airliner filled with passengers crash into the side of the second of the twin World Trade Center towers. The first of the twin towers was hit just 17 minutes prior at 8:46 am. Due to the rapidly unfolding events, cameras were rolling in time to capture the second airliner crash into the South Tower. It was a tragic day that affected many lives, most particularly those who were murdered that day and their surviving families and friends.

The airline industry started bleeding rapidly as demand for air travel plummeted. My airline was no exception. Management sought concessions from unionized employees, including our pilot group, and forced concessions on non-union employees. Union leadership was privileged to see the company's financials and encouraged our pilot group to vote to accept the pay cuts and other concessions if we wanted to save our airline and our careers. 1300 pilots were furloughed, 2500 pilots were offered early retirement and the remainder had lost significant gains recently negotiated in working conditions and pay. To persuade a yes vote from the pilots to accept these concessions (including a 32.5 % loss in payrates) was management's verbal promise that it would save the company and avoid bankruptcy.

Imagine my surprise when my company filed for bankruptcy less than 10 months later, with "notification of Section 1113(c) filing to reject the contract." This effectively meant they wanted to toss out the contract and pay whatever they deemed sufficient. I lost every ounce of respect for our management team that day. They didn't honor their word. Honesty builds trust and I no longer trusted our company's management team. Trust leads to loyalty, which is necessary when a company, football team or militia are facing difficult odds and those who are being led through a "trial by fire" must give their absolute best effort if they are going to succeed. Lack of loyalty almost guarantees failure. What followed were several difficult years as many employees lost confidence and trust in our management. Morale suffered tremendously. Passengers saw it too and our customer satisfaction hit all-time lows.

A good friend once shared a beautiful imagery of trust with me. He said, trust is accomplished by doing something small, a simple deed or carrying through with a promise, which is repeated over time. It is like putting a marble in a large mason jar for every good and honest deed until one day, that jar is filled with marbles. If you do something untrustworthy, it's as if you smashed that jar and all the marbles spill out. Trust is lost completely and will need to be earned once again, one marble at a time.

Honesty is the third pillar of good leadership.

The last pillar of good leadership is faith, but it may very well be the most important. The Apostle Paul taught that "faith is the substance [assurance] of things hoped for, the evidence of things not seen" (Hebrews 11:1). Alma (a Book of Mormon prophet) made a similar statement: "If ye have faith ye hope for things which are not seen, which are true" (Alma 32:21). Faith gives one power to do something they believe in. It is an action verb. Let's examine some examples of how faith can "move mountains."

Turning back the clock of time to 1776, we find James Madison beginning his political career as a representative in the state of Virginia. The goal at that time was for the delegates to organize a new state Constitution, one no longer under British rule. This experience would serve as a steppingstone for his great and ambitious task of reorganizing the ineffective Articles of Confederation into a more powerful federal government. In the Constitutional Convention of 1787, it was Madison's "Virginia plan" which described three branches of government that became the foundation of our present Constitution.

He not only shaped the Constitution but wrote a series of essays to help persuade the states to ratify and adopt it. This was no small feat, as there was much opposition to it, particularly since the states had just thrown off an oppressive national government. James Madison had faith in his idea of a strong national government bound by restraints codified in its Constitution. To persuade those who opposed its adoption, amendments were promised that addressed the concerns many citizens had. These amendments were written by none other than James Madison. It was Madison's faith in an idea that steered this nation from a bickering group of thirteen loosely tied states into arguably the greatest nation in the recorded history of man.

Skipping forward a century, let us examine another visionary man, Thomas Edison. Among a multitude of inventions, he is most famous for the incandescent lightbulb. While he didn't come up with the idea, he persisted in finding the best filament that could be used that was neither costly nor had a short lifespan. It has been suggested he tried hundreds if not thousands of times to find the best material. His success led to replacing burning oil in lamps with the electricity we use today. Edison was a man of vision; he believed in his ideas and persistently pursued them until he succeeded. It was his idea, or faith in his ideas, that was the driving force behind his success.

Every successful idea, invention, or cause is powered by faith. Some people might label it visionary, but that's a matter of semantics. Faith motivates that leader through every obstacle that may arise because they believe in the idea and will see it through to fruition. Faith is the fourth pillar of a good leader.

In summary, good leaders can be taught, but to some, it comes naturally. They respect others, they are humble and teachable, impeccably honest and are driven by faith that they can and will succeed.

Chapter 10

NAVAL ACADEMY TRAINING, SIR!

It was a Wednesday evening, May 31st, 1978, when I delivered the "Welcome Address" to guests and students at Flour Bluff High School's Class of '78 graduation. It was the culmination of an exciting year. I had taken the Homecoming Queen to the dance, and we were honored as the senior class favorites, Mr. and Miss. FBHS. I served as the president of the National Honor Society, and was smart enough to graduate with honors, but not disciplined enough to graduate at the top of our class. I had even tried out for the football team but was hopelessly unsuited for it and didn't pass the first cut. My prom date was a beautiful woman a few years older who just happened to be my good friend's sister. It was a great senior year!

My father, a career Naval aviator and Commanding Officer of VT-27 at Corpus Christi NAS, had persuaded me to apply to the Naval Academy. My interests were in becoming an architect. A Navy career hadn't occurred to me. When my good friend (whose sister I had dated) and I both received appointments to the Naval Academy, I reconsidered attending. At least I'd have a friend there. Little did I know I would not see him for the entire six-week indoctrination period. I was about to transition from a year of glorious recognition and fun to one of obscurity and misery.

On July 6th, 1978, barely a month after our high school graduation, I reported to the Naval Academy for induction. I received a presidential nomination. It was nothing extraordinary. When I hadn't received a congressional nomination, my father's active-duty status as a Naval Officer provided the opportunity for my name to be placed on the unlimited number of applicants for a presidential nomination to be reviewed once more by the admissions department. I was fortunate to receive a nomination because of my father's active-duty status, yet I would still need to prove myself.

A word about my father. He was a hard man with high expectations of his children. My older sister and next younger brother do not have any fond memories of our upbringing because our father had a lot of issues. I won't get into that. I was the first-born male, and in my father's world, that meant everything to him. I was privileged to experience a side of him that none of my siblings experienced. The day my parents put me on an airplane to fly to BWI to report to the Naval Academy, my mother observed my father quietly move to a seat overlooking my flight on the tarmac and place his shades over his eyes and bury his head in his hands to hide the tears rolling down his face. She later told me that was only the second time she had ever seen him cry. The first was at his father's funeral. When the six-week plebe summer indoctrination period ended, he flew up to spend parent's weekend with me to show his love and support. He was a proud father.

Figure 7: 1982 The Lucky Bag

July 6th, 1978, was a busy day for me and the approximately 1600 other plebes. I was assigned to an upperclassman that guided my group of eight across the campus for uniforms, haircuts, marching lessons, and drill instructions among other things. He sure was helpful that day, but I learned early on that I had only 5 responses that were acceptable to him: "Yes sir; No sir;

Aye-aye sir; No excuse sir; and I'll find out sir." They hated sea-lawyers, someone with an excuse that would accompany an answer. I learned not to be a sea-lawyer.

At the end of the day, we were sworn in at a large gathering in Tecumseh court with spectators and parents observing our commitment to honorably serve as the newest class of midshipmen. When we were dismissed at the end of that ceremony, all hell broke loose. That helpful upperclassman along with his cohorts corralled us in our dormitory hallway and proceeded to give us a real tongue lashing. This came unexpectedly for most of us, but I was used to it from our father, others were not. Lined up along the bulkhead (wall) we stood in a braced position—at attention with our back, neck, chin and head pulled back in our best attempt to have our spine parallel to the wall. It was uncomfortable to say the least. About 10 upperclassmen assigned to

Figure 8: 4737 –Incoming Plebes Taking Oath of Office 1978. N.p., 1978. Print.

Figure 9: 1982 The Lucky Bag

our company of 44 plebes each paraded back and forth taking aim at each of us for what seemed like hours.

We had learned some basic facts throughout our first day and we were rigorously getting tested. If you failed to answer a question correctly, you received 5 demerits. Accrued demerits required extracurricular marching drills to expunge them. This exercise in our group of 44 was being repeated in the other 35 companies throughout Bancroft Hall, our dormitory. All I could hear was the echoing of hundreds of yelling voices at these unsuspecting classmates of mine. Then, as it began to wind down, the company commander barked out, "Now plebes, look to your left." In unison we all turned our heads to our left, followed by, "Now look to your right," which we all complied in sync. He continued, "one of those classmates will wash out! He or she will not graduate with you!" Statistically speaking, he knew it would be true. Whereas approximately 1600 midshipmen are inducted, usually only about 1000 graduate four years later.

Two of my company classmates quit at the end of the plebe summer. A total of 15 quit altogether from among my little group of 44 over the next two years. Quitting isn't an option after you start your junior year, unless you didn't mind serving as enlisted personnel somewhere within the Navy's fleet. Quitting prior to the beginning of junior year had no such obligation, so most people would endure for as long as possible before "punching out."

Five of those 15 endured two full years of academy life. Many believed they chose to do so to get the college credits, some even admitted as much.

Mealtime was unique. It always began with a formation either outside, or within Bancroft Hall during inclement weather, whereafter we would dutifully march to King Hall to dine. Feeding the approximately 2000 midshipmen and officers during plebe summer 3 meals a day was an orchestrated masterpiece in logistical precision. Considering that number would approximately triple during the academic year, and anyone with half a brain would come to appreciate the amount of work necessary to pull off such a feat. During every meal, carts of food would be wheeled out to every table at the same time. Each table consisted of about 10-12 midshipmen and the entire brigade of midshipmen would dine together, with hearty food fit for royalty, hence the

Figure 10: 1982 The Lucky Bag

name King Hall. That would be fitting for its origin, but King Hall was actually named after Fleet Admiral Ernest J. King, a 1901 graduate and Chief of Naval Operations during World War II.

It was at mealtime when plebes were most vulnerable to hazing or harassment from upper class students. I had managed to escape receiving any demerits throughout plebe summer and our upperclassmen were on the hunt to find any such as I. As soon as I and a handful of others were discovered, they began the drill of asking questions we were expected to know the answers to. On induction

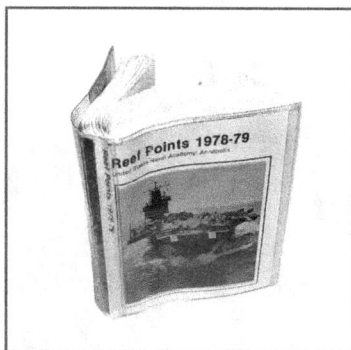

Figure 11: My personal Reef Points

day, we were issued a small, pocket size book titled "Reef Points." It included a multitude of Navy and Marine Corps facts, past and present, such as ranks of both officers and enlisted of all the armed forces. Other factoids included the names of the president's cabinet members, Secretaries of the Armed Forces, and the Joint Chiefs of Staff. Our daily study included current events, and oddly, all the items on the menu for the given and subsequent meal.

I was a likeable fellow—they told me as much—so they put on the kid gloves as they went round robin to ask me the questions that I was expected to know answers to. The exercise concluded when they finally found a question that I didn't know the answer to. I received my first 5 demerits, but one classmate eluded them for a while longer. We all secretly cheered him on, it felt good to witness his skill at parrying off their questions with ease. If he was nervous, it didn't show.

Plebe summer concluded with Parents weekend, and as I previously mentioned, my father flew up to show his support. The rest of the Brigade would return after that weekend to begin the Fall semester.

The hardest part was over, but the hazing would continue in a milder fashion until graduation week in May when plebes would participate in their rite of passage ceremony, climbing the 21-foot Herndon monument.

Figure 12: Herndon Monument

Figure 13: Herndon monument from '82 Lucky Bag

The Herndon monument ceremony is quite a sight to behold. The ceremony falls early in the events of Graduation Week, or more formally, Commissioning Week. Preparation by upper class students is performed to make the experience more challenging.

It has evolved over the years, but during our plebe year the surrounding ground was muddied up and the monument was greased. Upon a signal throughout Bancroft Hall, plebes rush to the monument to scale it. The goal is to replace the "dixie" cover (cover means hat) worn during the plebe summer with the more formal midshipman cover. The time it takes to build a human pyramid to scale the monument has been recorded for the history books since the early 60's.

The fastest time was less than two minutes (the year it wasn't greased or muddied) and often can last for hours. To witness this spectacle, just type in "Herndon climb" in the YouTube search field to get a better visual of this rite of passage.

Figure 14: 1982 The Lucky Bag

Figure 15: 1982 The Lucky Bag

The remaining three years were filled with rigorous academic study, sports, marching, and a tightly structured schedule designed to push and test the limits of each midshipman. It isn't for everyone, as witnessed by the punch out rate of approximately 33%. The reward of succeeding is well worth it.

From day one in plebe summer and woven throughout the 4-year experience, the word "honor" was emphasized. The mission of the Naval Academy is to build leaders for tomorrow's Navy, and honor is an essential component in the development of that leader. I quote from the "Reef Points" about the Honor Concept woven in the development of the midshipman experience.

Figure 16: Mustering for afternoon parade

"Honor is a quality which renders a person unable to say anything less than absolute truth in any situation, regardless of the outcome, and it leaves him incapable of any action which would bring reproach upon his

integrity. John Paul Jones is reputed to have said, 'It is by no means enough that an officer of the Navy should be a capable mariner. He should be as well, a gentlemen of liberal education, refined manners, punctilious courtesy and the nicest sense of personal honor.' It is this 'personal honor' that is the foundation for the Honor Concept at the United States Naval Academy."

"Honor, personal integrity, and loyalty are fundamental characteristics essential to every naval officer. To develop or enhance these attributes in a midshipman is to create in each one's mind and conscience lasting awareness of what is right and honorable as opposed to what is wrong and dishonorable. Through such indoctrination, midshipmen will both by habit and by conscious thought, choose the honorable course of action in every situation encountered."

"Each midshipman must understand, therefore, the need for complete honesty and truthfulness in word and actions. Each must come to know that false or misleading statements or acts in the stress of combat situations could endanger lives and military success; and that training and noncombat situations develop habits and traits that determine a person's response under more demanding conditions. Through acceptance and practice of the highest standards of personal conduct, an officer's word has become his or her bond, his or her signature a verification of truth, and their actions assumed to be straightforward and above reproach. It is thus requisite that each graduate—and each midshipman—be a person of infallible honor at all times under all conditions."

Figure 17: Graduation, May 26th, 1982
(My mother, Jane & grandmother, Anne Borcik)

The four-year experience I had at the United States Naval Academy was invaluable in so many ways. It helped refine who I was and who I was becoming.

When I say that I had an experience in the Washington D.C. temple whereupon I heard the voice of the Lord command me to "Run for President," you can be certain that I understand all the consequences of such a bold statement, and I will defend that truth until I die.

Chapter 11

PRIORITIES AND BALANCE: A LESSON FROM MY WIFE

In 1995, President Gordon B. Hinckley along with the other remaining 14 members of the First Presidency and the Council of the Twelve Apostles of The Church of Jesus Christ of Latter-day Saints, shared a proclamation to the world titled, "The Family." In this proclamation, they define the values and principles of the family as designed by God. Today, by man's definition, family and marriage has changed. But to God it hasn't. In this proclamation it states, "fathers and mothers are obligated to help one another as equal partners."

While the Church may seem patriarchal in nature, and that is a harsh criticism levied by many, I've always viewed my wife (and all women) with nothing but admiration and respect. To appreciate your spouse and their strengths is important if a marriage is to grow into something lasting. As Latter-Day Saints, it is our doctrine and view that the marriage compact endures beyond the grave, and not "until death do you part." A wise bishop once provided the following counsel when he drew this diagram out for us. He explained, when you each draw closer to God, you will narrow the gap between yourselves.

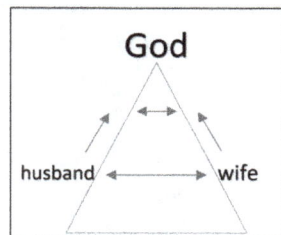

Figure 18: Marriage Triangle

Marriage between a man and a woman is ordained of God and always has been, but to succeed, you ought to keep God in it. He is the perfect partner and will help you to succeed.

My bishop was right too. Every relationship will get strained, it's inevitable because you each come from quite different backgrounds which will lead to challenges. My wife and I had childhoods that left emotional scars and that baggage doesn't get left at the church entrance when you say, "I do." Keeping God as a partner has always led to self-reflection instead of pointing fingers when our marriage encountered challenging moments of different opinions.

I met my wife in October 1982, after reporting to Pensacola for training to become a Naval Aviator. I had recently completed Aviation Indoctrination at NAS Pensacola and had reported to Whiting Field north of Milton, FL for basic training as a student pilot. I was living a few miles from my parents in a small apartment by the University of West Florida. The local grocery store manager where I did my shopping had a propensity to hire attractive cashiers. I dated a few, but there was one young girl who caught my eye because she had a glow about her that I could not fully appreciate at the time. I later came to understand what it was.

Christ, in the New Testament, taught his disciples,

> *Ye are the light of the world. A city that is set on a hill cannot be hid.*
>
> *Neither do men light a candle, and put it under a bushel, but on a candlestick; and it giveth light unto all that are in the house.*
>
> *Let your light so shine before men, that they may see your good works, and glorify your Father which is in heaven.*
> (Matthew 5:14-16, *KJV*)

My wife, at the tender young age of 17 when I first met her, had that light as a disciple of Christ. If you are not a Christian, you may have difficulty understanding it, but chances are you have experienced it in your lifetime. If you ever come across a person in your circle of influence who just seems too nice, ask them this penetrating question: "Why are you so nice?" Most will gladly share with you about their walk with God and Christ.

At the time when I met my wife to be, I didn't understand this "light," but within a few years of marriage, it began to reveal itself when she started attending church while I was away on deployments. While I couldn't comprehend her Christian faith for the first few years of our marriage, I had a deep yearning to spend the rest of my life with her.

My wife had a "born again" experience when she was about nine years old. A local church would send out a bus to pick her and other congregants up who needed transportation to attend church. She fondly recalls the joy of attending church and Sunday school as a young girl. As she grew into adolescence, her church attendance dwindled to naught, yet the seed had been planted and was later nourished during those lonely days that accompanied our separation when my Navy squadron was deployed.

We are not a perfect couple and still have moments where we don't see eye to eye, but just as our good bishop predicted, that gap has narrowed over time, and we are more "one" than ever before. I love my wife unreservedly, and I'm not the only person who does. Over the course of our lifetime, she has nurtured strong relationships with dozens of people who simply admire, respect and love her for the person she is.

I would like to share a beautiful story about how my wife touched the heart of a friend in our church who happened to be having a miserable day. My wife woke up on a rainy, winter day in Georgia and humbly asked Heavenly Father, "Who do you need me to serve today?" The name of a friend came to mind and my wife immediately went to work preparing a meal for this friend and her family. In the words of the friend, these were the events of that day.

> *"It was a very rainy, dreary February morning and I was 4 days overdue with Gabriel. I was beyond miserable in my discomfort and anxiety about the upcoming (and seriously delayed, from my perspective) birth. London's school bus came at an early 6:30 a.m. and on this rainy day, she was early.*

> *While we were running across the street in the rain to catch the bus, she drove off, much to my utter dismay. We got drenched while running to the car, loaded Emma in her car seat and started chasing after the bus. We caught up with her and started running in the rain to get on just as she once again started driving off. This continued for 3 more bus stops. London and Emma were both bawling, as well as myself.*

> *We were soaking wet, embarrassed to keep running to the bus only to be left behind, especially me in particular with my waddling and awkward pregnant body. I was furious! I finally gave up and drove London to school, which was a time-consuming process, given the rain and traffic. I got home and called Jim, who was quite upset at the bus driver. I was a mess! I could not stop crying! This felt like the last straw for me. (My emotions were admittedly out of whack.) I was truly feeling down in the dumps.*

> *Low and behold, around 10:00 a.m., I was still in my pajamas crying. I just could not get control! Suddenly, much to my horror, the doorbell rang, and I knew I couldn't escape as the windows beside the door revealed my lack of absence. I was humiliated, but it seemed that there was nothing to do but answer the door. I*

opened it and found my sweet visiting teacher standing there with a full dinner for our family. She exclaimed that she had woken up that morning and prayed to know what our Father in Heaven would have her do that day, and He told her that I needed her. This simple act of service brought home the reality of my individual worth in our father's eyes. I knew that my trivial and insignificant problems were noticed and felt by my Father in Heaven. I knew that He loved and cared for me and my small world.

He was able to use my visiting teacher hands as His own, in great part because of her faith and diligence in asking and then listening for a reply. The meal was wonderful, but the message she delivered as an angel from above is one that I'm reminded of frequently. My Heavenly Father loves me and is aware of me!

He is actively supporting me and trying to express His love. It is often up to us to be the deliverers of those messages for Him. If we take the time to listen, we can be instruments in His hands. I am forever grateful to Sister Borcik for listening on that day for me."

That is my wife—someone who understands that other people need help. She serves others every day. It can be a simple text message: "thinking of you." She might receive a prompting to call a friend or one of our adult children to check on them. She will often post a positive "comment" on a friend's or family member's FB post. No matter how she serves, she is always looking for ways to brighten someone else's day, and often it is mine. She is wise too!

I am a Type-A personality. I am driven and often focused to give one hundred and ten percent of my time and energy to whatever project is my primary focus. I don't like failure, and I especially don't like to be reminded of my failures. It is a curse and a blessing. This is who

I was. My wife helped me understand that the curse of this type of personality can damage relationships.

When my wife and I joined The Church of Jesus Christ of Latter-Day Saints in 1992, we embarked on a path that helped us become different people, more well-rounded, empathetic, caring and loving. Because we believe our marriage covenant will extend beyond the grave, we are cognizant of the need to nurture that relationship. Most often, lessons learned in life are from those closest to you as your differences must be resolved if your relationship is to endure. My wife chastised me once, which sank deep into my soul causing me to reflect on my Type-A personality.

I was leading a fundraiser for my younger two sons' elementary school. It consisted of a night of fun activities and food. I had spent months planning and preparing for it. I was driven and had made up my mind it would be the best fundraiser the school had ever seen. On the night of the event, I was dressed as Springy the Clown (in honor of Spring Hill Elementary). Springy had been promoting the event for several weeks on the school's morning closed circuit broadcast hosted and run by the students. While I was circulating among the event's attendees, both parents and children, one of my sons came to me seeking help. I blew him off by telling him I didn't have time. My wife saw this and felt my son's disappointment. Here was his father, loved and admired by all the children because he had created a persona of fun and excitement for the past several weeks, ignoring his own son. When we got home that evening, I heard all about it.

I loved my children immensely, and still do. When my wife helped me understand our son's disappointment, I was devastated, and rightly so. It was a huge lesson that needed to be learned and my loving wife helped me clearly see the importance of balancing family and work.

I won't say that was the last time I learned a valuable lesson from my wife, but it was probably the most important one. Our actions should reflect our beliefs, and when they are not in harmony, something needs to change. (This disparity is called cognitive dissonance.) As Latter-Day Saints, we believe family is important. In fact, it is the most important thing in our lives because it is the only thing in this life that will survive after death. It reminds me of the time-honored adage, "You've never heard anyone on their deathbed exclaim, 'I wish I had spent more time at the office.'"

Yes, my wife is a saint and I'm lucky to have found her and it is my privilege to be married to her. She taught me how to balance my family and my work.

Chapter 12

AVIATE, NAVIGATE, COMMUNICATE

During our senior year at the Naval Academy, our class members participated in "Service Selection" night where each soon to be graduating midshipman would choose his or her career path upon graduation. The midshipmen were ranked by academic scores, and I fell squarely at the tail of the top third of my class with a 2.89 (or B-) cumulative score going into our final semester. Beginning with the midshipman ranked number one in the class, followed by each successive classmate in order of ranking, we would report to the location on campus where we would make the ultimate choice that would define the next 5 years of our lives and potentially the next 30 years.

The main choices were simple, Marine Corps officer or Naval officer in the ship community, aviation community, or submarine community. There were other needs of the Navy and Marine Corps that had to be met, but for me, I was comfortable knowing I was ranked high enough to get my first choice, aviation. My father was a career naval aviator and it had always been my desire to fly too.

My father's duty station during my 4 years at the Academy was Pensacola, Florida, the place I visited during vacations and called "home," albeit I hadn't grown up there. I would soon be returning, but for entirely different reasons than a break from school. After graduation in May of '82, I reported to Pensacola for my first assignment as a newly commissioned officer to begin Aviation Indoctrination, the first in a series of challenging academic, physical and hands on training experiences carefully designed to produce some of the finest aviators in the world, or at least that is what we were told. "You are the cream of the crop" we were told, and that naturally inflated one's ego. Life has taught me otherwise, that there are plenty of people more intelligent, more successful, and more driven than I am, but flying suited me and I was determined to do my best. It was a challenging program, and because it was, I studied hard, listened carefully to my instructors and learned my procedures well. One thing that I remember to this day is a lesson that was drilled into new students, "Aviate, navigate, communicate!"

"Aviate, navigate, communicate," is a mantra that has served me well. Simplistic, yet profound, it is a lesson that warrants further discussion. In the world of aviation, your aircraft is a dangerous piece of equipment that has the very real potential to kill its occupants as well as any within its path, and that includes innocent bystanders on the ground in rare emergencies. My father warned me of the dangers of aviation when he once told me he had lost several friends throughout his career due to aviation accidents.

My wife and I, early on in our marriage, experienced the death of a friend due to an aviation mishap. My wife received a phone call from the Navy liaison personnel asking her to accompany and assist them when they had to notify our friend's wife that she had lost her husband that morning due to a tragic and fatal accident. Aviation is, by its very nature, dangerous, and lessons learned throughout its history have taught the community the importance of always remembering to "aviate" or fly the aircraft, first and foremost.

It seems obvious to the reader that "aviate" should be the number one priority, but there are always situations that can distract the pilot's focus and pull his or her attention away from that duty. The most common type of distraction is the abnormal situation. An abnormal situation can develop quickly, taking the focus and attention away from the primary duty of flying this deadly projectile.

Abnormal situations can be as benign as a light bulb that has blown. Let's explore this for a moment. Here we have a photo of a cockpit with three green lights, each light representing one of the three landing gear positions of a tricycle system (the wheels of the aircraft). The upper light indicates the forward gear under

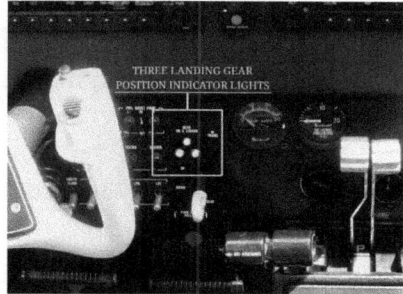

Figure 19: Aircraft cockpit

the nose of the aircraft while the left and right light indicate the gear under their respective wings near the fuselage. When the green lights are illuminated, they indicate the gear is locked in the down position.

Imagine, if you will, that on final approach and just minutes from landing, one of those green lights doesn't illuminate when you position the landing gear control handle down. Is the bulb burnt out? Or, perhaps, the respective gear is not fully locked in the down position?

An inexperienced pilot, especially a student pilot, could easily fixate his or her mind on the problem and forget that they are near the ground on the approach, at slower and more dangerous airspeeds. Slower speeds mean the aircraft could stall, losing the lift necessary to keep the aircraft flying. What could be a benign problem (a potentially burnt bulb) could develop into a significant problem if the pilot doesn't remember that simple mantra, "Aviate, navigate, communicate." There are several good ways to troubleshoot this problem, but the most important thing to remember is to continue to fly the aircraft!

In a multi-pilot aircraft, something that most of the aviation industry has, the solution is always to have one pilot focus on flying the aircraft while the other pilot troubleshoots the problem. In a single pilot aircraft, something I have far fewer hours in, the solution remains the same, don't forget to aviate while troubleshooting. In the above example, a single pilot should abandon the approach and fly a few thousand feet higher above the ground and at a higher airspeed to provide a greater margin of safety (airspeed and altitude) while troubleshooting the issue, always remembering to focus on flying.

The mantra, "Aviate, navigate, communicate" reminds the aviator that the single most important task at hand, whether in an abnormal situation, an emergency, or just simply normal operations is always to fly the aircraft. The terms, "navigate and communicate" have importance and could be elaborated on, but we will save that discussion for another day. The purpose of this discussion about aviation is to help the reader understand that this simple life lesson has not only served me well in my career as an aviator, but also has applications for life in general.

Let's explore, for a moment, how the principle to "aviate" first can be applied in your life too. For this experiment, I invite you to observe how often you witness other drivers on a multilane highway handling their phone while driving. Perhaps you are the offending person, reaching for or texting on your phone while driving in traffic. Using our phones while driving distracts us from the importance of paying attention to the road and the traffic around us. I remember watching a public service announcement on social media showing the dangers of texting while driving. It was eye opening to see how an accident can occur in the split second that we become distracted by our phones while driving.

The US DOT's National Highway Traffic Safety Administration reported that distracted driving accounted for 3,142 fatalities in 2020.[13] If we each applied the principle I learned as an aviator in our daily driving habits, we could save thousands of lives a year, even perhaps our own.

"Aviate, navigate, communicate" reminds me that our attention should be focused on what matters most. Author Stephen Covey wrote about the same principle in his book titled, "First Things First," focusing on things that matter most! All too often we get distracted by things that are of little importance in life, leaving us less time for those things that matter most. This principle can best be taught by an object lesson I've seen often and shared with our children when they were young.

It begins with a large glass jar and some rocks, pebbles, and sand. The jar represents our time. The rocks represent the most important things in your life such as your relationships with God, family and friends and your health (spiritual, mental,

Figure 20: Priorities object lesson image

emotional, and physical). The pebbles represent important but less meaningful things like work. The sand represents everything else, unimportant distractions. We can get easily distracted in life and fill our time with unimportant things.

The interesting thing about this object lesson is that if you fill the jar first with sand, then pebbles and finally the rocks, you run out of room for all the rocks, but if you change the order by filling the jar with rocks first, representing the most important things in your life, followed by pebbles, then sand, you will be able to get them all in the jar. There are several YouTube videos that demonstrate this principle.[14]

"How does the idea of putting important things first relate to the office of President?" We, as a nation, have tunnel vision on certain issues and we miss the weightier matters, particularly when it comes to political discourse on a national level. When billionaire businessman and independent candidate Ross Perot entered the presidential race in 1992, he beat the drum continually on the federal debt and the importance of balancing the budget. The federal debt when he ran in 1992 was slightly over $4 trillion.

In 2022, just one generation later, the federal debt is over $30 trillion, approximately 750% higher than when Mr. Perot was sounding the alarm in 1992. The tragedy of a growing national debt results from our elected government officials lacking the discipline to balance the budget each year (excepting 1998-2001 and some post WWII years) by spending more than they take in revenue. Just one generation prior to Mr. Perot, in 1962, the federal debt was about 1% of what it is today at only $298 billion. In 1932, just 3 generations ago, the federal debt was $20 billion, or .065% of what it is today.

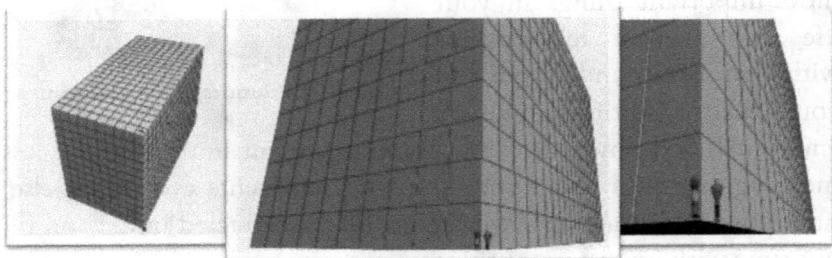

Figure 21: $30 Trillion

Let's put that $30 trillion national debt into perspective. One million seconds equals about 11 ½ days (11 days, 13 hours, 46 minutes and 40 seconds to be exact). 30 trillion seconds is more than 950,642 YEARS. If you are a visual person like me, perhaps the following images will help. The entire set of blocks stacked on each other represents $30 trillion. Each of those individual blocks represents 12.5 billion dollars carefully stacked with bundles of $100 bills. The small blip in the lower corner is two people of average height.

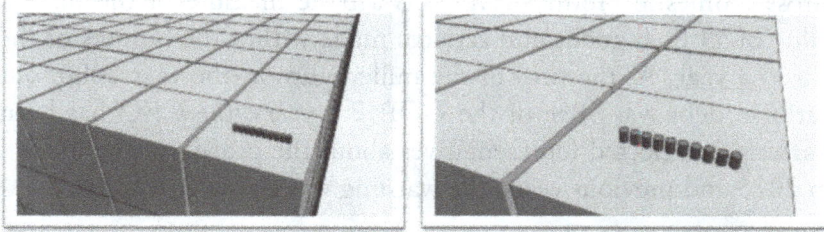

Figure 22: $30 Trillion

Lastly, as we zoom into the top corner, we see ten containers, each about the size of a grocery bag, stuffed with stacks of $100 denominated bills. Each small cylinder container represents one million dollars.

While my drawings are rudimentary, in June of 2017, Visual Capitalist did an *EXCELLENT visualization* of the then $20 Trillion in debt.

It can be found here at https://www.visualcapitalist. com/20-trillion-of-u-s-debt-visualized-using-stacks-of-100-bills/

Let's look at this looming crisis in different terms. If you take the national debt and divide it by the number of US citizens, which includes you and your children or grandchildren, me and my grandchildren, and every child or person born before the

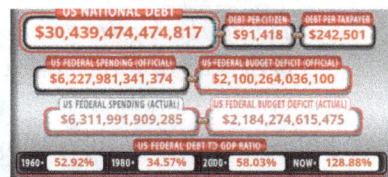

Figure 23: US National Debt-May 2022

2020 census, our share (and your children's and grandchildren's share) of that debt is more than $91,400 as of May 2022 (Figure 23). It increases about $5 a day. **It's immoral to straddle our children with our debt.**

Let's examine our national debt in other sobering terms as seen through the eyes of the Congressional Budget Office (CBO). Our

Gross Domestic Product (GDP) is a basic measure of the market value of all final goods and services made within the borders of the US in **a year**. At the turn of the millennium in the year 2000, our national debt was 58% of the GDP. For years, the CBO has been warning our elected representatives about the growing federal debt. In 2015 and previous years, the warning was similarly worded,

> *"If current laws remain generally unchanged, federal debt held by the public would exceed 100 percent GDP by 2040 and continue on an upward path relative to the size of the economy—**a trend that could not be sustained indefinitely**."* [15] (Emphasis mine)

That warning continues to fall on deaf ears and today (in 2022) the national debt is 120% of GDP, 18 years ahead of the CBO's 2015 warning. The annual warning from the CBO now includes an additional phrase with ominous implications. In 2016, the CBO warning read,

> *"If current laws remained generally unchanged, the United States would face **steadily increasing federal budget deficits** and debt over the next 30 years—reaching the highest level of debt relative to GDP ever experienced in this country."* [16] (Emphasis mine)

That phrase, "steadily increasing federal budget deficits," is the succinct way of saying the debt is getting out of hand. In other words, the cost of maintaining that debt, meaning interest payments, (which is part of the federal budget), will continue to rise so much that the interest payments alone will become the highest budget item and will eventually be unsustainable.

As of this writing in May 2022, the largest single annual federal budget item is $1.3 Trillion for Medicare/Medicaid. A close second in the annual federal budget is Social Security at just over $1.1 Trillion, and Defense Spending comes in a distant third at just over

$725 Billion. The interest on the debt is over $432 Billion and comes in as the fourth largest annual budget expense and is currently 1/3 the cost of Medicare/Medicaid, but those numbers will soon change.

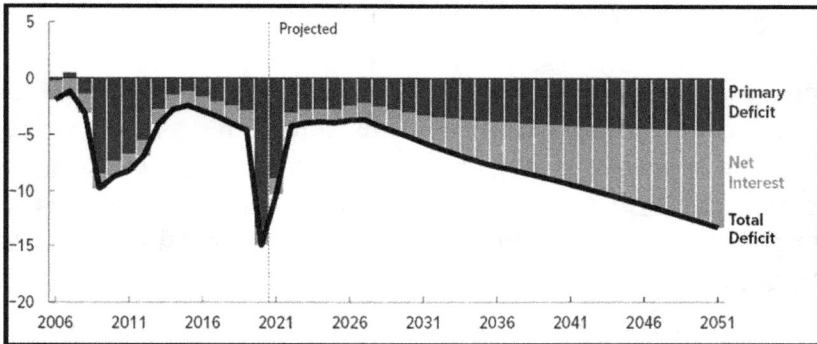

Figure 24: https://www.cbo.gov/publication/57038

This graph from the CBO's March 2021 report shows projected interest payments for the next 30 years. In less than one decade, the interest payments on the federal debt **will be the fastest growing federal expense and ultimately unsustainable**. The time to solve this problem was yesterday, not tomorrow. Ross Perot warned Americans in 1992 and today the problem is far worse. In the words of Abraham Lincoln,

> "As an individual who undertakes to live by borrowing, soon finds his original means devoured by interest, and next no one left to borrow from—so must it be with a government."

Let's talk briefly about that deep trough in 2020-2021 we see in Figure 24, the US government's response to COVID-19. As the COVID-19 pandemic fades in our rearview mirror, we are paying the piper for it today. The US government's response was more deficit spending, money they do not have in their treasury. Of the $4.6 trillion budgeted towards COVID-19 loans, grants, direct payments and other awards; to date, as of this writing, the government has spent $3.7 trillion (added to the national debt, of course) in the form of payments from 308 federal checking accounts thru 44 federal agencies to about 14.82 million recipients including insurance companies, state governments, businesses—small and large (airlines having received in the billions), universities, and a multitude of other entities.[17] Economists, (those that aren't Keynesian students) will tell you that those extra dollars circulating in the economy, (after our general recovery from COVID-19) are diluting the value of the pre-pandemic aggregate supply of currency. **<u>The inevitable result is a rebalancing of prices as goods and services chase the increase in the supply of money. This rebalancing we see is in the form of rising prices.</u>**

Notably, there are a variety of factors that cause inflation, but an increase in the supply of money to the tune of $3.7 trillion is the underlying cause of the inflation we see today. One only needs to look back to 1930—when my grandparents were young adults about to get married—and compare prices of homes and other commodities to understand the relationship between money supply and the prices of goods. In 1930, the average price of a home was $3,845.00. Yes, you read that right! The average price of a new car was $600.00, a gallon of gas, 10 cents, a loaf of bread 9 cents and a pound of hamburger meat 12 cents.[18]

The average American knows that they are paying more at the pump for gas and more for food at the grocery store than they did a year ago. Unfortunately, too many Americans don't understand why. Why is it that my grandparents could buy a house for under $4,000 while the average price of a home today is over $400,000? We will address the *why* in greater detail in Chapter 17. That *why* is the most important topic of this book—one that every American needs to understand.

When I turned to my friend Paul in 1995 and told him of my experience in the Washington D.C. temple, in addition to studying the Constitution, Paul suggested I read a well-researched book on the Federal Reserve titled, "The Creature from Jekyll Island" by G. Edward Griffin. As a matter of fact, he handed me a copy of the book! I've read it several times and worn out its pages. The one most important thing I've taken away from the book is the seriousness of the problem that lies at the root of nearly all our economic problems, not just in our country, but the world at large.

The seriousness of the problem hits close to home, too. It's been said that in a marriage there are several stressors that strain the relationship. Finances is in the top 5 of most lists of stressors and is often ranked as the number one stressor in a marriage relationship. As this book goes into circulation, American households will be experiencing the stress of another recession, and for some, their first.

The $30 Trillion national debt held by the Federal Government is just half of the problem we need to fix if we are to survive as a nation. Our government's national debt and the role of our Central Bank, the Federal Reserve, in facilitating the government's deficit spending, combine to create the boom and subsequent bust cycles in the economy.

The health of our national economy directly affects your lifestyle and whether you get a pay raise or whether you get fired, whether you pay more at the gas pump, or whether you can afford to go on a vacation; therefore, it is incumbent that you understand the primary forces that wreak havoc on it. Our number one priority should be to fix our fiscal and monetary policy. It may seem complicated with too many moving parts, just like flying an aircraft with its several integrated systems, but the simple solution is to remember to "aviate" first. That will require us to focus on fixing the broken fiscal and monetary systems. Chapter 17 explains the systemic problem of our monetary system and the government's role in compounding the problem that affects every American household.

Chapter 13

THE HUMAN EQUATION

Attending Navy flight training in and around Pensacola, Florida was both challenging and exciting. In 1982, "Primary" flight training was conducted at one of three squadrons at Whiting Field near Pensacola, or at a fourth squadron in Corpus Christi, Texas, where my father served as the Commanding Officer during my senior year of high school. Although aviation might have been in my blood, my inner ear and stomach were less agreeable.

Our training aircraft was the Beechcraft T-34C with a tandem seat unpressurized cockpit. Most maneuvers, such as acrobatics, were demonstrated by the instructor who sat in the rear seat. It was during these demonstrations I questioned whether my body was capable of the intensity of a fighter pilot career. I had picked up the nasty habit of smoking in my senior year at The Academy and was far from being physically fit. Being at the controls and flying the acrobatics was fun, but when the instructor demonstrated each maneuver, I felt nauseas. I decided a fighter pilot career wasn't for me. That decision left me with only two options as a Naval Aviator, either the "prop" pipeline or the "helos" pipeline.

Helos, or helicopters, fly off ships. I had experienced two summers as a midshipmen onboard Naval vessels as part of midshipmen training and had determined I didn't care for the shipboard life, for a variety of reasons (one of which was nausea during inclement weather). My father's aviation career was primarily in patrol aircraft, which were land-based aircraft. That became my de facto choice after Primary flight training. As in all assignments within the Navy, if you rank high enough in each assignment or training, you usually get to choose your next assignment, provided there is a need for it in the Navy. So, I worked hard in my Primary training at Milton, FL to ensure I could choose the advanced training for the prop (propellor driven aircraft) pipeline at Corpus Christi, TX.

It was during my primary training at Milton's Whiting Field that I met my bride, Chandra. We dated and it didn't take long before I knew I wanted to marry her. She was young, almost five years younger than me, and that choice to be married led to some harassment, both to her and myself during our early years. But she was worth it. She has been a great friend and companion throughout our lives. We married at the end of my training at Milton, and we packed our humble belongings in a small U-Haul trailer and headed west to my next training assignment in Corpus Christi, Texas.

After I completed flight training in Corpus Christi and was officially "winged" a Naval Aviator in January 1984, six of us were assigned to plowback as instructors in a new program for Naval Flight Officers (NFO's) in Pensacola, Florida. Our assignment was to teach brand new students who were beginning their training as NFO's. The platform for this new program for NFO's was the same T-34C we used in Primary training. It was a dream assignment for a pilot because the students were NOT learning how to fly, they were learning how to be "co-pilots" such as navigators, tactical coordinators, radar intercept officers and electronic warfare specialists.[19] The basic training we provided had some fun flying and you didn't have to worry about the student unwittingly "trying to kill you" because they weren't learning how to fly.

Each successive assignment in the Navy became an experience that taught me that I liked working with people. When I was the student, I knew I learned best in an environment that encouraged and rewarded success. When I became an instructor, I tried to teach in the same way that promoted successful learning for myself. I was moving into the real Navy with squadron assignments and opportunities to apply leadership skills that we were taught at the Naval Academy. Working with people, whether in my squadron assignment, or as an instructor suited me. My next assignment provided even more hands-on training, but not before the Navy invested more money to 1) teach me to fly a new platform, the P-3 Orion at Jacksonville, Florida, and 2) attend a Navy Leadership course (LMET) in Norfolk, Virginia.

After leaving the two-week Leadership course in Virginia, my wife and I headed to Brunswick, Maine for what would be my final assignment in the regular Navy. I did a short stint in a Reserve squadron after Brunswick, but my 3 years in Brunswick at VP-8 was my last opportunity to receive the hands-on training that the Navy had to offer before moving into civilian life.

While at VP-8, we had two deployments that lasted six months each, and about a year between deployments to train and prepare for the next deployment. While serving in VP-8, I had many opportunities to observe leaders at all levels, from each of the three Commanding Officers, the Department Heads, and several aircrew mission and plane commanders. The plethora of opportunities to observe leadership in action can't be overstated in active duty—real world squadron experiences where the primary function of the squadron was to remain prepared to fight a war against enemy combatant surface or subsurface vessels should we be called upon by our nation's leaders.

It was a sobering thought, wondering whether one day I would have to kill some poor b@$#*rds stuck in some metal tube below the surface of the ocean because of their leader's umbrage towards mine. This possible reality vexed my mind often when I participated in maritime patrol of Soviet submarines during my tenure at VP-8. Nevertheless, it was the experiences of observing human interactions and behaviors that fascinated me the most. How does one person in a position of authority inspire loyalty and dedication to duty when compared to another person? I had plenty of examples to observe and learn from during those 3 short years at VP-8.

My time at VP-8 and my tenure as a Naval Officer was about to end in December 1988. I decided during my preceding deployment that I didn't want to keep missing our newborn child's experiences. My wife recorded him on videotape, and we would get mail runs every 10 days on deployment, allowing me to watch our baby boy on the lounge TV in our living quarters. I yearned to be a part of his life and decided that a lifetime of service in the Navy wasn't for me. My instructor assignment back in Pensacola, Florida introduced me to several pilots who were eligible to discharge from the Navy and had applied to the airlines for employment. I still owed the Navy several more years at that time, and it hadn't occurred to me then that I would choose anything but a Naval career.

Becoming a father changed everything for me. After careful consideration and an Executive Officer who tried to persuade me to reconsider, I submitted my request for discharge. I began the process of applying to the airlines with the help of friends who made the transition 3 years earlier, and on December 15, 1988, I reported to my new employer.

The airline industry is fraught with large swings during economic cycles of booms and busts. During the tough times, layoffs and/or pay cuts are common. We experienced a few during my time as an airline employee. Pilot salaries are the largest payroll expense and company management always seeks concessions from pilot groups during downturns in the economy. The rhetoric between the pilot union's leaders and the company's management team with whom they would conduct negotiations, is a rich experience in human relations.

Much of the rhetoric is public and is a great opportunity to learn what drives or motivates people. In this case, it was all about money. It was clear that the personalities at the top of both management and the union were at play. When two strong personalities, each "wanting to be right" were involved, negotiations were always stalled. On the other hand, there was a time when our airline was in serious trouble and both management and the union were able to work together despite the demands for huge pay cuts and needed concessions. The point I want to drive home is that the different outcomes were shaped by the "human equation."

What exactly is the human equation and why is it important? The human equation as defined by Merriam-Webster is *"the factor of human strength or weakness that needs to be considered in predicting the outcome of any social, political, economic, or mechanical process operated by human agency."*[20] In every experience I discussed earlier, it was evident that the human equation played a vital role in outcomes. It didn't matter if it was a 1.5-hour sortie where I was the student pilot, or whether it was months of negotiations between union leaders and management, the human equation played a pivotal role in the success or failure of desired outcomes.

I mentioned earlier that I chose to leave the Navy because I had become a father. Three years later we had our second child. Raising children is a great teacher, not only about children, but about yourself as well. Several years later we decided to have two more children born a year apart. In total, we had four sons, each with a unique personality, different talents, and challenges as well. My role as a parent was to help prepare them for life as adults. I learned from each child about the nuances of the human equation and how it affected both my parenting skills (or lack of) and their individual personal growth. We read several parenting books and tried many techniques to help them learn what we believed were important principles. If we had to do it over again, we would certainly be better than we were, but I did have one major take-away during my experiences with my children, discipline.

The word discipline can have negative connotations, such as "*control gained by enforcing* obedience or order;" however, a definition I prefer is "*training that corrects, molds, or perfects the mental faculties* or moral character."

With that in mind, we would try to discipline our boys to help them eventually become men of strong moral character. The major take-away during all those years of instructing our boys was that negative emotions can have an unfavorable impact on that training, whether it was mine or theirs. For example, if, as a parent, I became frustrated at something they did, and if I allowed my frustration to become anger, the boys never learned, they were just simply afraid. I brought to my parenting skills everything I observed as a child, and it wasn't good. Fortunately, God had a way of teaching me to become a better parent and to learn how to bring love into the equation.

The Church made several videos that were instrumental in teaching good parenting skills. One such video showed a mother running down the sidewalk in house slippers trying to stop her 3-year-old from crossing a street corner. She was frantic and concerned for his safety. She scolded him and in a firm voice stated, "How many times have I told you not to go to the street corner!" His innocent reply was instructional, "Mom, what's a corner?" She was remorseful for the tone she used. Nothing is more instructional about the human equation than the lessons we learn from raising children. When my children were upset and emotional, no amount of discussion or discipline would prevail in teaching a principle. We had to wait for them to calm down. People by nature, and children especially, make decisions that are guided by self-interest. When a child has an emotional meltdown, it is usually because they don't get what they want: a treat, a toy, or something they feel they urgently need. Raising children helped me immensely understand the human equation.

I had a multitude of experiences as a pilot that taught me adults can have emotional meltdowns too. When an airline is running on time, the expectations of passengers are met. When on-time performance is impacted, some passengers can get emotionally ugly. It's simply a part of the human equation. There are several factors that impact on-time performance, some within the control of the airline, and other external factors beyond the airline's control. Most gate agents and flight attendants are not as knowledgeable about weather and the nuances of how it impacts our flights.

They are taught to simply state, "It's a weather delay." Pilots, on the other hand, not only understand the weather and its impact, but can mitigate the frustration passengers feel because they are still sitting at the gatehouse waiting to board a flight that is already 30 minutes or more late. A simple PA (Public Address) at our gate could solve many problems. I knew as a captain it would not only help our gate agents who had to interact with frustrated passengers, but it would help our flight attendants to have a better experience with those same passengers when the time did come to board for departure.

Because I viewed our passengers as my true source of income, I felt it was my duty to keep them informed, good or bad, but especially during situations that were out of the ordinary that negatively impacted them. PA's both in the gate house and on the plane became an important part of my arsenal in mitigating problems as well as to assuage many concerns our passengers might be having.

I learned the importance of informative and honest PA's when I was a copilot. The year was 1998 and I was approaching my 10th anniversary with the company. We were flying our last leg of the day from Atlanta to Palm Beach International (PBI) and had received an in-flight notification that we were going to have an additional leg added to our day. The captain was already feeling fatigued and wasn't sure he would be able to fly from PBI to the new destination in Hartford, CT (BDL), over two hours away. Due to our familiarity with Atlanta, better weather, and fresh aircrew on alert for standby, we persuaded crew scheduling to reroute us to

Atlanta instead. We knew it was the safer choice, considering it was already approaching midnight.

When we arrived at the gate in Palm Beach to take the passengers to Atlanta, I discovered the passengers had been waiting for more than 4 hours after their original plane had a mechanical problem. In the station manager's written report of the incident, when the passengers learned they would be making a stop in Atlanta before continuing to Hartford, many "became extremely irate." I had never experienced that level of palpable anger in my cumulative to date, 10 years of flying for the airline. I asked the agent for his microphone and felt compelled to give an explanation to the passengers about our situation, specifically our concern for safety due to the length of our duty day and impending fatigue. In the words of the agent from the report, the "copilot...stayed in the gate area and answered the many questions he was being asked. I had never seen this done in the past by a crewmember, and once the passengers realized their safety was an additional issue, they became calm. By taking the initiative Chris took to explain the further delay to our customers made a very uncomfortable situation into an understanding one." The gate agent thanked me.

I share that experience because it was a pivotal moment in my airline career that helped me learn to be a better captain. It's also important that I share the following tidbit of information, so that the reader will understand exactly who I am. In my mind I am just the "Average Joe" trying to get by in life, and by worldly standards, I am just an average Joe. However, I had learned by then that I should trust the impressions that God gives me. This was one of those times in my life that I had the compelling "inspiration" that I should make that PA. God impressed my mind to give the PA and the words simply flowed, primarily because they were the truth. It became a pivotal moment in my career, the importance of communicating to our passengers to mitigate problems and alleviate concerns. I give God the credit for my successes, especially the ones where I recognize His helping hand. I am constantly thankful and in awe of His unwavering help.

I had 20 more years in the airline industry, 16 as a captain, where I had the chance to observe and apply the principles of the human equation and hone my skills to mitigate problems. It seemed that rarely a week would go by without some incident that I was either learning a new skill or applying one to reduce passenger anxiety, help solve a problem or provide a positive experience above and beyond expectations. I viewed my role as a pilot as a cog of a much larger team of gate agents, ground agents and flight attendants who all shared the same goal. That goal was to provide our passengers with a uniquely positive experience of air transportation from A to B. Fortunately for me, during most of my tenure as a captain, our management shared that same goal. I treasure my years in that industry and am grateful for the multitude of experiences that taught me the importance of understanding "the human equation."

During most of those 30 years as an airline employee, I had a parallel life in another social setting, that of being a Latter-Day Saint. As previously mentioned, my wife and I joined The Church of Jesus Christ of Latter-Day Saints in November 1992. What many people do not know outside of The Church is that we are a type of "lay ministry." On a local level, the congregations are led by people who have jobs outside of The Church, within society at large. The local congregation has a variety of positions that help the unit function, both administratively and spiritually.

For example, we have Sunday School lessons that are taught to every age group ranging from adults, young adults, teenagers, and children. Additional positions within a local congregation include leaders of the different age groups, such as young women and young men leaders for teenagers and, of course, leaders of the entire congregation. The teenagers also have leadership roles within their own age brackets. All told, there are up to 50 or more positions that are filled by lay people, without pay or other compensation. While the main goal of The Church is to build and strengthen an individual in their spiritual journey, we are a group that "bears one another's burdens."

Latter-Day Saints study and apply the teachings of Jesus Christ. As we study Him, we want to emulate Him but sometimes life's challenges can derail people from that path. Life's challenges can be so overwhelming that they can be discouraging, and hopelessness often casts a large shadow over us. It is during these times of despair that other Saints might step forward and help bear the burden of their fellow Saint. We all need help from time to time and the phrase, "It takes a village" has great application within a community, whether it be a church congregation, or perhaps even a village. It has been my community of fellow Latter-Day Saints where I learned even more about "the human equation."

There have been a few occasions when I was on the receiving end of help from other Latter-Day Saints, and one incident almost always comes to the forefront of my mind. It was early on during our new journey as members of The Church when I had gotten in an argument with my wife. She left the house and went to seek solace from our friends who had introduced us to the Church. I felt extremely alone and had my own "pity-party." I hadn't had the chance to enjoy my pity-party very long before the doorbell rang, and a fellow church member stood at my door with some of his infamous home-baked bread. It was Bob's signature way of showing his friendship towards others and it immediately snapped me out of my funk. I was incredibly grateful to Bob and his kindness when I needed it most and we became good friends. I don't know if Bob realized he had received inspiration to do what he did at that time, but God was aware of me, and Bob's kind gesture was perfectly timed.

It became my mission to pay it forward, not just to Bob, but to any fellow member when I felt the impression to show kindness. The human equation is a force, that when understood, pays huge dividends in achieving positive outcomes and turning negative experiences into manageable ones, and my 30 years of Church experiences taught me many lessons about it.

One more example about the human equation comes to mind that I believe is worth sharing. One of my sons loved to play soccer. When he was young, I often coached his recreational team until he was about 12, as far as my expertise could take him. He continued to pursue the sport as he got older and managed to land a position on his high school team. Once, when they were about 9 or 10, if I recall correctly, the league's governing board attempted to shut down the screaming and yelling heard from the parents by instituting a "silent" day for all the games that were to be played throughout an entire Saturday of competitions. Coaches and parents agreed to the idea, and we came to that game day committed to honor that agreement. What ensued was simply astonishing and the lesson sank deep in my soul.

Our boys had been taught how to play the game of soccer, knew ball handling skills, understood teamwork, and how to set up plays. On this "silent" day, not one parent or coach could be heard on the sidelines screaming at the children on the field. It was B-E-A-utiful! What could be heard were the boys on the field communicating with one another and it was one of the most exciting games I had the privilege of watching in all my years of coaching. It was unfortunate that most of the parents and the league didn't walk away from that experience with the desire to have "silent" days during every competition, but for me and I'm certain others, it was a great lesson on the negative impact of yelling at our children, no matter how good our intentions might be.

Having our own compass guiding us, particularly when we've been trained or taught well, is often far better than a single person in authority (such as a parent or coach) telling each player what they should or should not be doing. This principle can translate from the soccer field to the field of life—as I can attest to as a pilot, both in the Navy and for the airlines. We were trained and taught how to conduct our missions.

We were given the responsibility to execute those missions, or in the case as an airline pilot, each flight. At no time did we have someone dictating how or what to do. We were given the authority to execute our responsibilities to either complete the Navy mission or execute our commercial flight. Any goal (whether a Navy mission, airline flight, or any objective) is best achieved when those tasked with the objective are given the authority to make all decisions relating to that objective. Let's explore this with an example most of us should be familiar with.

You are a young adult, early 20's, and your parents are coming to visit from out of town. You pick them up at the airport, in your car, and drive them to your new place, where you've been living for the last year. You haven't driven 10 yards from the pickup location before one of them points out the traffic that they think you do not see. Their "backseat" driving continues the entire 20 minutes enroute to your new place. A similar experience could be played out between husband and wife, or perhaps several friends in the car. If you've never had a "backseat" driver as a passenger, your time will come, but I'd wager a guess that probably every person who reads this has had this experience. Predictably, this is irritating to the driver, but why? Simply put, the person with the authority and responsibility of driving the car should be the one making the decisions, not the passengers. That includes the parents who, at one time, were the authority in their children's life, but not anymore. This is the human equation at work, in the most basic situation.

How does the human equation relate to government and politics, you might ask? Imagine you are now running a small business and you've been quite successful because you are honest, your customers respect you, and your product and/or service is something they desire. You've filled a demand in the market, life is good! One day a government bureaucrat comes to enforce a new law, one that negatively impacts your business, and he chooses to shut down your business until you can become "compliant." This story is played out often in our country.

The human equation, when understood, helps us recognize our failures as a nation when it comes to government intervention that is destroying the health of our nation, and I don't just mean economic health. Place yourselves in the shoes of the business owner previously cited and ask yourselves if the situation would induce significant emotional stress, particularly if they couldn't afford to be "compliant." When government leaders seek to single handedly impose what they believe are good intentions on an entire nation (or individual state) as was witnessed with our national response to COVID-19, the previous scenario was played out throughout the nation and devastated countless lives. The government's solution was, of course, to throw money at those whose lives they disrupted, creating another entirely new problem, inflation.

The human equation must be understood if we are going to heal our nation and move from an angry dysfunctional polarized society to one where we are able to respect one another and try harder to live in harmony. It begins with recognizing that we are each responsible for our own well-being, a role that has been taken on by the government. Predictably, if you give a man a fish, he will have his hand out for another, but if you teach him to fish, he will be equipped to feed himself for life.

Chapter 14

SAFETY FIRST: A LESSON FROM THE AIRLINES

January 2019 was a busy month for me, but also one that changed the course of my life. I had my semiannual FAA medical exam scheduled, my church assignment was keeping me busy, a trip to Atlanta with my wife to visit the grandchildren and their parents was planned, and I had my usual work schedule with the airline. As part of the semiannual FAA medical exam with my AME (Aviation Medical Examiner), the FAA required me to submit a status report on my OSA, or Obstructive Sleep Apnea. This status report was only required once a year, so prior to my FAA medical exam, I would schedule an extra visit to my sleep doctor asking her to write up an assessment of my treatment's efficacy to forward to my AME.

Twenty-one-years prior, in 1998, I had transitioned to wide body flying as a copilot based in Atlanta. Many of our four-day trips ended with a final leg flying from the west coast to Atlanta on what we termed an "all-nighter." This "all-nighter" trip began with daytime flying and on the third day we would finish before noon somewhere west of Denver, inclusive. We would have the mandatory 12 hours of rest at the company provided hotel and the departure would leave somewhere around midnight local time, give, or take an hour, only to arrive in Atlanta between 5am and 6am.

This routine (three dayshifts followed by backside of the clock flying) eventually wore on my body and over the next several years I discovered I was tired more often than I wanted to be. I sought medical help and that was when I discovered I had Obstructive Sleep Apnea.

The FAA permits pilots to fly with OSA, but they carefully monitor your status and the efficacy of the treatments. Annual reports, once they determine your treatment mitigates sleepiness, are required. It became a way of life for me, regular Maintenance Wakefulness Tests (MWT's) ordered by the FAA, along with new sleep studies to assess and or tweak my therapy. The typically prescribed therapy is a CPAP machine during sleep. CPAP machines utilize a prescribed amount of air pressure forced through a tube affixed to a mask you wear over your nose or nose and mouth. Any patient who uses CPAP therapy will tell you it is exceedingly difficult to get used to wearing something over your face while you sleep.

To make matters worse, if the mask and headgear are too tight, it is uncomfortable; too loose and it leaks air which will wake you up. It's difficult to get used to, but effective if all the parameters are just right. Once, while travelling on vacation with my CPAP in tow, a friendly TSA agent began to expound the virtues of getting surgery (he too had OSA and had empathy for my plight: the confiscation of my CPAP machine to "test" it for bomb residue). The idea of never having to lug that machine through airport security both for work or leisure travel was too appealing and I opted for the UPPP surgery in 2007.

UPPP is the acronym for Uvulopalatopharyngoplasty. It had a two-to-three-week recovery period that was quite uncomfortable. Nevertheless, it succeeded in mitigating my OSA and its symptoms for several years. After those years of CPAP-free sleep, my symptoms resurfaced, and I had to return to CPAP therapy which I continue to this day. In January 2019 during the consultation with my sleep doctor, we agreed that another Polysomnogram (sleep study) would be beneficial as it appeared that the subjective "Epworth Sleep

Assessment" showed worsening symptoms. She also decided to run a follow-on Multiple Sleep Latency Test (MSLT) the next day, the standard test for narcolepsy. The results were forwarded to my AME who informed me that I had narcolepsy, which abruptly ended my aviation career.

Safety is always the paramount concern in aviation and my diagnosis of narcolepsy left no alternative for the FAA but to deny my medical permission to fly. I completed more MSLT's and tried different therapies, but narcolepsy is incurable. Drugs are the only treatments to mitigate symptoms and their use is not authorized by the FAA to fly. Thirty years as an airline pilot was a good run, and I can't complain. I enjoyed the entire experience and all the lessons learned. One lesson worth expounding upon is this very topic—safety—for which my career abruptly ended.

Safety is the overarching theme when it comes to commercial aviation. Military operations might have the overarching theme of completing the mission, particularly in times of war, but in commercial aviation it is always safety. Every flight, every procedure, every decision during abnormal or emergency events required us to prioritize safety if there were two competing objectives. One example I previously mentioned can be found in the chapter, "Aviate, Navigate, Communicate" regarding the burnt-out landing gear indicator light. The safest choice for the single piloted aircraft was to execute a missed approach if you recall, to fly up to a higher altitude and greater airspeed before troubleshooting the problem.

There are countless examples of how pilots prioritize safety when it comes to commercial aviation, but I will share just a few. Let's begin our first example by examining jet fuel. Jet fuel is a kerosene-based fuel used by the airline industry with different properties than the gas we use in our cars. A maxim in the industry is "fuel is life."

If you run out of fuel, and it has happened, you better hope you are good at gliding and that there is a runway in range—or in the case of Sully, a smooth strip of water. (Note: Captain "Sully" Sullenberger lost both engines due to a flock of birds destroying his engines and not a loss of fuel, but the end result was the same, the jet became a glider.) Because fuel is life, you need to ensure you have adequate fuel, but if you carry too much, it becomes excess weight, which reduces efficiency, in other words, you'll burn more fuel to carry more fuel, which increases your unit cost per mile. When planning a flight, you only want to carry enough fuel to get to your destination, plus a reserve amount. If the weather is forecast to be below a certain threshold at your destination, you will need to have enough fuel to fly to an alternate destination (with better weather) should the need arise. Therefore, monitoring your fuel burn and status throughout every flight is paramount to safety. Another safety concern for pilots is turbulence.

When I fly as a passenger with my wife, she often clutches my hand for security when we encounter turbulence. Turbulence occurs when air is disrupted, and the disruption can occur from a variety of meteorological events. That's why it is important for pilots to understand weather phenomenon and why meteorology is studied in flight school. Because weather conditions are foremost in a pilot's mind, it is also why you will often hear a pilot expound over the PA about weather conditions either enroute, or at the destination. Turbulence, sometimes, is unavoidable, but in many instances, it can be mitigated. Turbulence causes anxiety among passengers, and sometimes it has been known to cause severe injury to flight attendants.

I remember once flying with a flight attendant who had recovered from a severe injury caused by turbulence. She was forthcoming with that information for fear that it could easily happen again. I assured her that I always did my best to mitigate turbulence by staying abreast of pilot reports ahead of my aircraft to avoid flying into areas of known turbulence or I would ensure crew and passengers were seated if it was unavoidable.

Often, at cruising altitudes, turbulence is associated with the jet stream or particularly when crossing through the edge of the jet stream. Jet streams can be advantageous while flying transcontinental from west to east, but detrimental when flying east to west. Winter jet streams can be as high as 200 knots (knot = nautical mile per hour[21]), making a flight from the west coast to the east coast take as little as 4 hours, if the flight takes advantage of the jet stream. Conversely, if the flight cannot avoid the jet stream flying from New York to Los Angeles, it will take several hours longer. The jet stream can be your friend, but crossing into it often causes turbulence. Safety is paramount for our passengers and flight attendant crew, so it is always necessary to be aware of turbulence, whether it is associated with the jet stream or other phenomena.

Safety is always the number one priority when pilots are engaged in their work, both before, when flight planning, and during the flight. Due to the nature of the business of flying and the speed at which events can unfold, pilots will review all their flight data before beginning a flight, including the topics of fuel and weather as previously mentioned. Both the captain and first officer will review all the aspects of the flight to ensure "no stone is left unturned" so that they are both as familiar as possible with all the aspects of the flight. Unfortunately, the industry has had mishaps and accidents and it is always the goal to learn from those events to improve safety as much as possible. One example comes to mind that occurred about 3 years before I was hired.[22]

In 1985, an accident occurred because of a weather phenomenon, not at cruising altitude, but near the ground. This weather phenomenon was a "microburst," a significant downward burst of air that occurs when a thunderstorm can no longer suspend the core of precipitation

Figure 25: https://www.ntsb.gov/investigations/AccidentReports/Reports/AAR8605.pdf, pg 32

in the thunderstorm. The sudden downward core of air that hits the ground is usually short in duration and small in diameter, and it has nowhere to go but spread out (see Figure 25).

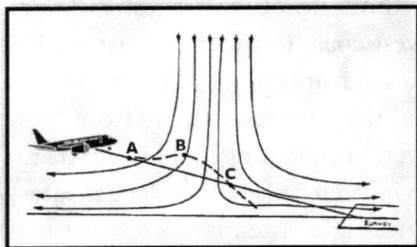

Figure 26: Aircraft on
approach thru windshear

The accident I am referring to occurred during an approach into Dallas/Ft Worth Airport (DFW), where thunderstorms are common. As a plane flies into the microburst with the air being forced towards the front of the aircraft, they will experience a sudden increase in airspeed and lift (see Figure 26 "A"), which will cause the aircraft to get above ("B") the designated glide path aligned with the landing threshold of the runway. The natural reaction for a pilot would be to reduce thrust to reduce airspeed and pitch the nose down to capture the glidepath ("C"). As the aircraft moves into position "C" the wind is shifting to behind the aircraft, reducing the airspeed further and causing a loss of lift. This reduced airspeed and loss of lift is concurrent with the pilot's compensation of nose down pitch and thrust reduction (between "B" and "C").

If the pilots are not aware of what is happening due to the microburst, they may have trouble flying safely out of the situation, which is what occurred during this accident in 1985 at DFW when the plane impacted the ground well short of the runway. Of the 163 passengers and crew, only 29 survived the accident.[23] This accident, like all other accidents in aviation history, precipitated changes that made the industry safer for the future. Of the many changes incorporated to prevent a similar accident, an onboard system to detect windshear was developed and all commercial aircraft now have them. Additionally, pilots receive routine simulator training to help them recognize and fly out of windshear situations that are caused by microbursts or other severe weather phenomenon.

Safety is always the number one priority in the airline industry and something every pilot is cognizant of and something that cannot be overemphasized. When operational procedures, such as aviation regulations, economy of flight, or perhaps passenger comfort challenge safety, safety trumps those guidelines or procedures. For example, if a pilot declares an emergency, all aviation rules may be suspended in the interest of safely getting the aircraft on the ground and the passengers evacuated. Air traffic controllers will clear the airspace of other air traffic to allow an emergency aircraft unfettered access to the airport of its choice and runway of choice.

How does the priority of safety translate to the office of President you might ask? There are absolutely some things that should always take precedence when fulfilling the office of President. Just as safety in aviation is the supreme governing objective, the overarching rule that should always take precedence in executing the office of president is the supreme law of the land, The Constitution. When governing, or when suggesting laws, or even when signing bills into law, the president should always determine if the law passes the litmus test— is it Constitutional.

If a law doesn't pass the Constitutional test, it is unlawful. I would argue that the Framers would suggest a great many laws of the land are adulterated and unconstitutional. I believe many constitutional scholars would also agree. We will discuss in further detail the need to return to constitutional principles in a later chapter, but suffice it to say, a good president understands the importance of prioritizing the Constitution while governing. After all, it is the "supreme" law of the land.

Chapter 15

GOVERNMENT 101 FOR DUMMIES

I love the colorful yellow and black *For Dummies* books and I have had several in the series. I enjoy the format, easy to read material and how it is presented in a non-intimidating way for the average person. I chose this chapter title to convey in a non-intimidating way, what I believe are essential characteristics of good government. We will explore various ideas, visit historical examples, good and bad, and discover together what are the principles of good government.

Let's begin with Merriam-Webster's definition of government: "*the body of persons that constitutes the governing authority of a political unit or organization.*"[24] "Political unit" can be summed up as the society living within a geographical boundary. An "organization" can be a smaller unit of society such as your Homeowner's Association, your Parent-Teacher Organization, or your employee union. Each of these organizations has a group of people that govern the organization.

We elect these governing groups, at least here in the US. We have governing bodies of persons for "political units" such as city councils, county commissioners, state legislatures and governors, and of course the US government, each governing a successively larger group of society. There are political units that govern across national borders as well, but we won't explore those in this book. Our goal is to understand what constitutes good government principles so we may evaluate our own country's government and make any necessary corrections.

Let's explore a hypothetical story. Our story begins with two families that have become stranded on a remote island. Each family has a mother and father and one daughter and one son, just to make things even. Neither family knew each other before becoming stranded.

We need to make a few assumptions to begin with, 1) they are civil to one another, 2) they have an innate desire to live and survive and hence they follow the same "family" unit pattern they are familiar with (children marry and become a new family) a mother and father, and 3) the island is rich in resources: an abundant supply of food, fresh water, and everything necessary to provide shelter. Because each family is civil, and there is an abundance of resources, they do not need to compete with one another to survive. Assuming birth control isn't available, families are expected to be larger, much like they were two centuries ago averaging seven to eight children.[25]

If each daughter marries a son from the opposite family, the next generation of two families would have conservatively 6 children each for a total of 12. The third generation of 6 families would have a conservative total of 36 children, enough to have 18 families. The fourth generation of 18 families would conservatively have 6 children each, or a total of 108, and when paired together, would produce half that or 54 families.

The formula would look something like this $F=(\frac{C}{2})^{(g-2)} * 2$. F is the number of families, g equals the number of generations from the first generation, and C equals the average number of children per family.

We divide C by two because it takes 2 children to produce one family and we subtract two from g because the first two generations didn't have 6 children each but only two and we multiply by two for that reason, we began with 2 families at generations one and two. Using our formula, we would expect the 4th generation to have 18 families.

$$F=(\tfrac{6}{2})^{(4-2)} * 2$$
$$F= (3)^2 * 2$$
$$F= 9 * 2$$
$$F= 18$$

The fifth generation should have 54 families and a grand total of 6 x 54, or 324 children. Let's check our formula.

$$F=(\tfrac{6}{2})^{(5-2)} * 2$$
$$F= 3^3 * 2$$
$$F= 27 * 2$$
$$F= 54.$$

When we multiply the number of families by 6, we have total children, when we multiply families by 2, we have total adults, thus the total population, "P," would be (F x 2) +(F x 6), or 2F + 6F, or 8F. In other words, the total population would be 8 times the number of families.

The formula for population would become $P=8[(\tfrac{C}{2})^{(g-2)} * 2]$.

Plugging into our equation the two variables of C and g, representing the number of children for each family and the number of generations away from the very first two families, we can see that our population would conservatively increase to nearly one million just 10 generations from the original two families.

$$P=8[(\tfrac{6}{2})^{(12-2)} * 2]$$
$$P=8[3^{10} *2]$$
$$P=8[59,049 * 2]$$
$$P=944,784$$

If we add one more generation and increase the number of children to seven instead of six for each family, the population would be greater than 15 million! If the first two families had more children, let's say two more each, then these figures would be twice as high.

The population of the United States in 1776 was estimated at under 3 million. I realize there are other factors that affect population, but for the purpose of this hypothetical story, it is necessary to see that **eventually, the population would exceed the available resources on the island.**

Let us return to our hypothetical story with just the two families on the deserted island and recognize that as each generation passes and as population grows, the society will recognize there is a finite supply of some of those rich resources and demand will eventually catch up to supply. How will this growing society deal with this and other problems that will occur and remain civil?

I hope we can recognize that as the population increases, disputes and disagreements will occur over resources and boundaries among other things, and there will be a need to mitigate those disputes; otherwise, the society will degenerate into disorder and mayhem. Wisdom dictates that a growing society will establish compacts before disputes ever arise. For example, the first two families might agree to a compact that one half of the island will be occupied by one family and the other half to the other family. Trade between the two families might be necessary to exchange resources that might not be available to one or the other family. As each generation increases in population, the island would likewise be subdivided in equal portions.

As areas on the island increase in population, more compacts would be necessary to mitigate disputes. Governments grow out of the need to enforce compacts. At first, a government could simply be a judge who reviews the compact and ensures both or all parties honor those agreements (picture Moses after the Israelites began their 40-year wandering journey). The judge would need to be wise, impartial, and trustworthy if all parties are to accept him or her in that position. Perhaps the judge would be authorized by all parties to enforce the compact and mete any punishment affixed to a party that breaches the terms of the compact. **The key point is that to avoid disorder, societies institute governments.**

Governments should be chosen by the parties they govern.
Today we have elections for that purpose. Representatives should
represent the concerns of their constituents. Lastly, the compacts,
or agreements that the society is willing to abide by should originate
from the people at large, not the government. This fundamental
principle, that governments are by the people and for the people,
was recognized by the Framers of the Constitution. Even though the
Framers drafted the Constitution, they still sent it to the people for
their ratification. The people accepted that document, albeit there
were serious reservations which were mitigated by the inclusion of
the Bill of Rights—the first Ten Amendments.

Author W. Cleon Skousen, in his landmark book, *The Making of
America, The Substance and Meaning of the Constitution*, explains the
difference between anarchy, where there is no law, and the opposite
end of the spectrum, "Ruler's Law." He diagrams[26] the difference
which you can see in Figure 27.

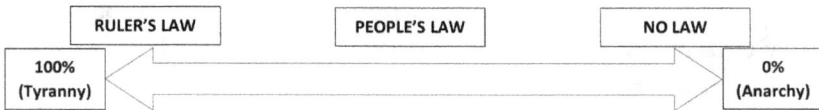

RULER'S LAW	PEOPLE'S LAW	NO LAW
100% (Tyranny)		0% (Anarchy)

Figure 27: People's Law

He further defines Ruler's Law as, "a form of government which
allows total authority and power to rest with the central government.
The ruler or ruling group makes the law, interprets the law, and
enforces the law."[27] "Ruler's Law comes under different names,"
ranging from monarchy to aristocracy and oligarchy to dictatorship.[28]
"This was [James] Madison's definition of tyranny."[29] Madison said,
"The accumulation of all powers, legislative, executive, and judiciary,
in the same hands, whether of one, a few, or many, and whether
hereditary, self-appointed, or elective, may justly be pronounced the
very definition of tyranny."[30]

As Skousen suggests and the Founders sought to achieve, the key to good government is the right balance between too much government and too little, or as Skousen describes it, "People's Law." As governments move away from the proper balance towards Ruler's Law, the effect is always more legislation, more bureaus to enforce or administer those regulations, more taxes, and more oppression. Good government recognizes there is a proper middle between too much government and too little. How do we determine what good government is when it comes to evaluating our present systems? I contend that it is easier to determine than you might think by asking one fundamental question. Do the people have adequate influence in the government process? Let's explore this fundamental question.

When determining if any system of government is functioning properly, the very first question we need to ask is, "Do we have a choice who governs?" If the answer is no, we've moved away from "People's Law" towards tyranny. If one *believes* the answer is no, then again, we may be moving toward tyranny. We know we have elections for that very purpose, to choose who governs, but if we believe, as many citizens do, that their vote doesn't really matter (on a national scale) then the result is the same. They choose not to vote and only those who vote are electing candidates that represent their interests, not the population at large.

We then have government representatives who are more biased or at least skewed to represent only the interests of those who elected them to office. What about those who choose not to vote and why do they believe their vote doesn't matter? There are various reasons that affect voter turnout, such as lack of interest,[31] alienation, and voter fatigue.[32] These reasons can be summed up as voter apathy. I contend that voter apathy can be attributed to two underlying factors, 1) constituent to representative ratio, and 2) function. Let's explore each.

You are invited to your neighborhood party planning meeting. The neighborhood has 50 households, and each household sends one representative to the planning meeting. The party is for the 4th of July celebration, which will involve a cookout, games or other activities and fireworks (if approved by local ordinances). In the neighborhood are children of all ages, young adults, many parents in their thirties and forties and some empty nesters. The household reps are of different ages and different ethnicities. The goal is to plan an event that is affordable, fun, and builds harmony. Positions are chosen from among the participants to help the meeting succeed, including a secretary and presiding authority. During the meeting all 50 participants may chime in to provide ideas and concerns. At the end of the meeting, activities and a budget are voted upon.

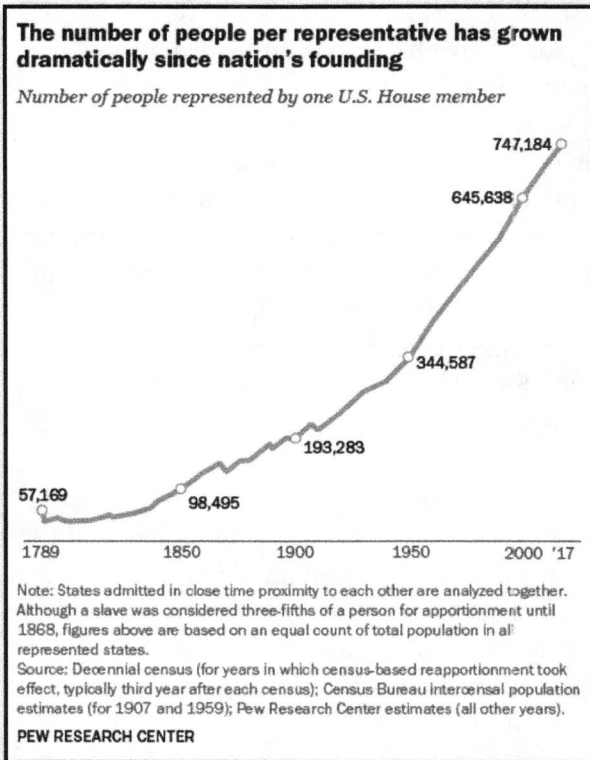

The number of people per representative has grown dramatically since nation's founding

Number of people represented by one U.S. House member

747,184

645,638

344,587

193,283

57,169

98,495

| 1789 | 1850 | 1900 | 1950 | 2000 '17 |

Note: States admitted in close time proximity to each other are analyzed together. Although a slave was considered three-fifths of a person for apportionment until 1868, figures above are based on an equal count of total population in all represented states.
Source: Decennial census (for years in which census-based reapportionment took effect, typically third year after each census); Census Bureau intercensal population estimates (for 1907 and 1959); Pew Research Center estimates (all other years).

PEW RESEARCH CENTER

Figure 28: Constituents per House member

The question we need to ask is, do you think our voice in this 50-person meeting can have an impact? Now, imagine, we are in a meeting of 35,000 people. Does our voice have the same impact? What about a meeting of 700,000? These last two figures are the approximate historical values of the number of citizens to each U.S. House of Representative in 1793 and 2020, respectively. Figure 28 shows the growth of the number of people each U.S. House member represents according to a 2018 Pew Research Center article.[33]

Is it any wonder why people are increasingly apathetic when it comes to elections? Is it even possible that the "people's" representatives (House members) can know the will of more than 700,000 constituents? If a U.S. House member were to work 12-hour days, 365 days a year to give his or her undivided attention for one hour to each constituent to hear their concerns, it would require 159 years to do so. Is it even possible that House members truly represent the concerns or needs of even a fraction of those constituents? To put it another way, when we take our example from the party planning committee, our voice represents 2% of those in the meeting. As a constituent trying to influence our elected members of the House, our voice represents 0.000134%. This huge ratio, the number of citizens each member of Congress represents is, in my opinion, the primary reason for voter apathy. A close second underlying reason for voter apathy is function.

Returning to our example of the 4th of July party planning committee, let's explore function a little further. The function of the party is to build community harmony through a fun and affordable activity. Unless you are a recluse or had other plans, it is safe to say most residents would want to participate in the activity and nearly as many would participate in the meeting, particularly if it required an assessment (think tax) from each household to fund the activity. Why would most residents choose to participate, either in the planning meeting or the event? The function, or event in this case, is something of interest to most, if not all the residents.

Now, let's examine some of the agenda items in the House of Representatives which can be found at: https://www.house.gov/legislative-activity.

I selected 9 events from a total of 33 events over the course of 2 ½ days from their June 2022 calendar.

- *Hearing: On the January 6th Investigation*
- *Business Meeting: H.R. 7666 Restoring Hope for Mental Health and Well-Being Act of 2022; H.R. 5585 Advanced Research Projects Agency Health Act; H.R. 4176 LGBTQI Data Inclusion Act*
- *Hearing: Tackling Toxic Workplaces: Examining the NFLs Handling of Workplace Misconduct at the Washington Commanders*
- *Hearing: Investigating the Nature of Matter Energy Space and Time*
- *Markup: H.R. 7900 - National Defense Authorization Act for Fiscal Year 2023*
- *Hearing: A Growing Threat: How Disinformation Damages American Democracy*
- *Markup: Fiscal Year 2023 Commerce Justice Science and Related Agencies Appropriations Bill*
- *Hearing: "Congress Technology: Modernizing the Innovation Cycle"*
- *Hearing: SBA Management Review: Office of Government Contracting and Business Development*

Do you have any interest in any of the above agenda items? The point is, the function of much of the work done in Congress these days is of little concern to many Americans. **To make matters worse, I believe that much of the work that Congress tackles should be of no concern to them either.** Why should Congress need to *"Investigate the Nature of Matter, Energy, Space and Time?"* Why should that national body of representatives concern themselves over the *"NFL's Handling of Workplace Misconduct at the Washington Commanders?"* Seriously?

Aren't we adult enough that we can allow the parties involved to work through the issues, and if not, take it to a lower court to determine if laws or other workplace rules were violated? Not only does Congress usurp the authority of lower jurisdictions, but they have the arrogance to believe they should! They are completely out of touch with the real world, something that term limits would quickly solve. Sorry, but I've digressed. The number two cause of voter apathy is that the function of government is of little interest to many of our citizens. Perhaps, if we were to reduce the scope of what Washington DC is responsible for, then voters might have a greater interest in what is going on and whom they should elect. Oh, right, we already have a document that limits the scope and function of our federal government, and it's called the Constitution. We will explore this topic in a later chapter.

Although we do choose our House representatives through elections, the concerns of constituents have been diluted over time by the House member/constituent ratio and increased usurpation of government power. Try this simple experiment by writing to your congressperson and see if you don't get a canned response that sounds something like this, *"I appreciate your concern. Thank you for writing. We will look into it."* Do the people have adequate influence in the government process? I believe the answer is a resounding, No! In other words, as author Skousen suggests, we are moving away from "People's Law" towards tyranny. I wholeheartedly agree.

The government should be "right sized" in relation to the population and the role it plays. In other words, the larger the society, the fewer responsibilities the government should have. The responsibilities should be commensurate with the interests that are common to that sector of society. For example, the national government should be concerned with sovereignty issues that affect the nation at large, such as maintaining border integrity, national defense and international trade. Another function of the national government should be to protect individual rights. Liberty is fundamental to a free, prosperous, and happy society.

Monetary policy, because it affects the entire nation, should also be under the purview of the national government. If we scale down our society, perhaps to a local community, its government should also be "right sized," and the responsibilities should be commensurate with the interests of that sector of society. For example, a local community may be concerned with adequate education for their children or recreational facilities. The community may be concerned about after-hour noise, vandalism, or perhaps rising crime. The local government should address issues that are of concern to their community or sector of society.

The principle that a government should be "right sized" cannot be overemphasized. We touched on the reason when we explored voter apathy. The citizens ought to have an adequate voice in the process of their government and the functions it performs. It's my contention that our national government is no longer satisfactorily influenced by the citizens of this nation but by other interests. While we could author an entire book on what those other interests are and the impact they are having, we will save that for another time. Somehow, we've moved from a national government that once understood its role and limited function to one that infringes on individual rights, has become an entity without restraint, and will move rapidly towards tyranny if we don't course correct soon.

When the Founders created the Constitution, their goal was to create a national government that was strong enough to handle the needs of the nation but limited in scope to prevent the very abuses they experienced from Great Britain. That's why they specified in the Constitution the function of the national government and its powers. The function, or powers delineated in the Constitution were limited and defined. James Madison had this to say about it.

> "*The powers delegated by the proposed Constitution to the federal government, are few and defined. Those which are to remain in the State governments are numerous and indefinite.*"[34]

165

Returning to Skousen's work, we can see an expansion of his earlier diagram (Figure 27) with the inclusion of government powers as seen in Figure 29 below[35]. The shape of the pyramid represents what I consider "good government." The further away from the people, the smaller the government should be, namely its authority and responsibilities. The governments in the hierarchy should also be accountable to the lower government and not vice versa; otherwise, the powers of lower governments will be usurped, as we've seen in our country this past century. I will expound on this principle in greater detail in a later chapter, "Restoring Constitutional Principles."

In summary, good governments must be accountable to the people.

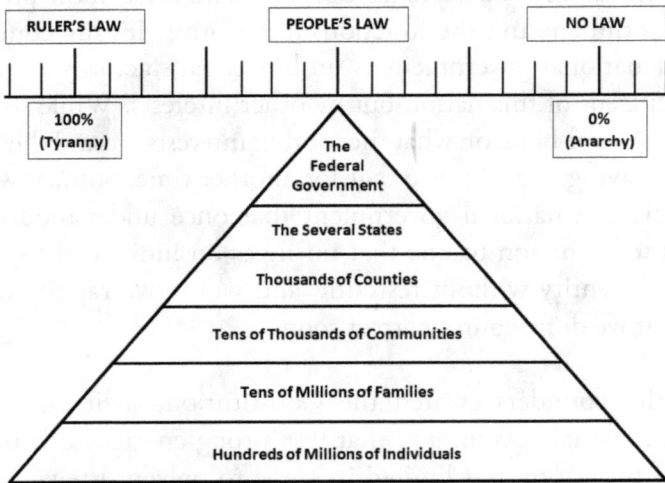

RULER'S LAW	PEOPLE'S LAW	NO LAW
100% (Tyranny)		0% (Anarchy)

The Federal Government

The Several States

Thousands of Counties

Tens of Thousands of Communities

Tens of Millions of Families

Hundreds of Millions of Individuals

Figure 29: Government Pyramid-from W. Cleon Skousen, "The Making of America"

Chapter 16

GOOD, BETTER, BEST

In October 2007, a leader in our church gave a profound talk titled, "Good, Better, Best."[36] The occasion was a semi-annual Church conference broadcast from the Church Conference Center dedicated in 2000 by then Church President, Gordon B. Hinckley. The 21,000-seat auditorium was filled with people five times over the two-day conference to listen to Church leaders.[37] The conference addresses are also broadcast over a Church satellite system to areas throughout the country and the world. Remote locations throughout the world will receive recordings to view the conference addresses at a later date.

With the advent of the internet, people can view the broadcasts on YouTube and the Church's streaming channel. As a member, I find many of the talks immensely helpful and the talk on this subject stuck in my mind.

I won't regurgitate the talk, nor hit on any of the fine points Elder Dallin H. Oaks made but will point out that it had an influence on others as well. Other Church leaders have referred to the theme when sharing their insights. The title of the talk appropriately encompasses the principle Elder Oaks was teaching, and that is, we can fill our lives with good things but possibly miss the boat on what is better, or best. For church members, he also gave examples of what might be a better use of our time or resources, even though we might be using our time to do "good" things. I haven't memorized the talk, I only remembered the title because of the principle it taught me.

From the time I first heard the talk and having reviewed it on occasion, the principal lesson he taught has stuck, mostly because the title says it all and is easy to remember. When faced with decisions in my life, I often remember those words: good, better, best. As a person who believes whole heartedly in God, and the mission of Jesus Christ, and the idea of living beyond the grave with the familial relationships we enjoy here on the earth, the concept of good, better, best may have an entirely different application in my life than it might for others. I hope I can adequately convey my thoughts.

Let me begin with my relationship with my wife. As in most marriages, we start off with high hopes and a strong commitment to make the marriage a success. However, we each come to the relationship with our own ideas about finances, budgets, raising children, forms of entertainment, vacations, where to live, etc. and sometimes those ideas will not agree with our spouse's. How do we navigate through those differences? Because of our spiritual beliefs (the doctrine that our marriage extends beyond the grave), my wife and I will work together to find a solution to any differences we may have on any subject. If we can't agree, we will table it, and ponder over it individually. Our guiding principle was, and always is, to try and keep peace and harmony in our relationship.

The idea of keeping harmony would be an example of the "best" solution to any problem or disagreement in our marriage. Sometimes things have a way of working out and by tabling a problem, the solution might become clearer later. The advantage of having God in our relationship, which I touched on in Chapter 11, is that He often helps us see more clearly the solution, but His influence cannot be felt when we experience highly charged emotions that often accompany two people who don't see eye to eye. Placing my wife's emotional wellbeing at the top of any disagreement was an important lesson

I CANNOT COME DOWN

for me to learn, a lesson reinforced by the talk of "Good, Better, Best." The same principle of seeking harmony in a relationship is applicable with extended family members, friends, and coworkers and has served me well.

In the New Testament, Jesus taught:

> *And thou shalt love the Lord thy God with all thy heart, and with all thy soul, and with all thy mind, and with all thy strength: this is the first commandment.*
>
> *And the second is like, namely this, Thou shalt love thy neighbor as thyself. There is none other commandment greater than these. (Mark 12:30-31)*

This second commandment, if applied throughout the world, would solve any and every problem we face. We would be anxiously engaged in working through our differences, trying for resolutions (the "Best" solution) that all parties could accept. Unfortunately, we are all individuals with weaknesses, biases, and selfish natures from time to time. It is practically impossible to "love our neighbors as thyself" when we each come to the table with our own shortcomings, or perhaps we judge others' shortcomings without a full comprehension of their extenuating circumstances.

I once served as a counselor to our bishop in our congregation. The bishop is the ecclesiastical leader of the congregation. He had assigned me the duty to assist the Primary organization of our congregation. The Primary organization is the organization that provides instruction and learning to the children of the congregation from ages 18 months to 11-year-olds and is led by a presidency of three women in the congregation. The Primary president was concerned about one of her teachers that wasn't showing up to church occasionally and the president (or one of her two counselors) would have to scramble to find a substitute and it was frustrating to the president. She asked me to "do something about it."

I arranged a meeting with the teacher. My first inclination was to ask the teacher why she couldn't simply give forewarning if she wouldn't be able to teach that Sunday. I received a spiritual prompting to just listen to her, and so I did. That was a great teaching moment for me. This good woman who was missing her teaching assignments was incredibly stressed and experiencing overwhelming problems in her life. After hearing her concerns, we were able to work towards a solution that would help solve the problem. My take-away was simply to "get understanding." Having empathy and listening to gain understanding is a "Best" solution for many conflicts.

Applying the counsel given by Elder Oaks by seeking "Best" practices extends beyond finding solutions to problems or conflicts. Seeking "best" practices can have applications in every aspect of our lives. For example, one of our sons enjoys running and staying fit. He has run several marathons and wanted to run the famous Boston Marathon. To qualify for running in the Boston Marathon, he needed to run a certified marathon elsewhere in under 3 hours. To meet the qualifying time, he researched and then executed over the course of six months what he considered the "best" training curriculum necessary to prepare himself to run under the qualifying limit. He succeeded in his goal.

Applying "Best" practices is a principle that parallels other principles we've already discussed in previous chapters, namely "Aviate, Navigate, Communicate" and "Safety First." These guiding principles have taught me that we need to focus on certain priorities first and foremost. Sometimes, after we solve the important problem, other less challenging issues vanish.

In our next chapter, _**we will explore an issue that affects every individual, every household, every family, every business, every sector of society not only in the United States, but throughout the world.**_ We are talking about money. Buckle your seatbelts, because, while this topic affects everyone, few people understand what I consider to be "THE MOST IMPORTANT" subject of this book and the need to understand it and fix it. It will be the "Best" and wisest use of our energy to fix it, but before we do, we need to understand how we got here and how destructive it truly is.

Chapter 17

MONEY DOESN'T GROW ON TREES

Figure 30: Money Tree

Growing up in the '60s and '70s seems like a world away. Nothing in society remotely resembles the period in which my peers and I grew up. One common idiom, however, has survived the decades and still exists today. It originated before I was born and was something my father would say when he wanted to emphasize the importance of hard work.

"You know son, money doesn't grow on trees. I have to work for everything we have." He was right, he had to work for his money. What if you didn't need to work for money? What if it did grow on trees? You might be surprised to discover that the absurdity of money growing on trees isn't far from the truth. In this chapter, we will explore money creation.

When my father was stationed in Jacksonville, Florida, he was thinking of leaving his career in the Navy. He went to an interview in Orlando for a job that would offer a huge pay raise and was excited about the prospect of earning $40,000 a year. At the time, I didn't know much about salaries, but the excitement in our household was unmistakable. The year was 1972 and he had served in the Navy for about 13 years advancing to the rank of Lieutenant Commander, or O-4. Finding his pay wasn't hard to do, thanks to the internet. Military Pay Scales can be found at https://veteran.com/historical-military-pay-rates/.

An O-4 gets paid the same, no matter which branch of service. There was monthly base pay at $1,176.30; basic allowance for quarters with dependents at $215.40; basic allowance for subsistence, $47.88; and aviation pay for crew (often called aviation hazard pay), $215.00.[38] The gross income my father received for his family of 6 was $1,654.58 per month. That is equivalent to $10.34 per hour for a 40-hour work week. Yet, in 1972, my father comfortably supported his family on an annual gross salary of $ 19,854.96. No wonder he was excited about doubling his income!

What has happened since 1972, where $20k could support a family of 6, but would be well below today's poverty level of $37,190 for a family of 6 as defined by the US Government's Department of Health and Human Services?[39] If you don't know the answer to that question, this chapter is for you.

We've all heard of inflation, but what is it really? In the previous chapter's conclusion, I emphasized that in this chapter we will talk about money because it affects every individual, every household, every family, every business, and every sector of society not only in the United States, but throughout the world. We need to understand it and we need to understand why my father's salary in 1972 is below today's poverty level. This chapter is THE MOST IMPORTANT subject of this book. If you don't read anything else, you need to read, and reread this chapter until you understand it.

Why is money worth less today than when I was growing up in the 70's? Did you know that money was worth less in my youth than when my father was born in 1935? We term this loss of purchasing power as "inflation." Millennials and Gen Zs are now experiencing real inflation for the first time. But the problem isn't President Biden, the problem is systemic and has been going on for more than a century.

Let's look at a few examples of "inflation" from the time when my grandfather was a young man.[40] They say a picture is worth a thousand words, so I plotted data found on ThePeopleHistory.com that illustrates the "inflation" trend.

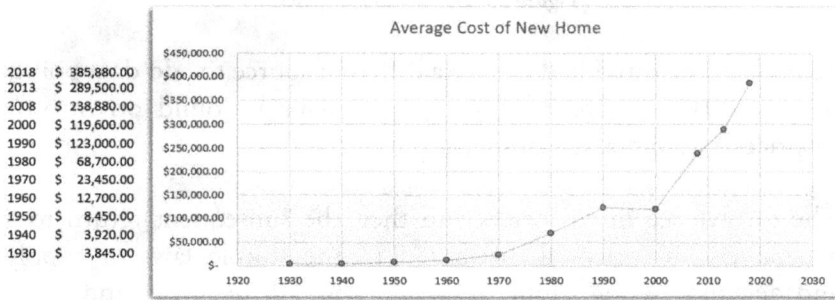

Year	Cost
2018	$ 385,880.00
2013	$ 289,500.00
2008	$ 238,880.00
2000	$ 119,600.00
1990	$ 123,000.00
1980	$ 68,700.00
1970	$ 23,450.00
1960	$ 12,700.00
1950	$ 8,450.00
1940	$ 3,920.00
1930	$ 3,845.00

Average Cost of New Home

Figure 31: History of Home prices

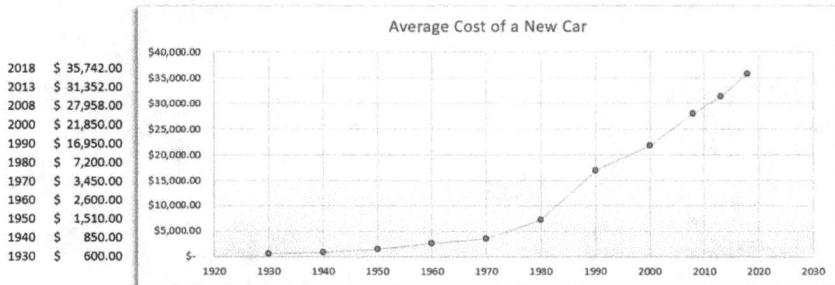

Year	Cost
2018	$ 35,742.00
2013	$ 31,352.00
2008	$ 27,958.00
2000	$ 21,850.00
1990	$ 16,950.00
1980	$ 7,200.00
1970	$ 3,450.00
1960	$ 2,600.00
1950	$ 1,510.00
1940	$ 850.00
1930	$ 600.00

Average Cost of a New Car

Figure 32: History of Car prices

One more example of inflation seems appropriate to illustrate: gas prices (Figure 33). Note that the data illustrates a drop in gas prices from 2013 to 2018. Since I hadn't plotted recent gas prices, we might wonder why we see the reversal in the upward trend.

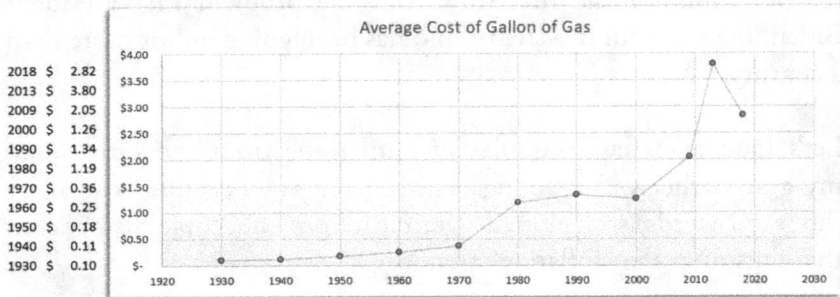

2018	$	2.82
2013	$	3.80
2009	$	2.05
2000	$	1.26
1990	$	1.34
1980	$	1.19
1970	$	0.36
1960	$	0.25
1950	$	0.18
1940	$	0.11
1930	$	0.10

Figure 33: History of Gas prices

To explain the dip, I had to find a different source to add data points beyond 2018. Figure 34 adds current data as found on https://gasprices.aaa.com and https://eia.gov.

The dip we see in gas prices and then the subsequent return to a general rise in prices is attributed to the simple laws of supply and demand. When supply increases, the cost decreases and when demand drops, so does the cost. Both forces were in play between 2013 and 2022.

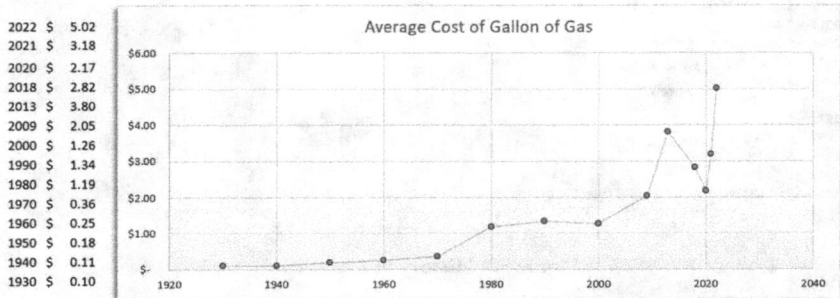

2022	$	5.02
2021	$	3.18
2020	$	2.17
2018	$	2.82
2013	$	3.80
2009	$	2.05
2000	$	1.26
1990	$	1.34
1980	$	1.19
1970	$	0.36
1960	$	0.25
1950	$	0.18
1940	$	0.11
1930	$	0.10

Figure 34: History of Gas prices (#2)

The steady increase of US crude oil supply more than doubled from 2011 to 2019 from just over 2 billion barrels of crude in 2011 to 4.48 billion barrels by 2019 thus significantly increasing supply and lowering the price.[41] When Covid hit and the economy was shut down, demand for travel (both work & leisure) plummeted, driving down the price even further in 2020.[42] We were traveling the country in our RV at the time and the average price of gas was around $2.00. One location in Texas was charging $1.55 (Figure 35). As

Figure 35: $1.55 per gallon

we came out of Covid restrictions, demand for gas increased, driving prices back up to previous levels, resuming the upward trend.

So, what is the systemic problem that caused the general rise in prices over time? **I hope to adequately explain the cause, why it has been systemic over the last century, how it affects every person, how it unfairly impacts certain sectors of our society, and the importance of changing it.**

Inflation is not understood by many Americans, and the truth is obfuscated. To prevent the average American from understanding inflation, it has been redefined as, *"the rate of increase in prices over a given period of time. Inflation is typically a broad measure, such as the overall increase in prices or the increase in the cost of living in a country."*[43] The truth is that **the steady long-term rise in prices is a consequence** of the true meaning of inflation. In other words, rising prices are caused by something else. Rising prices are caused by the "inflation" of the money supply. To "inflate" means to expand, or swell, thus the root cause of rising prices is the steady, chronic expansion of the supply of money, making each unit of currency less valuable. Even the U.S. Bureau of Labor Statistics (BLS) recognizes this in their definition of inflation:

> *"Inflation has been defined as a process of continuously rising prices,* **or equivalently, of a continuously falling value of money**. *"*[44]

In 1914, just months after the Federal Reserve Act was passed, the total money supply of the national banks and the state banks that would soon join the Federal Reserve System was $1.83 billion.[45] As of August 2022, the money stock was $21.7 trillion[46], a 1,185,692% increase in barely a century. The history of money is a fascinating story and entire books tackle the subject, but to understand the chronic problem of "inflation" as currently defined, we need a brief history lesson on money.

Figure 36: Gold bullion

Money, for the purpose of this discussion, will be defined as "anything which is accepted as a medium of exchange."[47] At the end of World War II, cigarettes were used as money in Germany because the German mark had become useless, and barter was common.[48] This type of money is referred to as **commodity money**.

Gold is also commodity money and has stood the test of time as an excellent choice for money because it has intrinsic value, is divisible, and fungible (*interchangeable; one part or quantity may be replaced by another equal part or quantity such as a pound of rice, or a bushel of wheat*). When not debased by governments or kingdoms, gold served to maintain price stability. Price stability translates to a healthy and stable economy.

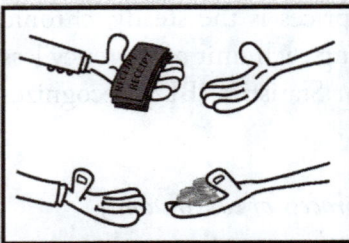

Figure 37: Receipt money

Receipt money is paper money that in the past was given in exchange by goldsmiths to store one's precious metal coins for a fee. The owner of the coins could withdraw their coins from the goldsmiths at any time by presenting the receipt.

Eventually, the owner could endorse his receipt to a third party who then could present the receipt to make the withdrawal. These endorsed receipts were the forerunners of today's checks.[49]

Fiat money is the final evolution of money into a form which we will later see is the cause of most of our economic troubles. The US dollar, along with most other major global currencies, is a fiat currency. Fiat money is defined as currency that is made legal tender by government decree (fiat) and is

Figure 38: Copyright: RomanR/ stock/adobe.com

not redeemable or backed by a commodity such as gold or silver.[50]

__The advantage governments have, by using fiat money, is that they can create as much as they need for their purposes.__ Let's dive into this last statement for a better understanding of the benefits of fiat money.

Let's suppose that "Carter the Counterfeiter" has a printing press in his basement from which he can create as many $20 bills that look, feel, and could pass for those issued by the US Treasury Department's Bureau of Engraving and Printing to his heart's content. Suppose Carter did business in his small town of 100 residents and used his newly "created" money to purchase all the goods and services he desired. Because Carter will be the first person to use this newly created money, he will be able to purchase whatever he desires and at whatever price he chooses.

In other words, *__those who can create money have the benefit of spending it to purchase whatever and however much they desire__*. *Prior to Carter's spending spree*, each merchant provided as much as their labor could produce and the free market set the price. For example, if one of the merchants was "Tim the Tailor" and he could only produce 50 suits (or dresses) a year, then on average, the residents would only be able to purchase a new suit or dress once every two years. Additionally, Tim the Tailor would set the price for the merchandise that he felt was reasonable and would sell the suits and dresses as fast as he could make them. If priced too high, then fewer people would buy, if priced too low, Tim couldn't keep up with demand. The free market set the price for Tim's labor. Each merchant would be similarly faced with the same forces that set the price of their goods or services, whether they were a farmer, carpenter, barber, or whatever.

Supposing Carter doesn't want to "wait his turn" for a new suit but wants to purchase five new suits at once because he has created the money to do so. Because Tim the Tailor had his suits priced "just right" and was selling them as fast as he could make them, he had no extra in his inventory. Carter tells Tim he will pay him extra to sell Carter the next five suits made. Perhaps Tim the Tailor works longer days or hires someone to assist him. If he chooses this course, more labor is required. On the other hand, maybe Tim chooses not to work harder, but bids up his selling price because Carter wants (or demands) the next five suits and is willing to pay beforehand as a show of good faith. Because Carter has created this extra money (albeit it's counterfeit), the price will get bid higher because that is the only variable that is available that will satisfy both the seller and buyer.

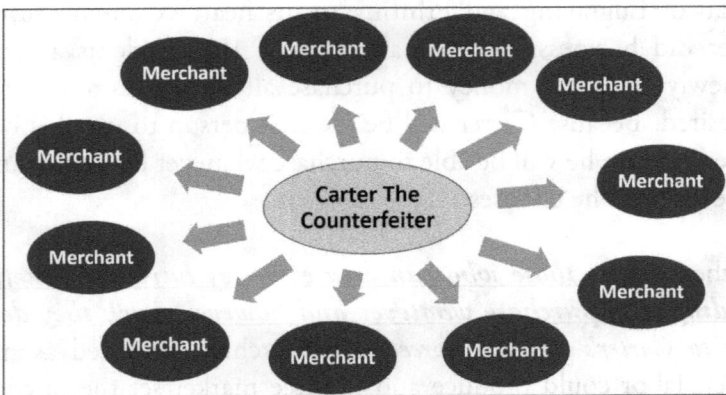

Figure 39: Carter the Counterfeiter

Imagine now that this same pattern is repeated with every merchant Carter does business with. They will either work harder to provide the goods or services Carter is willing to buy, or they will accept higher prices because they don't want to work harder. If the town is limited in its labor force (i.e., they have no more people to hire to increase production), they would of necessity have only two choices: work harder or accept higher prices. **Humans, by nature, take the path of least resistance and will not work harder if they can receive more pay for the same effort. Why should they?** Eventually, all the merchants (other residents) will be richer by the amount Carter was willing to pay higher prices. They will also be able to purchase more goods and services than before Carter went on his spending spree, until we reach an equilibrium in the market.

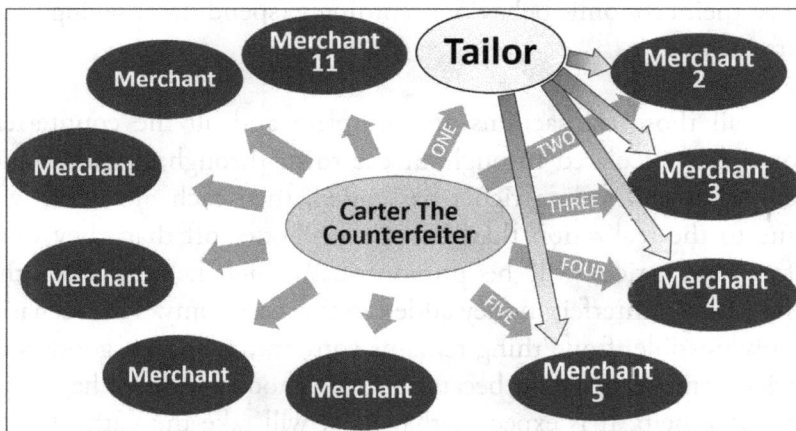

Figure 40: Tim the Tailor benefits first

Tim the Tailor, who received Carter's payments first, would have the benefit of extra income to purchase goods or services from all the other merchants at their previous prices. Suppose Carter spent his ill-gotten money in the order seen in Figure 40 beginning with the tailor and then progressing clockwise from Merchant 2 to Merchant 3, to Merchant 4 and so on, continuing until he negotiated with the last, Merchant 11. A secondary dynamic would occur. Because Tim the Tailor would be richer first, he would have the privilege of spending his extra income before all other merchants. He too could negotiate higher prices, or purchase more goods, but on a smaller scale than Carter could.

Tim the Tailor would have more purchasing power than other merchants but not as much as Carter. Suppose Tim went to each merchant in the same order as Carter to spend his extra income. Each merchant would be somewhat suspicious of a second customer with the ability to pay higher prices. As this plays out again and again, followed by Merchant 2, then Merchant 3, and so on, all merchants will soon realize they can not only raise prices, but keep them higher. Rising prices will continue until the market settles down and prices stabilize. Price stability will occur only after Carter the Counterfeiter completes his spending spree and all other citizens adjust their economic behavior accordingly (spending or saving their extra income).

Once all those transactions are complete and all the counterfeit money has circulated throughout the town through all hands and the euphoria of feeling richer has ended, then each merchant will come to the realization that they are no better off than they were before, but prices will be proportionally higher, relative to the amount of counterfeit money added to their economy. This scenario is only possible if one thing remains constant, supply of goods and services remains constant because no one chooses to work harder or hire more help. It is expected that most will take the path of least resistance, raising prices, because the extra money circulating in their town permitted them the opportunity to do so.

If we examine this phenomenon in classic supply and demand curves, we can see it in visual terms. Let us begin with the graph of our society where the X-axis represents the total supply of money in circulation before Carter begins his spending spree. It is a fixed amount, or constant, thus the supply of money = M.

Supply = M

Quantity of Money

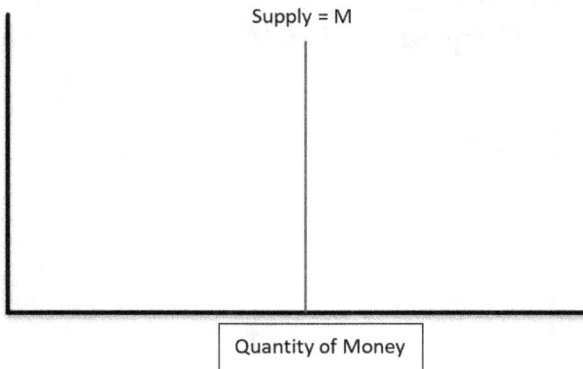

Figure 41: Money supply equals M

If prices are low, then the purchasing power of money is higher. To understand this, let's take a basket of items: a gallon of gas, a loaf of bread, a gallon of milk, and a pound of cheese. If we assign prices to each item (I pulled up prices from a well-known grocery store as of this writing) it may look something like this:

1 gallon of gas = $4.20
1 loaf of bread = $3.34
1 gallon of milk = $3.58
1 lb. of cheese = $3.88

Then, $15.00 would buy a gallon of gas, a loaf of bread, a gallon of milk and a pound of cheese. Let us cut prices in half for each item such that:

1 gallon of gas = $2.10
1 loaf of bread = $1.67
1 gallon of milk = $1.79
1 lb. of cheese = $1.94

Then, $15 would purchase twice as many goods. Therefore, the purchasing power of money (PPM) was doubled when prices were halved, thus PPM is the inverse of prices, and can be written as, $PPM = 1/p$ where P represents prices. We will place PPM on the Y-axis.

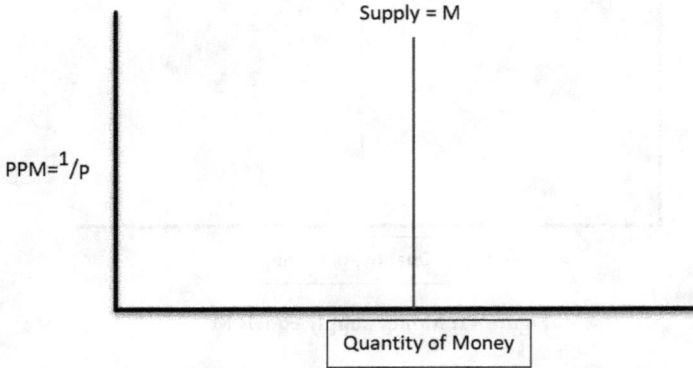

Figure 42: Purchasing power of Money is inverse of prices

The demand for money is related to prices. If overall prices are higher (meaning that PPM is lower), then the demand for money in our daily/weekly/monthly transactions would necessitate we carry a higher amount of cash balances (Higher Quantity of Money, or to the right on the X-axis), or Point A. If prices are lower overall (higher PPM), then the demand for money that we carry in our cash balances would be lower (to the left on the X-Axis), Point B. Thus, we can draw a "demand for money" curve 'D' on a diagram that would look like the following.

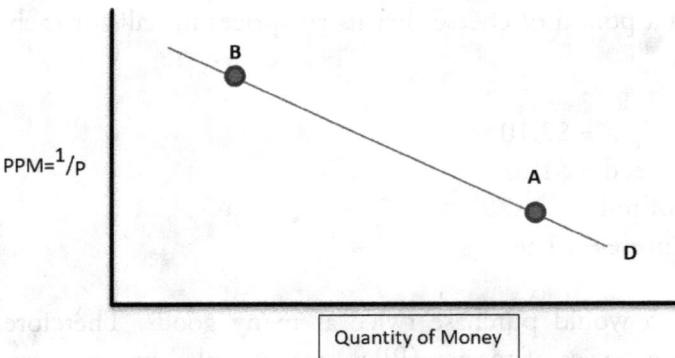

Figure 43: Demand curve for Money

Because there is a fixed supply of money 'M' in this fictional town (before Carter goes on his spending spree) we discover that when we overlay the supply of money, there will be an equilibrium for overall prices and purchasing power of money = PPM^A

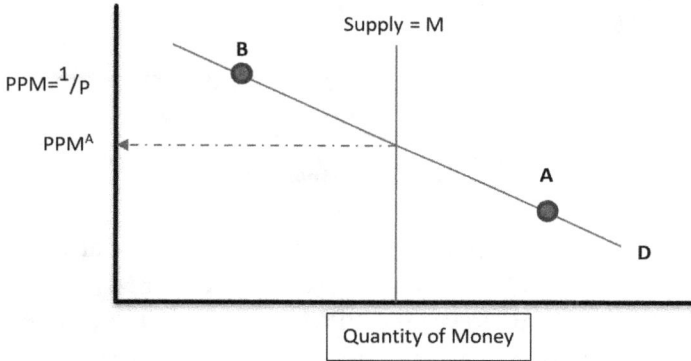

Figure 44: PPM^A at money supply, M

If you have followed along thus far, let's see what happens when we increase the supply of money. When we return to our fictional town where Carter the Counterfeiter has finished his spending spree after printing more counterfeit money, we now have an increase in the supply of aggregate money circulating in their town, which we will label M^2.

After a period when all individuals adjust their spending accordingly, the town will reach an equilibrium at the new PPM^B. As you can see, the PPM^B is less than the PPM^A.

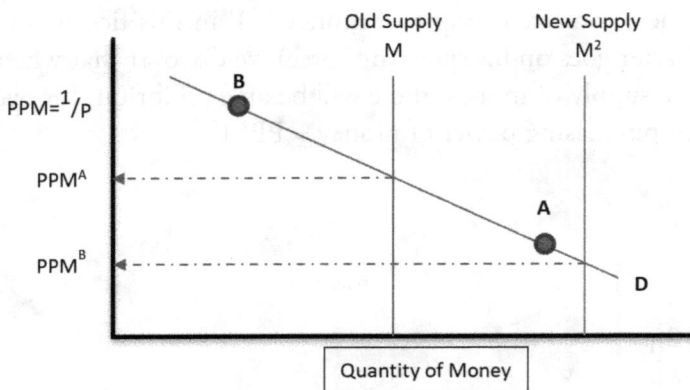

Figure 45: PPM^B at new money supply M^2

In other words, the purchasing power of money is less at M^2 than it was at M. Since the PPM is the inverse of prices (PPM = $^1/_p$ where P equals prices) then the lower the PPM, the higher the prices. Thus, we can see from basic economic graphs that an increase in the total supply of money will lead to an increase in prices. Let us return to our story of Carter the Counterfeiter and discover another anomaly that happens when money is added to the total supply.

It is important to understand that the first big spender, Carter, received the benefit of his ill-gotten money before all others. Yet each merchant whom he did business with, *in the order in which he did business with them*, also benefited. From the time they spent their extra income (before others could spend their extra income), they benefited from lower prices.

Each successive recipient of Carter's counterfeit money would benefit to some degree over others after them, provided they spent their extra income. However, as each successive merchant spends their extra income, subsequent merchants will begin to raise prices. The last merchant, the one who has yet to receive any extra business from Carter or others, will be unsuspecting of the events and of course will be the last to raise prices and the biggest loser in this inflationary economic cycle. In the real economy, the people who get their hands on the money last will be those who aren't skilled laborers. It will be the work force that we typically label as minimum wage earners. They will be the biggest losers.

In other words, _**as the extra money circulates in the economy, it benefits proportionally to those in the order in which it was spent**_. This is termed the "Cantillon Effect."[51]

This sample community where Carter the Counterfeiter increased the money supply is akin to the first step in money creation in the real economy. **It is important to fully grasp the concept that any increase in the aggregate money supply will drive prices up in the economy.** This is only true when the increased money supply is "spent" or passed into the economy. If it is saved, it isn't added to the economy. Money saved is withdrawn from the economy.

Some people might save the extra income for a rainy day, but it will add to the total supply of money circulating in the community in the future. Consequently, if they chose to save money, they will have lost purchasing power because prices will be higher in the future. **Savers are punished by rising prices. Retirees are also especially hurt!** So far, we see that inflation hurts those on limited income (people on the bottom of the pay scale such as unskilled labor and minimum wage earners) and retirees who must live off their life's savings.

Let us suppose that in our community of 100 residents that when Carter the Counterfeiter spent his counterfeit money, each merchant placed an advertisement in the neighboring town (which had high unemployment) to hire the needed help to meet the demand Carter placed on each merchant for their goods or services. Instead of negotiating higher prices, let us assume each merchant stepped-up production by adding those new workers to their business.

The new workers might migrate to the town and hire the carpenter and other craftsmen to build them a new home. They will purchase more goods from the farmer, and others, until such time as the economic activity settles down into an equilibrium state. This would be an entirely different scenario than described earlier where each merchant accepted Carter's offer of higher prices. The truth is, every merchant will respond differently to Carter's spending spree and ___in the real world, there will be increased production/supply as well as rising prices.___ This type of economic growth we label as a "boom" cycle.

Just as the increase in prices in our sample community was caused by an increase in the supply of money, in like manner, a reduction in prices will occur when the supply of money is contracted. As we learned from the previous paragraph, an increase in the supply of money had a two-fold effect, an increase in prices and an increase in productivity, including lowering unemployment. Conversely, a contraction of the money supply will slow economic activity, increase unemployment, and force prices lower. We often refer to a downturn in an economic cycle as a "bust."

As I am drafting this book, the Federal Reserve is implementing policies that are designed to decrease the money supply in circulation. The effect will be just as described—a slowing of the economy because they are attempting to arrest the "inflation" we experienced in 2022. The bottom of this "bust" cycle (also known as a recession) is yet to be seen. There are many factors at play, but the Federal Reserve's playbook has already forced our economy into a recession.

The symbiotic relationship between the US government and the Federal Reserve, as well as the commercial banks under the umbrella of the Federal Reserve System, affects the economy just as Carter

Figure 46: Shell game

the Counterfeiter did. When the government goes on a spending spree, they cannot simply raise taxes because the people would revolt and vote them out of office. So most, but not all, programs of the government are funded through a process between the Central Bank (Federal Reserve) and the government. It is like a shell game, so pay close attention!

The process begins when the government spends more than they take in tax revenues. We call this deficit spending. As I mentioned, raising taxes is political suicide; therefore, deficit spending is the preferred method by our illustrious federal government representatives and is funded by selling US treasury securities, or "treasuries" for short. Treasuries come in a variety of different packages. They can be sold to financial institutions, such as your commercial bank, or to individuals like you and me. With the advent of the internet and electronic banking, you can buy treasuries directly from the US Treasury at https://www.treasurydirect.gov after creating an account.

Figure 47: Series EE Savings Bond

Prior to electronic banking, treasuries were issued on paper, but today they can be purchased either electronically or on paper. My grandmother would purchase treasuries to give as gifts for significant events, such as my high school graduation, or for my children when they were born.

The most common forms of treasuries available to both institutional investors and individuals are:[52]

Treasury bills: securities with maturities ranging from a few days to 52 weeks.
Treasury notes: securities with maturities of 2, 3, 5, 7, and 10 years and pay interest every 6 months.
Treasury bonds: pay interest every 6 months and mature in 20 years or 30 years.

There are several more types of treasuries available to the public. Banks and other financial institutions can purchase treasuries. The Federal Reserve can buy and sell treasuries from the open market, but not directly from the US government, except for about a year during World War I (Oct 1917-Oct 1918, 1926-1927), and off and on from 1942 to 1979.[53] Treasuries can be redeemed at maturity or sold prior to maturity. Treasuries are backed by nothing but the public's confidence in the US government.[54] Presently, as of this writing, the Federal debt (outstanding treasuries) held by the public is almost $31 trillion ($30,751,828,000,000 to be exact on Aug 24, 2022. The Treasury publishes daily numbers[55]).

It's not important to know which treasuries are available, just understand that they are IOUs, and the government gets the use of money without having to tax you directly by selling treasuries to investors. However, these IOUs continue to add up and the federal government has a growing debt. In Figure 48, we see the Federal government's debt from 1792 through 2027 (projected estimates beyond Fiscal Year 2023). The US debt is the "base" money from which all the money in the system is "created." Prior to the Federal Reserve System, precious metals formed the base money and the only way to increase the supply was to mine the ores, which requires human labor. After the Federal Reserve was created, there was one significant event that completely severed gold as base money and has been termed, "The Nixon Shock."

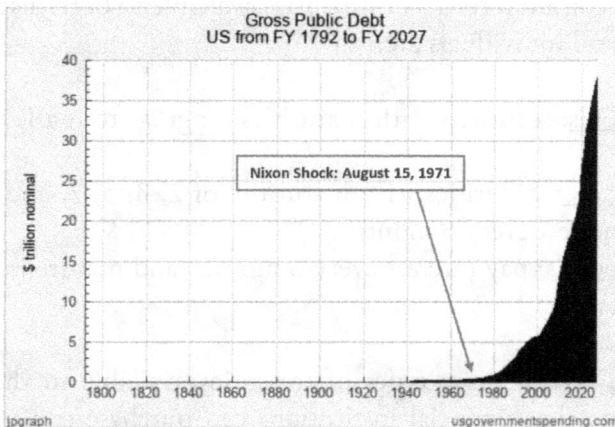

Figure 48: US government debt, 1792 to present

From that time forward, our money has been pure fiat. **Fiat currency can be inflated without any constraints**. It is a virtual printing press. As we explore this topic further, we will understand the factors that have driven the average price of a home from $3,845 in 1930 to $468,000 in 2022, a 12,000% increase in barely a century.[56] **This phenomenon of chronic inflation was made possible by none other than Uncle Sam, foisted on an unsuspecting public beginning with the passage of the Federal Reserve Act in 1913.**

> "*The US Treasury* [Uncle Sam] *issues trillions and trillions of dollars' worth of Treasury securities but does not appear to have a plan to repay any of it*" and the number of outstanding treasuries "*continues to grow at an accelerating pace.*"[57]

When the treasuries are sold it can have an inflationary effect. That is the first step in "money creation" we will explore. When the Federal Reserve purchases treasuries, it has an even greater inflationary effect, which we will explore later. Let's examine this first step in "money creation."

If several investors purchase, let's say, $1 billion in 20-year treasury bonds, the government immediately spends that $1 billion. It gets pumped into the economy to meet the deficit spending of the US government. If the investors had not purchased the treasuries, they would have either invested elsewhere, or simply saved the money. Money saved is money not in circulation.

However, because our currency is fiat, *and the supply continues to be inflated* (thus decreasing its purchasing power), **individuals eventually learn their "savings" need to outpace "inflation." They will look for ways to "invest" their money to outpace the rising cost of living.** Individuals who do not understand the chronic inflation problem simply save their money in the bank, where it loses purchasing power over time. Thus, we have "investors" and "savers," those who understand chronic inflation and those who don't. There are several types of investment opportunities, but let's look at an example we are all familiar with, Apple.

Suppose you chose to invest your savings in Apple by purchasing stock through a brokerage account. Apple might use this capital to grow Apple's production of iPhones that are in high demand (increased production translates to more jobs), and you could receive dividends (payments) on those stocks you invested in. Thus, money invested in the real economy (**capital**) helps grow the economy (including more jobs and lower unemployment). However, government spending usually does not go towards any increase in productivity in the real economy. Case in point, for the Covid-19 pandemic, the US government spent to date, $3.91 Trillion[58] (as of Aug 2022). Except for healthcare workers, much of the Covid relief went towards people and businesses that were negatively impacted by the pandemic, or worse, they were forced, due to government mandates, to close or restrict their businesses. In other words, the government began adding $3.91 Trillion to our nation's money supply while much of the real economy was shut down.

As the country (and the world) emerged out of Covid and the economy began to open, ***those trillions of dollars were added to the pre-pandemic levels of money, driving up prices***. Our response to Covid was an extreme example, and often the government doesn't resort to such measures unless there are crises such as the Great Financial Crisis of 2007-2008 or World Wars. Thus, deficit spending by the federal government can and often does have an inflationary effect. If, however, the economy is steadily humming along and the government chooses not to interfere with some boondoggle program (or finance wars), then the government's sales of treasuries have a minimal impact, if any, on inflation.

The federal government maintains its banking account with the central bank, The Federal Reserve (Fed). The Federal Reserve plays a significant role in the manipulation of the money supply. But before discussing the Federal Reserve, we need to understand banking.

The first concept in banking we need to understand is "**fractional reserve**" banking. I will illustrate it with another story—a night of poker. Let us assume that 5 friends get together on a Friday night to gamble by playing several games of poker. The owner of the house, Bill, just so

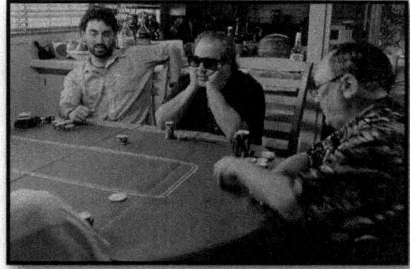

Figure 49: Poker night

happens to have poker chips in his game closet, to provide the aura of a Las Vegas experience. Each participant must exchange their money for poker chips. Assuming each player comes to the activity with $1000 in cash, the teller, Bill, exchanges the sum of $5000 to be warehoused for safe keeping in a wall safe for an appropriate amount of poker chips to each player.

Three distinctive styles of chips represent denominations of $10, $20, and $50, respectively. At the conclusion of the night's event, Bill exchanges each player's chips from their winnings (or losses) for the appropriate currency that was warehoused in the wall safe. The $5000 would be returned to the players as each chip gets exchanged for its equivalent value in cash and returned to Bill's game closet. After the settlement is complete, all chips have been returned to the game closet and the total of $5000 has been returned to the players.

Now, let us imagine that the following Friday, the same scenario is played out. $5000 in cash is safely stored in Bill's safe and the equivalent value of poker chips are used to enjoy a night of poker amongst the same 5 friends. Midway through the night, Bill's cousin, Bruce, interrupts the game and asks Bill if he can borrow $1000. Bill doesn't have any extra cash, so he reaches into the safe and takes his $1000 in cash from the warehoused currency to help his desperate cousin. The players commend Bill for his generosity and return to play.

This isn't Bill's lucky night; he loses every game, and they call it a night. At the settlement, Bill is short $1000 in cash and cannot pay the other players. The biggest winner of the night, Jack, holds onto the chips representing the $1000 until such time as Bill can pay him back.

The purpose of this story is to help the reader understand that deposits cannot be lent or borrowed without the consent of the depositors. The poker chips represented the cash in the safe and no matter how altruistic Bill's intentions were with his cousin, he couldn't lend any of it unless he first exchanged $1000 worth of chips before withdrawing the cash from the safe.

Fortunately for Jack, he was aware of the problem and held on to his chips representing $1000. If he hadn't, the chips representing $5000 would only be worth $4000 of cash in the safe. They would be worth a "fraction" ($^4/_5$ of their original value) of what they were worth before Bill lent his cousin the $1000. If you understand this paragraph, then you are well on your way to understanding "fractional reserve" banking.

Unfortunately, banks operate in a similar manner, lending deposits without depositors full understanding. We think our money is sitting in the bank and we can withdraw our deposits at any time, but it doesn't work that way. The process by which banks lend deposits is not understood by most of the population and it is the major reason we have a central bank and chronic inflation.

Let us begin by examining the banking practices of the 19th century by returning to our fictional town that had 100 residents, including our tailor and other merchants, only this time, we don't have "Carter the Counterfeiter," we have "Bob the Banker." Bob promises the residents that he will hold their deposits of silver or gold coins, or "**specie**" (which had been proven throughout time as an excellent form of money) in his big fancy vault and in exchange, gives them receipts, or paper notes that represent the specie in the vault (not unlike our poker friends receiving chips for their money held in the wall safe). In the course of time, our fictional town uses the receipt money in lieu of the specie they previously used that are now stored in Bob the Banker's big fancy vault.

Rarely is there a need to withdraw any silver or gold coins because the paper receipts are easier to carry and have been _trustworthy_ replacements as the medium of exchange that the residents now use as money. Bob recognizes that the coins are sitting safely in his vault and few customers come to redeem their receipts for their gold, so the temptation to profit from this "idle" money overcomes Bob. He will soon become a "counterfeiter."

Bob the Banker learns that Fred the Farmer wants to purchase 20 acres from his neighbor because he wants to add new crops to his growing farm. Bob sees this as an opportunity to make some money. Bob lends Fred $5000 worth of gold coins stored in his safe, coins that were deposited and belonged to other residents. Fred immediately returns the specie to Bob to safely store in his vault in exchange for "new" paper receipts, identical in appearance to those already in circulation.

Bob wants in return 10% interest for the borrowed money. Bob the Banker has just added $5000 in paper receipts to the aggregate supply of paper receipts without adding a corresponding $5000 worth of gold coins to his vault. Bob has just created $5000 worth of receipt money and like Carter the Counterfeiter, it was created illegitimately. Others hear about Bob's loan capacity, and they too reach out for assistance. Bob continues to issue similar loans to other merchants so that they too can expand their business and each loan he issues adds to the receipt money already in circulation. These loans of receipt money are used to purchase goods or services in our fictional town and circulate in their economy.

Just as Carter the Counterfeiter added money to the town which caused rising prices, so too has Bob the Banker added receipt money to the aggregate supply of receipt money. *If enough loans are made, the increase in the aggregate supply of receipt money will cause prices to rise.* This is a key point to understand, that ***the money supply in the form of receipt money has increased and*** if all other factors in the economy remain the same, ***it will cause prices to rise,*** just as it did with our story of Carter the Counterfeiter!

The receipt money no longer represents the amount of gold and silver coins in Bob's vault. Let us suppose that before Bob became a lender, the sum of receipt money represented $100,000 worth of gold and silver coins. Now suppose that Bob the Banker lent $50,000 worth of receipt money, thus adding $50,000 worth of receipts to the already circulating $100,000 receipts, now totaling $150,000 in receipts. Each $1 paper receipt no longer represents 1 silver dollar coin but is now worth $2/_3$ of a coin.

Divide both sides by 150,000 → 100,000 (dollar) coin(s) for 150,000 receipt(s)

And you get-----------------------→ $\dfrac{100{,}000}{150{,}000}$ (dollar) coin(s) for $\dfrac{150{,}000}{150{,}000}$ receipt(s)

2/3 coin(s) for 1 receipt(s)

Figure 50: One receipt is worth only 2/3 of a coin

Each receipt is now worth a fraction ($2/_3$) of its face value. The receipts became what is called *fractional money,* and the process by which they were created is called *fractional-reserve banking.*[59] This poses another problem in addition to rising prices.

As the prices rise, some of the citizens might become suspicious of the value of their receipt money and decide to exchange it back for the gold and/or silver coins they deposited with Bob the Banker. As word gets out, others might follow suit and withdraw their gold or silver coins. Once $100,000 worth of receipts are exchanged for gold or silver coins, Bob's vaults will become empty and the holders of the remaining $50,000 worth of receipts will be rather upset.

I CANNOT COME DOWN

This practice of loaning "demand deposits" created two problems, rising prices and potentially a "run on the bank." A run on the bank is when depositors lose faith in their bank and withdraw their deposits. **Bank runs will always result in bankrupting the bank and many depositors losing their money.** Unfortunately, the near universal (and immoral) practice of "fractional reserve" banking has been legalized by The Federal Reserve Act of 1913 for its "member banks." Banks have been "loaning up" throughout the decades and our sample fraction of $^2/_3$ (66%) we saw above, has become increasingly smaller and smaller as permitted by the Federal Reserve Act and subsequent amendments. The 1980 amendment allowed the Federal Reserve Board to adjust the fraction between 14% and 0%.[60]

> *"Effective March 26, 2020, the Board reduced the reserve requirement ratios applicable to all transaction accounts to zero percent, eliminating all reserve requirements."*[61]

Guess what else happened in March of 2020?

If you guessed that banking is a lucrative business, then you are beginning to understand this chapter. It has been my experience studying human behavior that the **"love of money" is an addiction** just like any other and the appetite of the wealthy isn't satiated (with rare exceptions), no matter how much money is to be made. It is this appetite for more money that has driven the evolution of the banking industry to what we have today. They have and will continue to do what they deem necessary to prevent "killing the goose that lays the golden eggs."

As our country expanded west and south, banks in those regions cut into the profits of Wall Street banks. The bigger New York banks had two problems: they wanted to protect their share of this lucrative business (lending demand deposits), and they needed to find a way to prevent not only runs on the bank, but also what is called a currency drain. Let's learn what a currency drain is.

A **currency drain** has the same effect as a bank run.[62] To understand a currency drain, we need another story that includes Fred the Farmer

and his other neighbor, Winona the Widow. Winona recently lost her husband and wants to sell her entire farm to Fred and move back to a neighboring town to live with her daughter and son-in-law.

Figure 51: Winona the Widow's Farm

Winona doesn't bank with Bob the Banker, but she and her late husband had been banking with the scrupulous and honest banker, Abraham. Abraham the Banker doesn't lend out other people's money, he maintains 100% reserves. Fred returns to Bob the Banker and asks for an additional $30,000 loan to purchase Winona's farm. Bob gives Fred $30,000 in gold who then turns around and deposits the gold whereupon Bob issues Fred $30,000 in paper receipts. With the aid of Larry the Lawyer, Fred and Winona complete the sale by exchanging the $30,000 paper receipts for the signed deed to the farm.

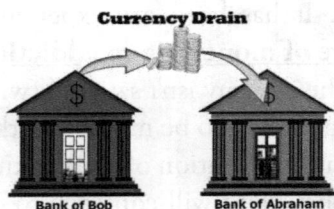

Figure 52: Currency Drain

Winona takes the $30k in "receipt money" to Abraham's bank to deposit it into her account. Abraham goes to Bob the Banker and demands $30,000 worth of gold and silver for the receipts that Bob had given Fred for the loan. This "bank to bank" transaction will reduce the amount of "reserves" held in Bob's bank. If Bob had made too many previous loans where receipt money was similarly deposited in other banks, subsequent "bank to bank" transactions will "drain" Bob's reserves completely, causing a bankruptcy to Bob's Bank just like a bank run does. Bank reserves today are in currency instead of gold and silver; therefore, we call these drains on the bank, a "currency drain."

The history of banking is fascinating, to say the least, but has been extremely disruptive to our economy. When banks continue to "loan up" by lowering their reserve requirements, it creates a "boom" cycle.

However, when households and businesses reach their limit on debt, we move, as a society, towards austerity by curtailing our expenses. This will decrease the demand for goods and services. Businesses will, in turn, need to tighten their budgets or begin cutting their expenses. Businesses often demand pay cuts or begin layoffs. Additionally, the B2B (business to business) expenditures will need to be reduced, affecting the other businesses' revenues, adding to the overall downward trend in the economy. Less & less money circulates in the economy creating a contraction of the money supply further compounding the problem. Startup businesses or those heavily in debt will go bankrupt, adding to unemployment.

This downward trend can rapidly bring the economy to its knees. Guess how we turn it around? The Fed will manipulate the money supply once again by injecting "fuel" (money) into the economic engine just as you would prime your two-cycle gas-powered weed-eater to get it to start. We call these downward trends in the economy a "bust" cycle. Unfortunately, the boom-and-bust cycle is the result of the expansion and subsequent contraction of the money supply, and since the Federal Reserve Act of 1913, many cycles can be attributed to the Federal Reserve's manipulation of the money supply.

For an in-depth explanation of how we got the Federal Reserve, I'll refer you to the well-researched book I've already alluded to in Chapter 12, "The Creature from Jekyll Island" by G. Edward Griffin. Figure 53 is a graph that shows every "bust" cycle, or recession, our nation has experienced since 1948 (the unemployment data points were only available from 1948 to present from BLS), 35 years after the introduction of the Federal Reserve system.[63]

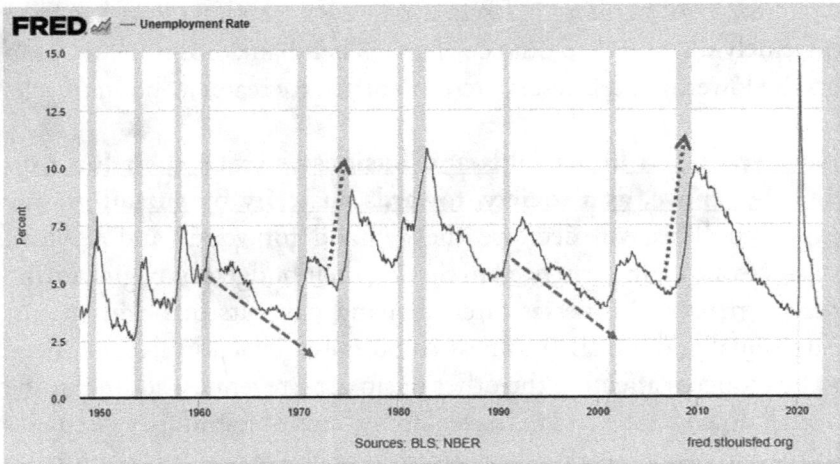

Figure 53: Unemployment Rate

Notice that every recession is preceded by a gradual decline in unemployment (as seen in the 1960s and 1990s downward sloping dashed arrows). Those are periods of economic growth or "boom" cycles. However, as a recession hits, the rate of unemployment increases more rapidly as seen by the steep rise (dotted arrows). How does the Federal Reserve combat recessions, you might ask? The same way they caused them—by manipulating the money supply.

The Federal Reserve has a few tools they use to manipulate the money supply. _**As the money supply increases it has a two-fold effect, prices rise, and economic activity rises,**_ creating a "boom" cycle, as we discovered from our Carter the Counterfeiter story. _**Conversely, when the money supply shrinks, it reverses economic activity, unemployment rises while general prices fall, and we enter a "bust" cycle or recession.**_ One is led to ask, why do we have a Federal Reserve System if they can't seem to meet their _"Congressional mandate to promote maximum employment and price stability?"_[64] It is my assertion that the purpose of the Federal Reserve is to protect the current quasi-monopolistic banking system at all costs and to pass to the unsuspecting public the system's failings through the hidden tax of inflation and government bailouts. How we got here is a subject that has been tackled by other authors.

When I use the term, quasi-monopolistic banking system, I am referring to the concept that all the "member" banks of the Federal Reserve are governed by the same rules. There is no competition among these 800+ member banks like you would see in any other industry. Understanding the importance of competition cannot be glossed over, so it is time for another story.

When my wife and I go shopping for items on Amazon or do a Google search to find a local restaurant for a dinner date or utilize my insurance portal to find a new primary care physician, we look at the ratings, evaluate the costs, and try to make an informed decision that meets our needs, wants, or desires. Competition affords us those opportunities.

Without competition, the general population is stuck with the services of only one provider (a monopoly), whether they be good or bad. When companies are allowed to compete for your business, there are generally two things that we as consumers are concerned about, the cost and the value of the goods or service we receive. The value of services has an element of subjectivity, how did we perceive we were treated: fairly, kindly, satisfactorily, etc. Additionally, the value of goods is determined by our perception of the quality relative to the cost. If we are happy with the cost and value, we will likely return as a customer. If not, we will move on and look from among the pool of other providers for the same goods or services.

Competition forces companies to meet the demands of consumers in both costs and value of the goods or services. Competition allows the better companies to grow, and weaker companies will eventually fall by the wayside. Additionally, as companies compete, supply goes up, which drives down costs, provided demand remains constant for that good or service. This concept of unfettered competition is the backbone of free-market capitalism that many unlearned folks seem to have an aversion to (capitalism being the "taboo" word).

When governments interfere with the free-market, they often prop up problematic companies (including banks) that might otherwise have failed if the governments had just let the free-market do its job. Additionally, over-regulation prevents innovation and change that is necessary to adapt to changing market conditions. A classic example of over-regulation occurred in my line of work, the airline industry.

The Federal government's regulatory arm for the airline industry from 1938 to 1978, the Civil Aeronautics Board or CAB[65], was preventing competition in the form of routes, fares, and market entry of new airlines. The result was higher prices and fewer passengers. Many factors in the 70's put pressure on Congress to examine the industry.[66] Wise heads prevailed and on October 24, 1978, President Jimmy Carter signed into law the Airline Deregulation Act.[67] There were growing pains, to say the least, as the industry adapted to deregulation. One example was the two-tier pilot pay-scale that I was hired into in 1988 which was necessary to help lower costs and appease the existing pilot labor force. Additionally, travel at peak times results in bottlenecks because the FAA still controls the management of air traffic. Free market solutions would help solve some of these problems, but overall, deregulation produced lower fares and an increase in air travel.

The problems we face in our country today are not because of the free-market capitalist system, but because governments continually interfere with it.

It was this very facet, the idea of eliminating competition, that New York bankers formed a cartel to "sell to Congress" the idea of the Federal Reserve System.[68] They wanted to "force all banks to follow the same inadequate reserve policies so that more cautious [banks] would not draw down the reserves [currency drains] of the others.

An additional objective was to limit the growth of new banks in the South and West."[69] Because bank failures were common, the public's trust in the industry was low. They would never have allowed the Federal Reserve Act to pass if they had known who was behind the secret meeting of financiers who crafted the idea for this new "central bank." It is estimated that the seven men who attended the secret meeting on Jekyll Island, where the Federal Reserve System was conceived, represented one-fourth of the total wealth of the entire world[70]. Not only was the Federal Reserve System conceived in secrecy, but the bill to sign it into law was passed by President Woodrow Wilson in obscurity (as poor legislation often is) when nobody was paying attention. It was signed during the Christmas holidays on December 23, 1913. Let us now return to our Federal Reserve System and explore how it can manipulate the money supply creating booms (and inflation) and busts (recessions).

The Federal Reserve, in its attempts to "promote maximum employment and price stability" (a smokescreen for its true purpose) has several tools to manipulate the money supply. One tool used was setting the "reserve" requirements of its member banks. Before getting into the mechanics, we need to understand how manipulating the "reserve" requirements of banks changes the aggregate money supply in our economy. If you do not understand "fractional" reserve banking, you will need to refresh your understanding by rereading the earlier pages.

Banks had learned, through their "fractional" reserve lending practices, that they could loan a significant portion of their customers' deposits and maintain only a fraction to be held in reserves. The "reserves" are used to meet day to day operations such as withdrawals of currency by customers, or a transfer of payment (for goods or services) from a customer's account balance to another business or individual who uses a different commercial bank. In bankers' terms, deposits held in an individual's (or business') checking or savings account are called "liabilities" because the bank is legally responsible (or "liable") to pay back that individual (or business) if they demand payment. Thus, to you and me, they are "demand deposits" but to banks they are labeled "liabilities" on the bank's balance sheet. If, for example, a bank has 100 customers who each have deposited $2500, then the bank's total of demand deposits would be $250,000 (100 x $2500). On the ledger, it would look like this:

LIABILITIES
$250,000 IN DEPOSITS

Figure 54: Bank ledger

Banks use the "double-entry" bookkeeping system (it improves detection of math errors) thus, the above "liabilities" are now considered "Assets" on the other side of the ledger and are reclassified as "Reserves." If assets equal liabilities, the books are considered balanced:

BANK WITHUS

ASSETS	LIABILITIES
$250,000 IN RESERVES	$250,000 IN DEPOSITS

Figure 55: Bank ledger

The $250,000 in Reserves, divided by the $250,000 in deposits equals 100%, thus the deposits are 100% backed by reserves. Reserves were formerly gold and or silver, but today they are strictly either fiat currency held in bank vaults or electronic entries in a computer. Banks historically lent more than they kept in reserves and that practice of fractional reserve banking became law when the Federal Reserve Act was passed. It is estimated that in 1900, the fraction of reserves divided by deposits was around 30%,[71] in other words, banks had "loaned up" 70% of their reserves. That fraction has been regulated up or down by the Fed numerous times, but the trend has been lower, and they announced on March 15, 2020, that the "Board" reduced reserve requirement ratios to 0% effective March

26, 2020. Let's examine how money is created when a bank "loans up" from 100% reserves towards the Fed's present 0% reserve policy.

Banks make money by selling loans to consumers or businesses, or in the case of some larger institutional banks, loans are made to foreign or local governments. Let's assume the Fed has set the "required reserves" at 10%. The remaining 90% of deposits ($225,000) are labelled as "excess reserves" and are eligible to be loaned.[72]

BANK WITHUS

ASSETS	LIABILITIES
$25,000 in "Required RESERVES"	$250,000 IN DEPOSITS
$225,000 in "Excess RESERVES"	

Figure 56: Reserves reclassified

Let's assume that "Bank WithUs" made loans to 10 customers at $5000 each for a total of $50,000. The $50,000 is "created" into existence the moment the loans are made. The balance sheet would look something like this:

BANK WITHUS

ASSETS	LIABILITIES
$25,000 in "Required RESERVES"	$250,000 IN DEPOSITS
$225,000 in "Excess RESERVES"	
+$50,000 in "LOANS"	+$50,000 Deposited in 10 Accounts

Figure 57: Loans created

$50,000 is added to both sides of the ledger to keep the books balanced. Loans are considered "assets" because the bank will earn interest as the loans are repaid. $50,000 is added on the "liabilities" side of the ledger as the money is deposited into the 10 accounts of the customers who received the loans, bear in mind that this is accomplished electronically, no new currency is printed, it is created by the stroke(s) of a computer keyboard. Those 10 customers didn't get a loan to let it sit idle. They plan on spending the $50,000 making the bank "liable" to make good on those payments when the customers spend the money.

The moment those customers spend the money, $50,000 is injected into the economy: $50,000 more than previously existed.

Let's assume that each of those customers bought a used car from Carl the Car Dealer who banks at Downtown Bank. Carl deposits the $50,000 in checkbook money into his account.

The teller will tell him the funds will be available in 2 days. This is because the two banks will now need to complete the transaction as follows:

1. Downtown Bank will demand payment from Bank WithUs
2. Bank WithUs will send the $50,000 from their "Excess Reserves" and reduce the amount in "Excess Reserves" by $50K from $225,000 to $175,000.
3. Downtown Bank now has an additional $50,000 in "Reserves."

DOWNTOWN BANK

ASSETS	LIABILITIES
$XXX,XXX in existing "Reserves"	$XXX,XXX in Existing Deposits
+$50,000 in "Reserves" transferred from Bank WithUs	**+$50,000 Deposited in Carl's Acct**

Figure 58: Bank reserves transferred

Now, Bank WithUs will look like this:

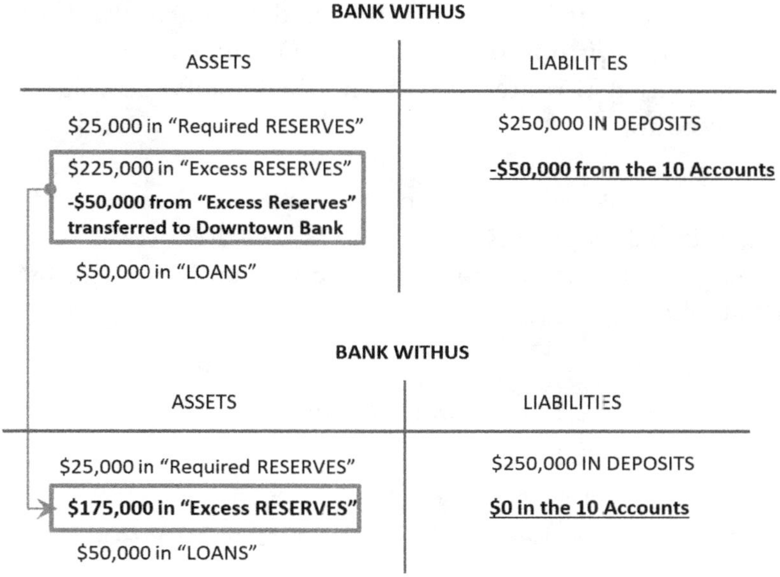

BANK WITHUS

ASSETS	LIABILITIES
$25,000 in "Required RESERVES"	$250,000 IN DEPOSITS
$225,000 in "Excess RESERVES"	**-$50,000 from the 10 Accounts**
-$50,000 from "Excess Reserves" transferred to Downtown Bank	
$50,000 in "LOANS"	

BANK WITHUS

ASSETS	LIABILITIES
$25,000 in "Required RESERVES"	$250,000 IN DEPOSITS
$175,000 in "Excess RESERVES"	**$0 in the 10 Accounts**
$50,000 in "LOANS"	

Figure 59: Reserves are now a fraction of demand deposits

Bank WithUs ledger is balanced where the assets total $250,000, the same as the $250,000 in total deposits; however, the excess reserves are $50,000 less and total reserves now equals $200,000 (Required: $25K + Excess: $175K). The fraction of reserves now equals $200,000/$250,000, or 4/5, or 80%. The remaining 20% in "Assets" are the $50,000 in loans.

What would happen if those 100 original depositors wanted to withdraw their $2500? It wouldn't be possible because the bank no longer has enough reserves to meet the demand. Can we see how this system is problematic? Yet, Bank WithUs will continue to loan up their "Excess Reserves." They will create new loans up to the amount of remaining excess reserves, $175,000. The total amount of loans they can make will be the original amount of "Excess Reserves" of $225,000. **Those new loans will add $225,000 to the aggregate supply of money circulating.**

The same pattern can be repeated at any other bank that receives deposits, including deposits that were the result of loans that became payments into someone's account, such as the $50,000 that Carl the Car Dealer deposited into his account at Downtown Bank. Let's see what happens at Downtown Bank and the $50,000 deposited into Carl's account.

Downtown Bank will take its new $50,000 in Reserves and will divide it into "Required Reserves" and "Excess Reserves" as follows, assuming it follows the same 10% reserve requirement set by the Federal Reserve.

DOWNTOWN BANK

ASSETS	LIABILITIES
$XXX,XXX in Existing "Reserves"	$XXX,XXX in Existing Deposits
$5,000 in "Required Reserves"	$50,000 in Carl's Account
$45,000 in "Excess Reserves"	

Figure 60: Reserves reclassified, pattern repeats

Downtown Bank only makes money when they lend it, so the $45,000 in excess reserves is the total amount from which they can "create" new loans. As soon as those new loans of $45,000 are spent, it will find its way into other banks where the deposits will get divided into 10% Required Reserves and 90% Excess Reserves and repeated once again. This pattern will be repeated over and over until all banks will "loan up" to the minimum "Required Reserve" set by the Federal Reserve.

The revolving deposits, loans, deposits, loans process will turn the original $225,000 in excess reserves into $2,250,000, a ten-fold increase. This is called the "money multiplier." The money multiplier is equal to the inverse of the minimum "required reserve," in our case 10%, or $^1/_{10}$.

If the "required reserve" minimum were 20% ($^1/_5$), then the money multiplier would be 5. Thus, if banks fully loaned up the remaining 80% of excess reserves, then the money supply would increase by 5 times the amount of excess reserves in the banking system. If the "required reserve" were reduced to 10%, the multiplier of 10 means that the money in circulation would be 10 times the amount of excess reserves.

A change from 20% required reserves to 10% required reserves increases the money supply from 5X to 10X (X= total excess reserves on the banks' ledgers), a doubling of the money supply. This process of changing the reserve requirements by the Fed was used to manipulate the money supply throughout the Fed's history as they attempted to regulate bank's liquidity and economic conditions. In 1907, the Wall Street Journal noted that reserves were around 21 percent of deposits.[73]

In 1917 after the Fed was created, reserve requirements on demand deposits were reduced to 13 percent, 10 percent, and 7 percent depending on the classification of the member bank.[74] This change in reserves from about 20% to about 10% would double the money supply. Author and economist, Murray N. Rothbard (1926-1995), also noted that the Fed lowered reserve requirements from 21% to 10% by 1917, thereby doubling the money supply at the advent of World War I.[75] The newly created central bank was well on its way to controlling the nation's money supply and setting the reserve policy was the first tool in its arsenal to manipulate the supply.

What, however, would happen if the reserve requirements for demand deposits were 100%, and banks could only loan customers' deposits if they were made aware that they could NOT access their money only until, or as loans were repaid? First, it would eliminate runs on the bank, because there would always be reserves available for the demand deposits.

There would be no "money multiplier" (it would be 1; 100% equals $^1/_1$) and ***thus no chronic inflation***. If the bank wanted to make money, they could 1) charge the customers a small fee for their demand deposits, or 2) make loans if, and only if, the customers knew they couldn't access their money for some period. This type of deposit to be used for loans is called a "time deposit" because the depositor doesn't have access to their money immediately.

Time deposits can be used by the banks to lend to borrowers, thus the liquidity (ability to convert to currency or cash immediately) for the depositor is limited. This type of banking would eliminate chronic inflation and we would not have the gyrations we see in the financial world nor the economy. It's a simple fix for a systemic problem. **Unfortunately, because those that benefit from the system have become extremely wealthy, they could, and would launch a massive advertising campaign to oppose this type of change if it gained popularity.**

Let us now return briefly to the topic of US treasuries and examine how the Federal Reserve manipulates the supply of money through what is termed "Open Market Operations." Lest we forget, the US Government funds its deficit spending operations through the sale of treasuries. Treasuries are considered assets by their owners, whether they are owned by you, me, or institutional investors (including banks). They are considered assets because they will earn interest (paid for by the US government), just like loans owned by a bank would earn interest (paid by the borrower). Treasuries would reside on the left side, or "asset" side of the two-sided bank ledger. Let's look at our hypothetical "Bank WithUs" once again. Returning to our previous balance sheet in the above example, let's explore treasuries a little deeper. The balance sheet of "Bank WithUs," after they transferred $50,000 in "Excess Reserves" to Downtown Bank, looked like this.

BANK WITHUS

ASSETS	LIABILITIES
$25,000 in "Required RESERVES"	$250,000 IN DEPOSITS
$175,000 in "Excess RESERVES"	
$50,000 in "LOANS"	

Figure 61: Bank Withus ledger

Let us suppose that Bank WithUs utilized the remaining "Excess Reserves" to purchase US Treasuries such as 20-year bonds which pay interest every 6 months. Their new balance sheet would look like this.

BANK WITHUS

ASSETS	LIABILITIES
$25,000 in "Required RESERVES"	$250,000 IN DEPOSITS
$175,000 in BONDS	
$50,000 in "LOANS"	

Figure 62: Bank assets include US treasuries

Bank WithUs would have no more "Excess Reserves" available to make new loans, and their $25,000 in "required reserves" would not adequately cover withdrawals from depositors in excess of that amount. Their assets exceeding the $25,000 in required reserves are not "liquid" or easily convertible to cash without, 1) calling in their loans, or 2) selling their bonds. This is where the Fed and "Open Market Operations" come into play. Bank WithUs can sell treasuries to the Fed during "Open Market Operations" to increase their "excess reserves." This provides, 1) more liquidity to the bank, to meet larger withdrawal demands from depositors, and 2) the ability to stimulate economic growth by offering more loans. As you might imagine, if the Fed chooses to purchase treasuries from other institutions, this provides more liquidity throughout the banking sector.

Imagine, if you will, that the Fed were to purchase $1 trillion in US treasuries from financial institutions. This new liquidity within the banking sector would provide $1 trillion worth of new "excess reserves" that could be used to provide new loans. Recalling how the money multiplier works, $1 trillion of new loans would ripple through the economy and multiply the money supply by the "money multiplier."

For example, if the "required reserve" ratio were 10% (or $1/_{10}$), the money multiplier could potentially increase the $1 trillion of excess reserves to $10 trillion of new money (provided all banks "loaned up" to the max). This process, the Fed's purchases of US treasuries from financial institutions, is how it stimulates growth in the economy, but the side effect is an increase in the money supply, which will cause rising prices.

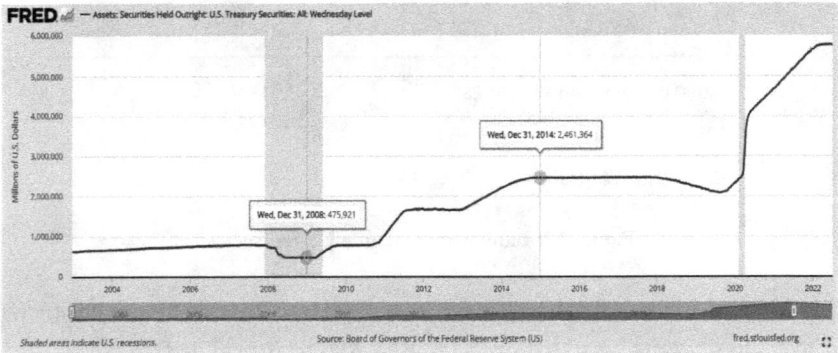

Figure 63: Board of Governors of the Federal Reserve System (US), Assets: Securities Held Outright: U.S. Treasury Securities: All: Wednesday Level [TREAST], retrieved from FRED, Federal Reserve Bank of St. Louis; https://fred.stlouisfed.org/series/TREAST, July 7, 2022

In Figure 63, we can see that the Fed purchased US treasuries at the end of the Great Financial Crisis in 2008 to the tune of $1.99 trillion from 31 December 2008 to 31 December 2014 ($2,461,364,000,000 minus $475,921,000,000). Note that from Dec 2014 through 2020, the Fed stopped purchasing US treasuries (their balance sheet remained constant through 2019 where it began to dip prior to Covid 19). The subsequent graph shows the growth of the money supply throughout the entire period. Notice how even though the Fed stopped purchasing US treasuries after 2014, the M2 money supply continued to steadily grow. This is due to the money multiplier effect as banks continued to lend their growing "excess reserves." From 2008 to 2020, the money supply nearly doubled from $8.2 trillion to $15.4 trillion.

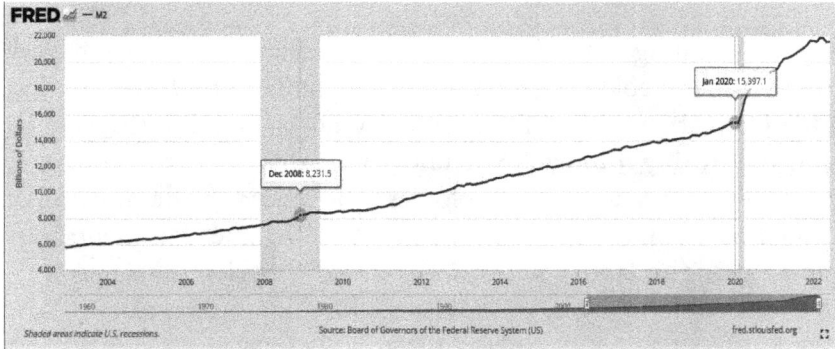

Figure 64: Board of Governors of the Federal Reserve System (US), M2 [M2NS], retrieved from FRED, Federal Reserve Bank of St. Louis; https://fred.stlouisfed.org/series/M2NS, July 7, 2022

The Federal Reserve has been in control now for over a century, trying to regulate the money supply and **_supposedly_** promote price stability, prevent bank runs and currency drains, and promote maximum employment with little success to show for it. As new problems emerged in the economy (or more accurately when those problems created demands on the banking system which could expose the fraudulent practice of "fractional reserve" banking) new legislation and/or Fed policies were implemented giving greater control of monetary policy to the Federal Reserve System and the US government. Let's examine just a few of those events.

As is often the case with most governments, wars are fought not just with spilt blood and the needless loss of limb and life but are costly in economic terms as well. The Seven Years War that originated in Europe in 1754 and spilled over into the Americas, known as the

French and Indian War, was costly to the British who wanted the American colonies to pay their fair share through various types of taxation schemes. Britain's attempts to tax the colonists and the colonists' concerns over "taxation without representation" motivated the colonists to seek independence from the British crown. What followed was the American Revolution and it was the first modern war of our nation that was financed by creating money from nothing.

At the beginning of the Revolutionary War in 1775 the total money supply for the colonies stood at $12 million.[76] **$650 million was added** over the course of the next 5 years **to pay for the war by simply printing money.** If you understand this chapter on inflation, you will understand that the colonies experienced the devaluation of that currency called the "Continental." In 1775, the Continental was valued at one dollar in gold. By 1779 it was worth less than a penny.[77] In a letter to John Jay in 1779, George Washington wrote,

> "In the last place, though **_first in importance_** I shall ask—is there any thing doing, or that can be done to restore the credit of our currency? The depreciation of it is got to so alarming a point—that a waggon load of money will scarcely purchase a waggon load of provision."[78] (Emphasis mine)

So repulsive was the colonists' experience with this inflation and having recognized the causality between money printing and rising prices, they wisely sought to prevent it, once and for all, when they drafted the Constitution. Article I, Section 8 reads:

> The Congress shall have Power...

> To coin Money, regulate the Value thereof, and of foreign Coin, and fix the Standard of Weights and Measures;

> To provide for the Punishment of counterfeiting the Securities and current Coin of the United States;

To drive the point home even further, in Article I, Section 10 they added:

> *No State shall... coin Money; emit Bills of Credit; make any Thing but gold and silver Coin a Tender in Payment of Debts*

The War of 1812 was not nearly as inflationary as the American Revolution, but it was paid for by money manipulation in the form of "fractional reserve" banking. The state banks had "created" enough money thru fractional reserve banking to purchase the government's war bonds, tripling the money supply and devaluing the dollar by about one-third of its former purchasing power.[79] By 1814, depositors caught on to what was happening and demanded their gold instead of paper and banks had to close their doors to prevent "bank runs" while hiring extra guards to protect employees from angry crowds.[80] This was the first experience where US government debt was financed by the inflationary practice of "fractional reserve" banking.

Each war thereafter has been paid for by some money scheme that inflated the money supply to finance the war. The Civil War saw an increase in the money supply by 138%.[81] The South saw the volume of money increase by 300% per year during the war.[82] Not long after the US entered WWI, the money supply (Federal Reserve Notes) in circulation increased from $2 million in November 1914 to $233 million in two years, an increase of 11,550%. By the time the war ended in November of 1918, the money in circulation was over $2.5 billion.[83] WWII saw an increase of approximately 380% from about $5.1 billion to over $24 billion.[84] Wars aren't the only crisis for which the monetary scientists at the Fed and the Fiscal policy wonks at the US government inflate the money supply.

As previously mentioned, the US government's response to Covid-19 added approximately $3.7 Trillion to the money supply. That didn't include the Fed's asset purchases to increase bank reserves and loans made, which added even more to the money supply. In Figure 65, the pre-pandemic money supply (M2[85]) was approximately $15.45 Trillion and by January of 2022 it was $21.65 Trillion, a 40% increase in the money supply. Thus, prices began following the increase in the money supply and would be at least 40% higher on average. This doesn't include the entire money multiplier of fractional reserve banking. If we take the $3.7 Trillion of new money spent by the government, set aside 10% for "Required Reserves," then banks could theoretically multiply the remaining $3.33 Trillion by the money multiplier of 10 (10% or $^1/_{10}$ "required reserve" produces a 10x money multiplier), thus inflating the money supply to an astonishing $37 Trillion (3.7 trillion + [3.33*10] trillion = 37 trillion) on top of the pre-pandemic amount of $15.45 trillion. This could theoretically increase the money supply 239%. **Prices of consumer goods would more than double if inflation were left unchecked**.

We could go deeper into the process by which the Fed manipulates the money supply, but I fear it will lose the majority of readers and I want to prevent that. Note that there are many tools the Fed uses at its disposal to either increase or decrease the money supply in its attempts to dampen business cycles, yet they continue unsuccessfully, because that was never its real purpose. Its true purpose is to protect the banking industry at all costs.

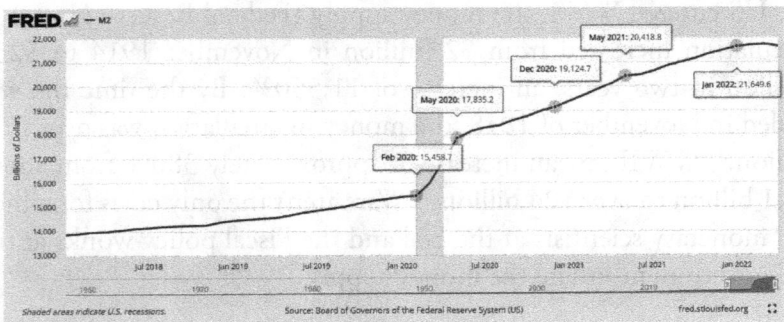

Figure 65: Board of Governors of the Federal Reserve System (US), M2 [M2NS], retrieved from FRED, Federal Reserve Bank of St. Louis; https://fred.stlouisfed.org/series/M2NS, July 7, 2022

During the "Global Financial Crisis" of 2007-2008, the Fed added new tools to its arsenal to "save" the banks and other financial institutions that had "loaned up" with bad "subprime" mortgages that were defaulted on, putting a strain on the entire financial system's liquidity. Think of liquidity as your ability to get cash or withdraw funds from your bank just to pay your bills and buy groceries and gas. The problem is systemic, as I previously mentioned, and the crisis spread throughout the world (much of the world uses US dollars). As previously mentioned, bank runs will always result in the banks going bankrupt.

If you were concerned that there was a financial crisis, wouldn't you try to withdraw your money from the bank? Absolutely! So, the Fed and the US government quickly went to work to "save" the economy, but in reality, they wanted to save their necks and the goose that lays the golden eggs. The Fed started buying assets (both loans and subsequently US treasuries as seen in Figure 63) from financial institutions to increase the banks' available reserves, meaning their "liquidity." They coined a new phrase along with this approach, QE, or quantitative easing. Where did the Fed get this money to purchase these assets? The same way banks create new loans, out of thin air.

The US government, by the stroke of a pen, increased the FDIC insurance from $100,000 to $250,000. This simple act is akin to the "misdirect" that magicians use to hide the sleight of hand used when performing a magic trick. The misdirection is meant to hide what is really happening. In this case, the change to $250,000 was to prevent runs on the bank, giving the depositors the "illusion" that their money was now "safe!" Let's talk briefly about the FDIC program.

A run on the bank will always result in the bank going bankrupt for the simple reason that they "loan up" and maintain only a fraction of reserves that make up the total of demand deposits in the system. Bank runs, even after the Federal Reserve Act was passed in 1913, continued. An average of more than 600 banks per year failed between 1921 and 1929.[86] 1,350 banks suspended operations during 1930.[87] About 2,300 banks suspended operations in 1931.[88]

Liquidity pressures on the banks during the winter of 1932-1933 forced banks to declare "bank holidays," thus preventing further runs on the banks. On March 4, 1933, when Franklin D. Roosevelt was inaugurated, every state in the Union had declared a bank holiday.[89] One of Roosevelt's first official acts was to declare a four day bank holiday beginning Monday, March 6th.[90] The "Emergency Banking Act" was rushed through Congress, legalizing the bank holidays while Federal Reserve Notes (our US currency) were printed around the clock to provide necessary liquidity to the system.[91] The Act, along with Roosevelt's fireside chats, helped calm the public's fears and banks were systematically reopened. Unfortunately for some depositors, 4000 banks never reopened.[92] Due to this period of financial uncertainty, the Federal Reserve Act was amended to include the creation of the Federal Deposit Insurance Corporation (FDIC) which Roosevelt signed into law with the Banking Act of 1933 on June 16.[93]

When a bank fails, the FDIC pays the depositors the sum of their balances in checking accounts, savings accounts, money market deposit accounts, time deposits such as CDs, Negotiable Order of Withdrawal (NOW) accounts and cashier's checks, money orders, and other official items issued by the bank up to the $250,000 limit. There are different "ownership" categories that the FDIC insures, such as a single account vs. a joint account.

If, for example, John Doe had a single account with Bank WithUs, and shared a joint account with his wife Jane Doe at the same bank, each account is insured separately up to the limit of $250,000. Supposing John Doe had a sum of $260,000 in his single account which included his checking, savings and CDs, then only $250,000 would be insured. If his shared joint account with his wife Jane had a sum of $400,000 in their checking and savings accounts, then each owner of the joint account would be insured up to $250,000 each. Thus, if Bank WithUs went bankrupt, Jane and John would each receive half of the $400,000, or $200,000 (which is below the $250,000 limit) from the FDIC, and John would receive $250,000 from the FDIC for the separate single account.

Don't be fooled by this program, it is still smoke and mirrors designed to obfuscate the truth. Banks are loaned up and any run on any bank will bankrupt that bank. The reality is, this "insurance" program is severely underfunded, proof that it was created entirely for one purpose, give the illusion your money is "safe." Sadly, even after the program was created, there have been hundreds of bank failures. From 1982 through 1991, more than 1400 FDIC insured banks failed.[94]

The FDIC requires banks to pay quarterly assessment fees, based on the degree of the bank's "risk" category. They also publish quarterly reports as part of their "transparency" efforts to mitigate the declining public trust of our federal government. At the end of the first quarter of 2022, the Deposit Insurance Fund (DIF) had a balance of $123.0 billion.[95] According to the same quarterly report, they insured 4,796 financial institutions, 40 of which were on the "Problem Bank List" with assets of $173.0 billion.[96]

The total "liabilities" of the 4,796 institutions equaled $23.97 trillion. The report candidly states that the $123.0 billion is only 1.23% of the insured deposits of $10 trillion.[97] Incidentally, that 1.23% reserve figure is below the statutory required limit of 1.35% and the FDIC has, amazingly, eight years to build the Fund back to the required minimum limit. In 1991, due to the previous decade of high bank failures, the Fund at that time (BIF for Bank Insurance Fund) had dropped below zero to a negative $7 billion.[98]

FDIC insurance coverage has increased on a few occasions throughout the decades. The first coverage was for $2500 when the FDIC was created in 1933. The coverage amount has been raised 7 times since. It was increased to $5000 effective June 30, 1934;

$10,000 in 1950; $15,000 in 1966; $20,000 in 1969; $40,000 in 1974 and $100,000 in 1980.[99] The latest increase was during the Great Financial Crisis in 2008 when it was temporarily increased to $250,000 on October 3, 2008.[100]

The temporary increase was extended on May 20, 2009, and permanently increased by law when President Obama signed the Dodd-Frank Wall Street Reform and Consumer Protection Act on July 21, 2010.[101] Again, **this entire program (FDIC) is simply an illusion, to signal to the depositors that your money is "safe" and is designed principally to discourage "bank runs."** What it does, unfortunately, is to perpetuate the problem of fractional reserve banking by creating "moral hazard."

The best definition I've ever seen of moral hazard is *"any situation in which one person makes the decision about how much risk to take, while someone else bears the cost if things go badly."*[102] The best examples of moral hazard are insurance companies. If you have insurance for your car or your health, the insurance companies pick up the majority of the tab should you need major repairs after an auto accident or require expensive therapies due to poor health. However, without car insurance, you might drive more cautiously. In the case of no health insurance, you might incorporate ways to reduce your medical bills, such as getting more exercise and eating healthier choices. Eliminating moral hazard puts the burden squarely on the individual, or in keeping with the theme of this chapter, the banks.

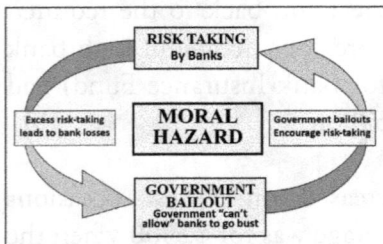

Figure 66: Moral Hazard

In banking, the creation of the FDIC, where the government takes on all the risks of depositors losing money should a bank fail, removes the banks' incentive to be more cautious in their lending practices. It is also another layer that protects the banks from the destructive, inflationary and immoral practice of fractional reserve banking.

Many economists and monetary scientists would have us believe that economic booms and busts are a normal part of the business cycle, and that the "elasticity" inherent in our present financial system of central banks, fiat currency and fractional reserve banking practices are necessary to mitigate the large swings of inflationary periods and recessions. However, my study of these problems leads me to conclude, it's all about the love of money and power, and these institutional systems and practices that we've discussed in this chapter are the problem!

We've discussed in detail how the supply of money impacts the economy and some history of money and its evolution to "fiat currency." We've discussed "money creation" and how it is achieved. We've also discussed the Federal Reserve System and, to a small degree, how it can manipulate the supply of money, impacting economic cycles. In my opinion, the creation of the Federal Reserve was entirely for the sole purpose of protecting the banking system and its inherent problem of "fractional reserve" practices.

We've explored how the federal government was used to help protect the banking system through the creation of the Federal Reserve System. We've also explored how amendments to the Federal Reserve Act, such as the creation of the FDIC, are used to prop up the system. What we haven't discussed is some of the other tools the Federal Reserve uses that either inject more money, or contract money from the aggregate supply, impacting our economy. We could go into great detail of how that is achieved, but that would be fruitless for the purpose of this book.

The purpose of this book is to highlight what I believe to be the greatest problem we face as a nation—unrestrained power. The power to create money gives the institutions, and by default those who run it, tremendous influence, or power. Money and power go hand in hand. Those with money yield tremendous power. Those who can create money yield even greater power, worldly power that is.

There are those who wield influence through their kindness and good deeds, but their influence is only limited to those lives they succor. I refer to these individuals as the "Mother Theresas" of the world. Most of us have known someone like that in our personal lives. But to wield worldly power, one only needs to throw money at it. Because everyone needs money to survive in our modern economy, most of us can be and are often influenced by money, whether it is in the form of compensation, rebates, gifts, government handouts, government subsidies, or government programs.

I'm always suspicious of those who throw large sums of money at a pet project without fully understanding the ramifications of it. For example, if you study the success of students in the classroom, the key factor to success is the teacher's ability to reach the student in such a manner that it inspires the student to want to learn. This is often achieved when the student believes the teacher cares about their success.[103] No amount of money thrown at the education system for state-of-the-art equipment or other ideas will work if we don't have an adequate supply of **quality teachers** in the classroom so that they can successfully reach the minds and hearts of these young people. If money isn't spent to hire an adequate supply of good teachers to lower the student/teacher ratio, money spent elsewhere is wasted. I believe it is important to examine an issue carefully when governments "talk" about spending money on it.

I'm always suspicious of the motives behind people in government who want to "spend" on some project. Spending is often double-speak for "I love power," or more accurately "I want your vote." This entire chapter has been void of any references to religion, but it seems appropriate to share a quote that most readers are unfamiliar with. The following reference can be found in a book that Latter-Day Saints use in addition to The Bible and The Book of Mormon. The following scripture can be found in Section 121 of The Doctrines and

Covenants (revelations received by Joseph Smith and his successors). I will quote from the scripture and expound on its meaning.

34 Behold, there are many called, but few are chosen. And why are they not chosen?

35 Because their hearts are set so much upon the things of this world, and aspire to the honors of men, that they do not learn this one lesson—

36 That the rights of the priesthood are inseparably connected with the powers of heaven, and that the powers of heaven cannot be controlled nor handled only upon the principles of righteousness.

37 That they may be conferred upon us, it is true; but when we undertake to cover our sins, or to gratify our pride, our vain ambition, or to exercise control or dominion or compulsion upon the souls of the children of men, in any degree of unrighteousness, behold, the heavens withdraw themselves; the Spirit of the Lord is grieved; and when it is withdrawn, Amen to the priesthood or the authority of that man.

38 Behold, ere he is aware, he is left unto himself, to kick against the pricks, to persecute the saints, and to fight against God.

39 We have learned by sad experience that it is the nature and disposition of almost all men, as soon as they get a little authority, as they suppose, they will immediately begin to exercise unrighteous dominion.

In no uncertain terms, God condemns those who have been ordained to the priesthood who use it to gratify their own pride or ambition. He warns that seeking the praises of the world and worldly possessions leads to the downfall of one who has been ordained to the priesthood. He also points out that most men who gain "positional" authority begin immediately to exercise that authority beyond the scope of the position. In simple terms, power corrupts.

We've spoken about presidential power, the human equation, and now money. They are interconnected. Because we have placed, as a nation, so much emphasis on the position of the President as being the most powerful person in the world and we have set high expectations for that position, most candidates will attempt to exalt their character to match the expectations of the nation. It's an impossible feat. No one can fulfill such lofty expectations. Anyone who tells you otherwise is fooling themselves. The next best method to magnify one's own stature is to promise the electorate they will spend money for this or that program. The greater the promises, the weaker the individual.

Money creation has become an artform, and the government's role in it by spending beyond its means, is all about gaining power. There is a solution to our monetary problems, and it begins with understanding the Constitution as it was framed by those who created it, the Founding Fathers. In our next chapter, we will examine the Constitution and the need to restore it to its true principles.

Chapter 18

RESTORING CONSTITUTIONAL PRINCIPLES

It was a Sunday evening, the night of April 29th, 1962, to be exact. The event was a dinner hosted by then President John F. Kennedy, affectionately known as JFK. The location was the State Dining Room and the adjacent Blue Room at his residence on 1600 Pennsylvania Ave in Washington, DC. The guests were a group of Nobel Prize recipients from the past along with the four most recent recipients. Additional guests included the Norwegian Ambassador, the Swedish Minister and other men and women from the arts, education, and science, including several university presidents.[104] All in all, the ***dinner guest list included some of the brightest minds of that time*** to honor the recent Nobel Prize recipients. In his welcome remarks, President Kennedy began,

> *"I think this is the most extraordinary collection of talent, of human knowledge, that has ever been gathered together at the White House, with the possible exception of when Thomas Jefferson dined alone."*[105]

JFK briefly extolled the achievements of his long-deceased predecessor, Thomas Jefferson, before continuing his welcome address. Who was Thomas Jefferson, and how is it he won the admiration and respect of his 20th century counterpart? Born in 1743, Jefferson was an astute learner and avid reader. He studied Latin, Greek, Spanish, Italian, and Anglo-Saxon and was very fluent in French.[106] At 16 years of age, he enrolled at the College of William and Mary where he continued his studies including philosophy, and mathematics. His keen mind was recognized by men his senior who continued his tutelage in politics and philosophy. He graduated from William and Mary two years later. He continued further studies in law to earn his law license while clerking for one of the men. He also had a love for the violin which he picked up while in his youth.

Most people today know him for his authorship of the Declaration of Independence written in 1776 at the young age of 33. There was probably no equal to Thomas Jefferson among his peers, and few today would match his abilities. Therefore, JFK could confidently suggest that the totality of bright minds during that April 1962 dinner could be matched by the singular mind of Thomas Jefferson.

Thomas Jefferson understood the Constitution as well as any person who ever lived and he understood its proper function in the affairs of our nation. He had this to say about it, *"In questions of power then, let no more be heard of confidence in man, but bind him down from mischief by the chains of the Constitution."* I have spoken about "power" in great length throughout this book. It is clear to me that Jefferson understood the near universal disposition of men to abuse power, that man must be constrained in his thirst for power by "chaining" him down with the limitations of the Constitution!

In Chapter 15, we were introduced to Figure 67. Let's revisit it briefly. As you may recall, I borrowed this figure from Cleon Skousen's work.[107] If we move governments left on the upper scale, we have too much government often resulting in Tyranny. Moving to the right on the scale, we have too little government resulting in Anarchy. Skousen suggests that good governments require the voice of the people, somewhere in the middle of the scale. The pyramid structure suggests that as governments move upward from the community level, they, of necessity, should be smaller in scope, or as Jefferson understood, have limitations—the limitations found in the Constitution.

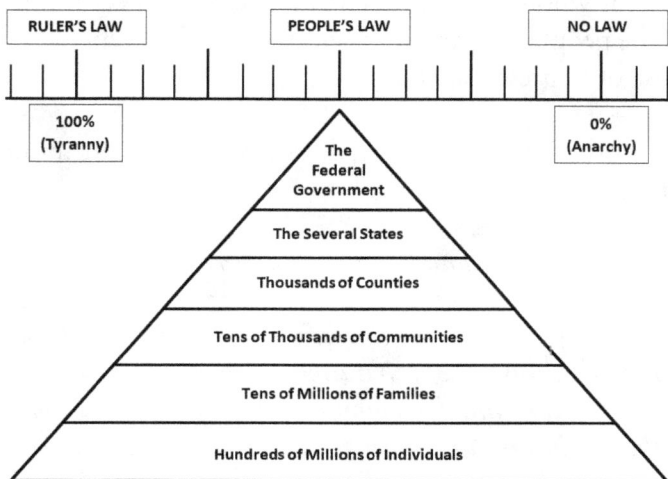

Figure 67: Government Pyramid-from W. Cleon Skousen, "The Making of America"

The Founders understood the differences between a republican form of government and the dangers of a direct democracy. If you've never heard the adage about the danger of democracy, it is worth retelling. The danger of a Democracy is best described as "two wolves and a lamb voting on what to have for dinner."

That's why the Founders designed a democratic republic. The people would vote for their representatives (the democratic process), who would in turn pass the laws and administer the government. Specifically, the voice of the people would elect one half of the bicameral US Congress, the House of Representatives. All other branches of the federal

Figure 68: Democracy?

government would be chosen by a body of individuals, but not the direct voice of the people. For example, the Supreme Court would be chosen by the president and the senators. The senators (the other half of the bicameral US Congress) would be chosen by the legislatures of the states for whom they represented. The only direct influence the voice of the people had was in the elections of their representatives to the House of Representatives.

There is another quote regarding democracy, whose attribution is in question.

> *"A democracy cannot exist as a permanent form of government. It can only exist until the voters discover that they can vote for themselves for the largest of the public treasury. From that time on, the majority always votes for the candidates promising the most benefits from the public treasury, with the results that a democracy always collapses over loose fiscal policy, always followed by a dictatorship. The average age of the world's greatest civilizations has been two hundred years."*

While we are not a pure democracy, our nation has fallen prey to the signs in the previous quote. We've passed the two-hundred-year mark and we continue to spend beyond our means. President Trump was hated, maligned and accused of being a dictator; President Biden, while meeker, uses the power of the pen (executive orders) and is no better (we will discuss Executive Orders in more detail later). Political and social unrest are all too common and the Founders republican experiment of freedom and liberty may be coming to an end. Is it any wonder we hear political slogans like "Hope and Change," or "Make America Great Again." ***Americans intuitively understand things are broken***.

The solution to our problems is the same as it was in 1776. We must throw off the yoke of an oppressive government. I'm not suggesting there needs to be a revolution, but I am suggesting we need to recognize we are moving along the scale, away from "People's Law" towards tyranny. Everybody recognizes we have problems; fewer understand the solution is less government, not more. The words of Benjamin Franklin aptly describe our day:

> *"Only a virtuous people are capable of freedom. As nations become more corrupt and vicious, they have more need of masters."*[108]

Our federal government is oppressive because it is unwieldly and has taken on too much power. One simple solution is to return the powers that once belonged to the States back to the States. In the progressive era from 1913 and later, the Federal government usurped more and more power from the States. This was made possible by one simple act of Congress, the passage of the 17th Amendment to the Constitution.[109]

Amendments to the Constitution have two sources from which they may originate, 1) from Congress and 2) from the States' legislatures. If from Congress, they need two thirds of both Houses (The House of Representatives and The Senate) to propose and vote on any suggested amendments. If a proposed amendment passes both Houses by the two thirds vote, then three fourths of the States' legislatures (or Conventions of three fourths of the States) must ratify the proposed amendment before it becomes "part of this Constitution."

The 17th Amendment changed the way the States elect US Senators. Prior to the ratification of the amendment on April 8, 1913, US Senators had been chosen by their respective state's legislative body. After the 17th Amendment was adopted, US Senators were elected by the people of the State.

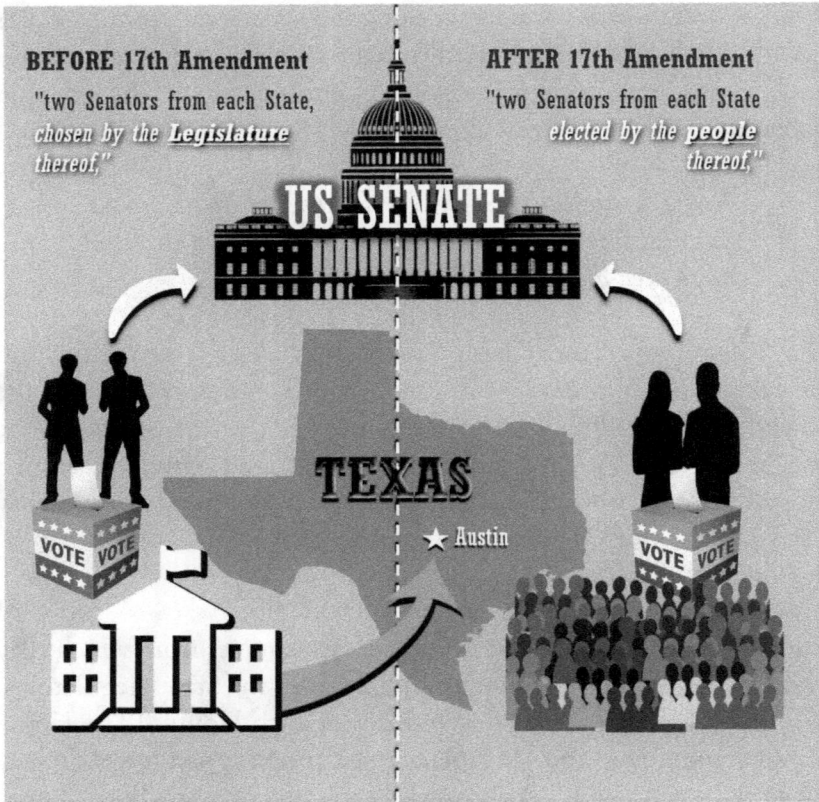

Figure 69: The 17th Amendment

The 17th Amendment completely eliminated the power of State governments to limit and restrain the Federal government. Prior to the passage of the 17th Amendment, any proposed legislation had to get past the US Senate, who essentially, by proxy, represented their state governments. If a proposed law infringed upon State rights, it could and would be rejected by the US Senate. After the 17th Amendment was passed, it removed this restraint, and the Federal government was well on its way to usurping more and more power from the States. The following graph adequately illustrates the unprecedented growth of the Federal government after the adoption of the 17th Amendment to the Constitution.

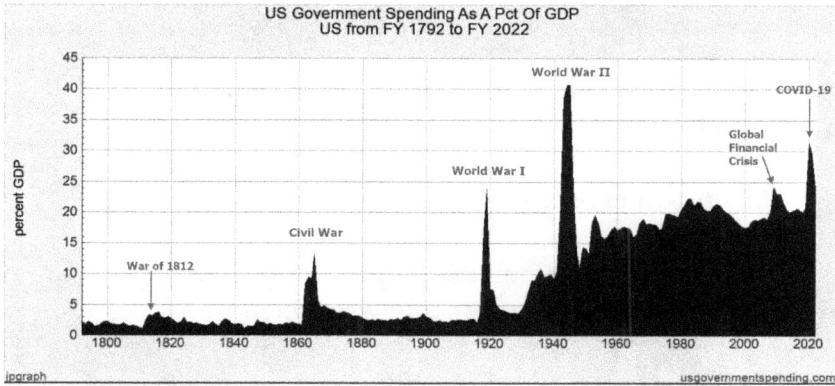

Figure 70: US government spending as a percent of GDP

The graph illustrates the spending of the Federal government as a percent of Gross Domestic Product, or GDP. Through 1913, spending was well below 5% of GDP except for the Civil War period, which we discussed briefly in the previous chapter. ***Since 1913, Federal government spending has grown almost 10-fold***. By abolishing the 17th Amendment, we could easily restore the restraint on the Federal government that existed during the first half of our nation's existence.

Step 1: ABOLISH the 17th Amendment.

Step 2: Term Limits!

Step 2 has gained popularity for decades and is part of my platform. There are many arguments in favor of it, and many arguments against adopting it. According to a national survey of 1000 respondents as recently as March 2021, *"An overwhelming 80% of voters approve of a Constitutional Amendment that will place term limits on members of Congress."*[110] Let us discuss some of the cons and dispel some of the arguments.

Cons:[111]

1. Not necessary, that is what elections are for, "It is undemocratic."

2. Loss of experienced lawmakers

3. "It means that politicians approaching their term limit no longer have to worry about what voters think."

While it is important to address each argument against term limits, bear in mind that we are discussing term limits for US Congress and not local or state governments, many of which already have term limits. The preamble to the US Constitution begins with "We the People;" therefore, if 80% of the "people" polled want term limits, the issue warrants the use of the Constitutional Amendment process with haste!

If elected, I would continue to encourage Congress to pass a Constitutional Amendment for term limits. Those in Congress who choose not to vote for the amendment run a significant risk of losing reelection. While Congress is at it, they might as well toss in another amendment, abolish the 17th amendment as discussed earlier. Let us now address each of the arguments against term limits.

1. **Term limits are undemocratic.**

This appears to be the most popular of the arguments against term limits. Incumbents enjoy name recognition, free mailers (at taxpayer expense), staff (at taxpayer expense) and travel allowance (at taxpayer expense) that tilt elections in their favor. Additionally, because long-tenured politicians have greater power and influence, "pork-barrel" projects find their way to their home district, increasing the incentives for political donors to back incumbents. ***These advantages to incumbents make elections less democratic***. Those who object to term limits and who cite many of the reasons against them are often those who benefit from the largesse that accompanies the growing power and influence of an out-of-control federal government. Term limits are specifically designed to remove them from power.

2. <u>Loss of experienced lawmakers.</u>

My proposal for term limits isn't the typical proposal. My proposal is founded on a principle I learned while serving as an instructor pilot at my airline. It simply works. Let me share that experience. The instructor pool of pilots is drawn from the entire pilot group. We call the group that flies the trips that carry passengers throughout the US and to other countries, "line pilots." Line pilots experience real world flying that involves things other than the "physical flying" of the aircraft (the only thing that can be realistically duplicated in a simulator). They interact with passengers, other crew, other employees such as gate agents and baggage handlers, and other supporting personnel. They experience real weather phenomena such as icing, snow on runways, windy conditions, heavy rains, thunderstorms and turbulence. They experience mechanical issues, delays, and late-night flying. All in all, "line flying" cannot be duplicated in the simulator where training is conducted.

When a pilot completes his month-long simulator training when advancing to another aircraft, he or she will be required to fly a "line trip" with a check airman before final certification. Instructor pilots are drawn from this pool and will lose touch with the nuances of line flying and the skills necessary to remain proficient at line flying if they remain away from it for any length of time. When I was serving as an instructor, our company had a policy that an instructor would serve two months as a teacher in the simulators, followed by a month of line flying.

This rotation is what I highly recommend when I suggest the need for term limits in Congress. Lawmakers are often given the moniker of "servants." To serve the citizens adequately, they must fully comprehend what it means to be a citizen. My idea of term limits would be to rotate lawmakers back to civilian life for a period before being eligible to run for election again. For example, a US representative could be eligible to serve 4 terms (for a total of 8 years) and be required to rotate to civilian life for half that time, or 4 years before being eligible to run for office again. This rotational idea for term limits will keep the lawmakers cognizant of the "nuances" of civilian life, ensuring they remain wiser, when and if they return to serve in Congress. It would not eliminate experienced lawmakers, just keep them relevant.

3. <u>"It means that politicians approaching their term limit no longer have to worry about what voters think."</u>

I find this to be the weakest of arguments. If you had to return to live among the same citizens for whom you represented, I can't imagine you would no longer be concerned about your constituents, or what they think, unless the purpose of serving in Congress was for your own personal gain to begin with. These are the individuals we are trying to expunge from Congress with term limits. When their entire agenda is for their own personal gain, they make promises to their constituents to get elected. Their motivation is always about their own power and prestige. When motivated by one's own personal gain, an individual usually lacks the wisdom or moral courage to do what is best. Sometimes, it is wiser not to have a government program to "fix a problem" because the new program will create another new problem, feeding the endless loop of a growing federal government.

Term limits are important for the reasons I mentioned, and my proposal is for it to be rotational (such as 8 years serve, 4 years off) for US representatives. I suspect that if we abolish the 17th Amendment, state legislatures who would then be responsible for choosing their US senators, would be more mindful of the need to rotate their choice as evidenced by the following statistics. For much of the 19th century (prior to the adoption of the 17th Amendment) the average prior service of Senators remained roughly constant at approximately four years.[112] At the start of the 117th Congress (January 2021), incoming

Senators averaged 11.0 years of prior Senate service (an increase of 175%).[113] Simply put, Senators served much shorter terms when chosen by their respective state legislatures.

Step 2: Establish term limits for US representatives and temporarily for US senators until we abolish the 17ᵗʰ Amendment.

Please note, what I am proposing so far, are amendments to the Constitution. To achieve term limits for Congress will take an honest effort by the electorate—that means you and me.

On my website, **https://RestoreAmerica.Today/renew-congress** you will find a map of the US House of Representatives and their districts. Each district shows its representative and their length of service. If we are serious about term limits, every person reading this sentence should email or call their representative and insist they vote for term limits before the next general election. Do not wait, do it now.

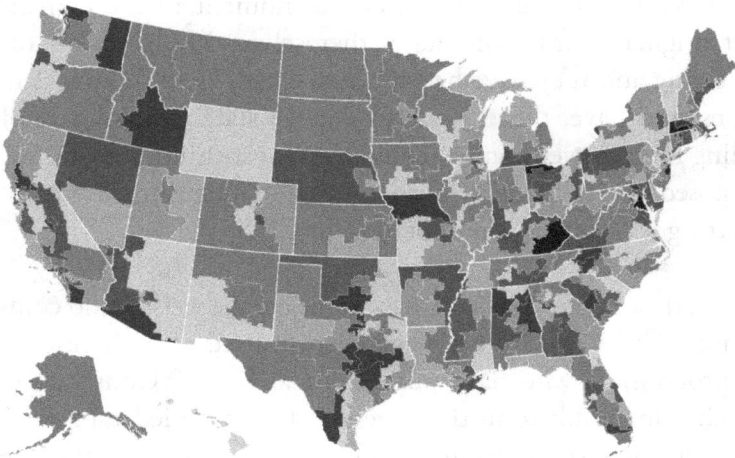

Figure 71: US congressional map

If your representative will not pledge to vote for term limits before the next election, then put forth a new candidate, possibly yourself, to run against the incumbent.

There are several movements across the country that are attempting to bypass Congress in what is termed an Article V proposal. As previously mentioned, there are two methods by which a Constitutional Amendment can take root,

1)   a proposal by Congress, and

2)   by an "application of the Legislatures of two thirds of the several States."

This second method requires a tremendous amount of coordination, people power and money to continually appeal to and influence the state legislatures to agree to a convention for the purpose of amending the Constitution. There is one group led by a constitutional scholar that has been working for several years to attempt what has never been accomplished in our country, an amendment to the Constitution that originated from the States themselves. My hat is off to them for trying and they have had much success. They are over 2 million strong and have, thus far, persuaded 19 states to pass a resolution calling for a convention to amend the Constitution for, among other proposed amendments, "Term Limits." The group to whom I am referring is "Convention of States," or COS.[114]

The next two issues we need to examine are the welfare and commerce clauses. These two clauses have been utilized over the last century by progressives who have pushed for a "living" Constitution, one which is malleable to fit their agenda, a growing federal government without limits or constraints. The purpose in sharing the anecdote about Thomas Jefferson was to emphasize his knowledge of the Constitution, that it isn't malleable, but that it has constraints and that we *must bind [man] down from mischief by the chains of the Constitution.*" What are those chains and how have they been broken?

To answer that question, we must take a closer look at two clauses in the Constitution. We will examine the "welfare" clause first.

The Constitution is divided as follows:

1) Articles (I – VII)
    a) Sections
        i) Clauses

Article I, Section 8. Clause 1 reads:

> *"The Congress shall have Power To lay and collect Taxes, Duties, Imposts and Excises, to pay the Debts and provide for the common Defence and general Welfare of the United States; but all Duties, Imposts and Excises shall be uniform throughout the United States;"*

Subsequent clauses in Section 8 continue with the phrase "To..." and end with a semicolon, ";" with the final clause of Section 8 also beginning with "To..." and ending with a period, ".". For example, Clauses 7 and 13 respectively read:

> *"To establish Post Offices and post Roads;"*

> *"To provide and maintain a Navy;"*

Article I. Section 8 is one sentence, and it should be taken as a whole. It is often referred to as the enumeration clause because it enumerates the powers of Congress, beginning with the "power to" tax. Clause 1 of section 8 gives Congress the power to tax and explains that that power is for the purpose of paying for:

1) "debts" of the federal government,

2) the "common Defence" of the nation, and

3) the "general Welfare" of the nation.

In other words, the power to tax is broadly for "defence" and "general welfare," but because the sentence structure is not completed, the broad terms for which Congress has power to tax are specifically defined, or "enumerated" in the remaining clauses of Section 8 of Article I.

This clear understanding of the limited or enumerated powers of Congress was the prevailing attitude among the Framers. To persuade the citizens to ratify the Constitution, a series of essays (later dubbed the Federalist Papers) were printed and circulated by Alexander Hamilton, John Jay and James Madison under the pseudonym, "Publius." James Madison, the "Father of the Constitution" had this to say in Federalist Paper no. 45,

> *"The powers delegated by the proposed Constitution to the federal government, are few and defined. Those which are to remain in the state governments, are numerous and indefinite."*[115]

Madison also had this to say about my analysis of the construction of Article I, Section 8 in his commentary in Federalist Paper no. 41.

> *"It has been urged and echoed, that the power 'to lay and collect taxes, duties, imposts, and excises, to pay the debts, and provide for the common defence and general welfare of the United States,' amounts to an unlimited commission to exercise every power, which may be alleged to be necessary for the common defence or general welfare. No stronger proof could be given of the distress under which these writers labour for objections, than their stooping to such a misconstruction."*[116]

Madison chastened his opponents to the Constitution, the "Anti-Federalist" writers in unmistakable terms, that they had stooped to "misconstruction" of the sentence structure. He goes on further and states,

> *Had no other enumeration or definition of the powers of the congress been found in the constitution, than the' general expressions just cited, the authors of the objection might have had some colour for it... But what colour can the objection have, when a specification of the objects alluded to by these general terms, immediately follows; and is not even separated by a longer pause than a semicolon?... For what purpose could the enumeration of particular powers be inserted, if these and all others were meant to be included in the preceding general power? Nothing is more natural or common, than first to use a general phrase, and then to explain and qualify it by a recital of particulars."*

Nothing could be clearer! The Constitution clearly spelled out the scope and limits that the newly proposed federal government would have. Progressives of the early 20th Century stretched the original meaning of the Constitution and greatly expanded the powers of the federal government. Many so-called scholars incorrectly cite the "welfare" clause as a broad, all-encompassing power to tax for the purpose of providing welfare in the form of government assistance, to include such things as Social Security benefits for over 70.5 million recipients.[117]

Let me be clear! I am not suggesting that Social Security benefits are not helpful nor necessary, I am emphatically stating they are unconstitutional! Generations have passed since the early days of progressivism and today's electorate is entirely ignorant of the large disparity between the Founding generation's practice of limited government and today's seemingly endless government expansion due to parsing of the wording in the Constitution to suit an agenda. If it were not for deficit spending funded by government IOU's that we discussed in the previous chapter, taxation to pay for the growing expansion of the federal government would be extremely onerous and Americans would have long since revolted.

Now that we have examined the "welfare" clause and how it has been misinterpreted, let us examine the second issue that has given the federal government greater power, the commerce clause. The commerce clause can also be found in Article I, Section 8. It reads,

> *"The Congress shall have Power… To regulate Commerce with foreign Nations, and among the several States, and with the Indian Tribes;"*

The use of the word "commerce" during the period of the 18th century leading up to the Constitutional convention could be easily interchangeable with our use of the words, "trade and exchange."[118] "To regulate" also had a narrower meaning, "to make regular." In other words, the Framers were attempting to aid and assist the trade between states, foreign Nations and the Indian Tribes, in part, by removing this regulatory power from the States, who had participated in discriminatory regulations on commerce.[119] In the Federalist Paper No. 42, Madison emphasizes this point,

> *"A very material object of this power was the relief of the states which import and export through other states, from the improper contributions levied on them by the latter."*

The Founders' intentions were not meant to restrict trade, but to ensure it thrived. Yet today, those powers of regulating commerce have been grossly expanded over the course of decades beyond the original intent of the Framers. The commerce clause now "justifies" federal government regulation of any activity which affects interstate commerce either directly or indirectly, such as fixing prices, wages, working conditions, health conditions and the retirement of employees. It also includes all aspects of manufacturing, selling, trading, and trafficking as well as interstate transportation. As discussed in the previous chapter, competition is paramount in fostering lower prices and improved services and/or products, but government's excessive regulations have often stymied competition, or driven some, such as major railroad lines, into bankruptcy.[120]

The original intent of the commerce clause was to promote trade, not burden it with excessive regulations that we see today. "By the 1830s, the late British economist Angus Maddison showed, American per-capita income was already the highest in the world."[121]

The Constitution's intended effect of protecting liberty, including promoting free trade, was a resounding success. We need to promote the free-market principles that fostered the tremendous growth and prosperity that propelled this nation to becoming the number one world economy, and that requires a returning to the Framers intended meaning of the "commerce clause."

We've explored a few principles that in total, are designed to reduce the size and scope of the federal government, simply by examining the Constitution as it was constructed, and not as it has been reinterpreted. Another significant principle found in the Constitution that needs to be examined is the meaning of the term "general" as found in both the preamble and again in Article I, Section 8. Understanding and applying the proper meaning will have a significant impact on future legislation. Let's briefly explore the term "general."

The term general meant the same during the Constitutional Convention of 1787 as it does today. Merriam-Webster defines general as: "involving, applicable to, or affecting the whole."[122] Cambridge dictionary defines general as: "involving or relating **to most or all** people, **things,** or places." Therefore, the intention was and always should be that the enumerated powers and any laws "necessary and proper" in support of those powers should be applicable to all people and/or places of the United States. In other words, the use of the word "general" was a limitation on the taxing powers, a restriction against taxing to pay for special interests or particular projects not beneficial to the population at large. To illustrate the Framers intent for this limitation, I quote from a publication that is instructive of this view.

> *"In the late 1790s Alexander Hamilton, an outspoken advocate of loose construction of the Constitution as well as of using the Necessary and Proper Clause to justify a wide range of "implied powers," became convinced that a federally financed system of what would soon be called internal improvements—building roads, dredging rivers, digging canals—was in the national interest. But, since each project would be of immediate advantage only to the area where it was located, none could properly be regarded as being in the general welfare. Accordingly, Hamilton believed a constitutional amendment would be necessary if internal improvements were to be undertaken. James Madison, in his second term as president, would veto a congressional bill on precisely that ground*[123]

Not surprisingly, we can find a multitude of projects that we (and generations past) have paid for with taxes that do not meet this strict limitation—to support, help, or improve the lives of the general (whole) population. For example, just off the top of my head, I can think of two projects: the Hoover Dam and the Tennessee Valley Authority that do not meet this limitation. The Tennessee Valley Authority, albeit it has been a success in providing electricity to all of Tennessee and portions of six surrounding states, was, nevertheless, created from government overreach beyond the Constitutional limits.

Likewise, the Hoover Dam benefits primarily southern California which receives 56% of the electricity generated by the dam followed by Southern Nevada, 25% and Arizona at 19%. The water from the dam, Lake Mead, serves 18 million people in those regions. Neither of these projects benefited the general population of the United States yet they were paid for by the federal government and were unconstitutional.

Today, the "earmarks" for special projects have reached new heights. Citizens Against Government Waste (CAGW), a private, non-partisan, non-profit organization representing more than one million members, has been chronicling these "unconstitutional" spending projects for over three decades. You can access their data base online at https://www.cagw.org/reporting/earmarks.

I did a quick search by typing "Boston" in the keyword search and the data returned 50 different earmarks targeted for institutions in Boston alone. The biggest offenders were Senators Kerry and Kennedy of Massachusetts in 2010 with 17 earmark projects totaling $19.4 million. Coming in a close second in "pork barrel" spending were Senators Markey and Warren of Massachusetts with 15 earmarks totaling $19.3 million in 2022. According to CAGW's *"2022 Congressional Pig Book"* report, they uncovered over 5 thousand earmarks totaling $18.9 billion! I quote from their report:

> *Earmarks continue to provide the most benefit to those with spots on prime congressional committees. In FY 2022, the 89 members of the House and Senate appropriations committees, making up only 17 percent of Congress, were responsible for 41.1 percent of the earmarks and 29.1 percent of the money. As the late Sen. John McCain (R-Ariz.) explained regarding those making the case for earmarks, "The problem with all their arguments is: the more powerful you are, the more likely it is you get the earmark in. Therefore, it is a corrupt system."*

> *Indeed, the most powerful legislators unduly benefited from the return of earmarks. Senate Appropriations Committee Ranking Member Richard Shelby (R-Ala.) received by far the highest dollar amount of earmarks. His 16 earmarks cost $647,936,000, which is $270,437,000 (71.6 percent) more than the legislator*

in second place, Rep. Brian Mast (R-Fla.), who received six earmarks costing $377,499,000.[124]

A complete turnover of Congress would easily solve this problem, but I'll settle for term limits. A return to the originalist understanding of the Constitution would quickly restore sound fiscal spending and eliminate the need for deficit spending. As you may recall, government deficit spending finds its way into the banking system, causing inflationary periods followed by recessions. Let's briefly revisit how this is accomplished.

When the government spends money that they do not have in the Treasury it adds "new money" to the money supply by finding its way into the banking system and ultimately is the basis for the "reserves" from which new loans are created. If you recall from the previous chapter, the fractional reserve banking process will multiply the amount of money by a factor of the inverse of the required reserve amount, which had been around 10% of the deposited money. New money is created when banks loan up to that reserve amount, creating new money for each loan made.

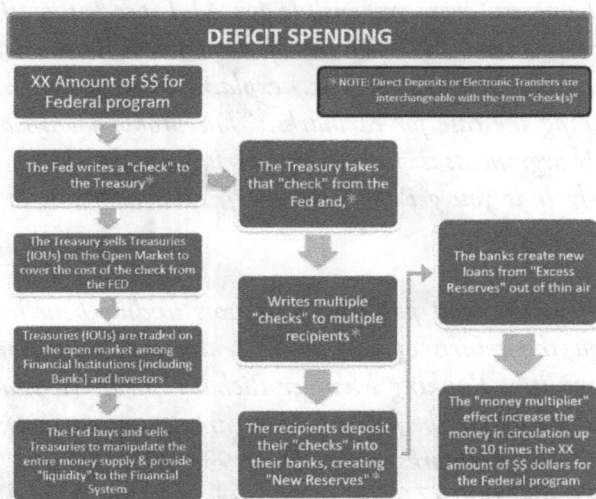

DEFICIT SPENDING

XX Amount of $$ for Federal program

* NOTE: Direct Deposits or Electronic Transfers are interchangeable with the term "check(s)"

The Fed writes a "check" to the Treasury*

The Treasury takes that "check" from the Fed and,*

The Treasury sells Treasuries (IOUs) on the Open Market to cover the cost of the check from the FED

Writes multiple "checks" to multiple recipients*

The banks create new loans from "Excess Reserves" out of thin air

Treasuries (IOUs) are traded on the open market among Financial Institutions (including Banks) and Investors

The Fed buys and sells Treasuries to manipulate the entire money supply & provide "liquidity" to the Financial System

The recipients deposit their "checks" into their banks, creating "New Reserves"*

The "money multiplier" effect increase the money in circulation up to 10 times the XX amount of $$ dollars for the Federal program

Figure 72: Deficit Spending

For Example, The Treasury borrows $4 billion. The $4 billion finds its way into multiple bank accounts. Each bank keeps approximately 10% in "Required Reserves" or $0.4 billion. The excess, $3.6 billion is loaned. The multiplier effect, (the inverse of 10%) multiplies $3.6 billion into $36 billion by the time all those new loans are made. The original $4 billion created from the "deficit spending" added to the $36 billion of newly created loans creates a total of $40 billion that didn't exist in the economy before the government spent money they didn't have. As the original $4 billion in IOU's is sold, then those IOU's take $4 billion out of circulation leaving an increase of $36 billion in the total money supply. When the government "borrows" in the trillions in today's dollars, then the increase in the total money supply results in rising prices.

Lest we forget, a dollar is worth less today than 20, 40 or 100 years ago. Therefore, the federal government has gone from borrowing millions to billions to now trillions.

The root of all our turbulent economic cycles begins with excessive federal spending beyond the "chains" of the Constitution, paid for by deficit spending which almost always leads to inflation. The Fed will, in turn, manipulate the money supply to dampen inflation, driving our economy into recessions. All this is caused by our governments excessive spending in the first place.

The two problems (monetary policy and fiscal policy) go hand in hand. It is why I addressed them in these two back-to-back chapters. We cannot solve the banking problem without first electing Congressional representatives who are willing to stop spending beyond the Constitutional limits the Framers intended. That won't happen until we remove the big spenders from office.

Term Limits and abolishing the 17th Amendment are critical components of the changes needed to solve this problem. After we remove the big spenders, we need to elect representatives and senators who are willing to abide by the Constitutional restraints we've discussed. Additionally, we will need to task them with examining the Federal Reserve System and the banking industry, primarily for the purpose of restoring real money in lieu of the destructive fiat money used today.

Let us return to our discussion on other abuses of the Constitution by examining the language, once again, of Article I, Section 8. Recall that Section 8 begins with *"The Congress shall have Power to..."* followed by all the enumerated clauses. The concluding clause (the one with the "period punctuation" that completes the entirety of Section 8) reads:

> *"To make all Laws which shall be necessary and proper*
> *for carrying into Execution the foregoing Powers, and*
> *all other Powers vested by this Constitution in the*
> *Government of the United States, or in any Department*
> *or Officer thereof."*

You may recall, Article I primarily established the Legislative Branch and its powers. There have been two abuses of the above clause. The first abuse I will briefly outline is centered around the ambiguity of the term "necessary and proper." There is a long history of scholarly debate over the ambiguity of "necessary and proper" and, not surprisingly one of the earliest debates includes my Constitutional heroes James Madison and Thomas Jefferson on the one hand and Alexander Hamilton on the other.

The phrase, "necessary and proper" as understood by Madison and Jefferson, meant that Congress could only make laws that were incidental to the enumerated powers. They had a more restrictive construction of the term. Hamilton argued, in defense of his proposition for the first national bank, that a more "liberal" view should be taken. It is this "liberal," or "discretionary" view that has prevailed throughout our history, especially this last century. Figure 73 illustrates the difference between the two viewpoints.

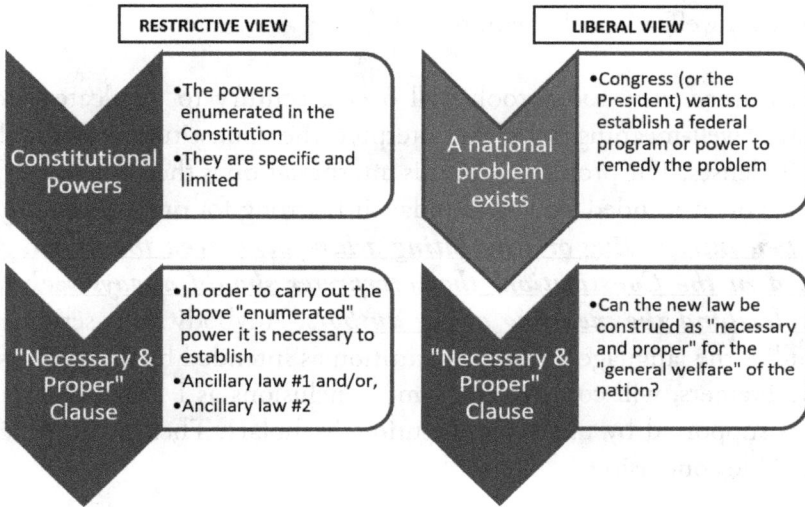

Figure 73: "Necessary and Proper"

During the congressional debates over the merits and constitutionality of the national bank proposed by Hamilton, Congressman James Jackson of Georgia had this to say:

> *"If the sweeping clause* [the earliest term used for the Necessary and Proper Clause], *as it is called, extends to vesting Congress with such powers, and necessary and proper means are an indispensable implication in the sense advanced by the advocates of the bill, we shall soon be in possession of all possible powers, and the charter under which we sit will be nothing but a name."*[125]

Jackson forewarned that stretching the meaning of the Necessary and Proper clause to advance the passage of the bank bill proposed by Hamilton would inevitably lead to an expansion of "all possible powers" to Congress and the "charter" (The Constitution) which was meant to limit Congress' powers would be "nothing but a name" with no constraints whatsoever. How prescient his comments were. The prevailing modern school of thought is that the Federal Government has no limits if a law or program is "necessary and proper" for the "general welfare" of the nation.

This broad view today took well over a century to inculcate, and many well-meaning scholars interpret the Constitution through these lenses. The problem with this interpretation is the same as every other open-minded view held today, it is wrong for one reason only. ***When interpreting or translating a language, even the language used in the Constitution, the interpreter should always seek to understand the meaning of the authors.*** Anybody who seriously studies the language of the Constitution as intended by the authors, the Framers, will come to the same conclusions as I have, which is also supported by many Constitutional scholars. There is no other possible conclusion.

There has been another calamity associated with the "Necessary and Proper" clause that has led to what has been dubbed, "The Administrative State." During the rapid federal expansion of the early 20th century, Congress passed the "Administrative Procedure Act" in 1946. The purpose of the act was to provide standard procedures for federal agencies to propose and issue regulations and adjudication. The act essentially gave the federal agencies in the Executive Branch "legislative" powers and "judicial" powers.

This defeats the entire premise of the Constitution's division of powers into the three branches of government (executive, legislative and judicial), for the sole purpose of preventing abuses of power by the federal government against citizens. Let us examine the "Necessary and Proper" clause once again, remembering that Article I, Section 8 is one continuous sentence and should be read in its entirety. It begins with "*The Congress shall have Power…*" and concludes with,

> "***To make all Laws*** *which shall be necessary and proper for carrying into Execution the foregoing Powers, and all other Powers vested by this Constitution in*

*the Government of the United States, or **in any Department or Officer thereof**."*

In addition to the clause above, Article I, Section I, plainly spells out,

"All legislative Powers herein granted shall be vested in a Congress of the United States, which shall consist of a Senate and House of Representatives."

The question we need to ask is, why should the legislative, or lawmaking power be given solely to Congress? The answer: accountability. Lest we forget, the intended experiment of the Constitution was to establish a national government accountable to the people (of the people, for the people, by the people). The House of Representatives is directly accountable to the people through frequent elections, every two years. The "Administrative Procedure Act" of 1946 gave lawmaking, or as it is termed in the Act, "rulemaking" authority (as well as "adjudicating" authority) to the federal agencies under the "Executive Branch," the branch responsible for executing and enforcing the laws. Although the "rulemaking" process is well defined and has a means by which it obtains "public opinion," ***there is no recourse for citizens to remove objectionable or oppressive federal agency bureaucrats from their unelected positions of power***.

The "necessary and proper" clause gives Congress the sole responsibility for making laws, or whatever name you want to call it such as "rules," "regulations," "policies," or "guidelines" in **"any Department or Officer"** in **"the Government."** Abolishing the "Administrative Procedure Act" and electing Representatives who understand the importance of the responsibility delegated to them in the "necessary and proper" clause to make **"all laws"** for the departments (and federal agencies) of the government would help solve the abuses perpetrated by out-of-control federal bureaucrats.

Can you imagine the flood of phone calls and emails your representative would receive, when they are once again tasked with the duty of establishing the rules governing the federal agencies? They will either be overwhelmed by the resurrected duty and quit (or not seek reelection), or hopefully rise to the occasion and correct the abuses of the out-of-control "administrative state." If resignation (or "retirement" in some cases) is the preferred choice by our elected officials, you can be certain there will be a cadre of liberty loving citizens ready to step up and fill the void. Either way, we would be restoring a significant amount of accountability to the government.

In like manner, the use of "Executive Orders" is a usurpation of power that belongs solely with Congress, particularly when an "EO" has the same effect as law. Let us briefly review Article II in the Constitution which defines the Executive Branch of the federal government to examine if the Constitution warrants the possible use of Executive Orders. Article II section 1, begins with,

> *"The executive Power shall be vested in a President of the United States of America."*

There are in total, only 4 sections that define executive powers, including how the president and vice president are elected, requirements to hold office, compensation, and duties of the president. The principal duties of the president are the following.

- *"Commander in Chief of the Army and Navy"*
- *"Commander in Chief of the militia of the several states, when called into the actual Service of the United States"*
- *"take Care that the Laws be faithfully executed"*

The president has shared responsibilities with the Senate. Article II, Section 2, clause 2 reads *"by and with the Advice and Consent of the Senate"* the president has the following duties.

- *Make treaties*
- *Appoint ambassadors*
- *Appoint other public Ministers and Consuls*

- *Appoint Judges of the supreme Court*
- *Appoint other Officers of the United States.*

Lastly, the president has secondary responsibilities, and of these, the most important one relates to the lawmaking duties of Congress. Section 3 reads:

> *"He shall from time to time give to the Congress Information of the State of the Union and recommend to their Consideration such Measures as he shall judge necessary and expedient."*

To provide this "feedback" to the Congress, the president *"may require the Opinion, in writing, of the principal Officer in each of the executive Departments, upon any Subject relating to the Duties of their respective Offices."*

The Constitution was carefully written to divide the powers and responsibilities between the three branches, and as previously discussed, lawmaking power belongs solely with Congress. The term, "Executive Order" is not found in the Constitution. Any Constitutional power that resembles an "Executive Order" is the power to order a subordinate to "take Care that the Laws be faithfully executed." Therefore, any constitutionally legal Executive Order is one that supports an existing law, it isn't a law unto itself.

When an Executive Order circumvents the legislative role of rulemaking, then it is unconstitutional. The evolution of Executive Orders took a significant turn towards a breach of constitutional limits under President Theodore Roosevelt. Teddy Roosevelt had this to say in his autobiography about presidential power.

> *I declined to adopt the view that what was imperatively necessary for the Nation could not be done by the President unless he could find some specific authorization to do it. My belief was that it was not only his right but his duty*

to do anything that the needs of the Nation demanded unless such action was forbidden by the Constitution or by the laws. Under this interpretation of executive power I did and caused to be done many things not previously done by the President and the heads of the departments. I did not usurp power, but I did greatly broaden the use of executive power.[126]

Roosevelt greatly expanded the power of the President because he believed it was his right to do "anything" unless it was forbidden by the Constitution or by the laws. This view is entirely wrong, and he set a dangerous precedent. It broadly expanded the powers of government which, in the wrong hands, leads to tyranny—the concern the Framers had when they put the reins of government firmly in the hands of the people's representatives in Congress. Roosevelt's overstepping flies in the face of the "Founders' doctrine of enumerated powers, which said he could do NOTHING except that which the Constitution authorized."[127]

While the term "Executive Order" wasn't coined until the 20th century, the founding generation of presidents clearly understood the limits of their powers as seen in Figure 74. The average number of Executive Orders prior to Roosevelt's term was under 12 per year. The Founding generation averaged less than one per year.

Teddy Roosevelt had 145 per year, commensurate with his misguided belief of the Constitutional powers he "usurped." Not to be outdone, his immediate successors expanded their use of Executive Orders. It didn't matter which party the president belonged to, the precedent had been set and we now have presidents that push the envelope and broaden their powers using Executive Orders.

Executive Orders have become a means to circumvent a non-compliant Congress to follow the recommendations or "measures" that the president believes "necessary and expedient." They are an infringement (or better still, a usurpation) of the rulemaking, or lawmaking powers that belong with Congress. It takes considerable restraint on the part of a president to abide by the Constitution and not abuse their powers with Executive Orders for the purpose of overriding Congress, but that was the reason the Founders divided the powers between the 3 branches of government in the Constitution in the first place: to restrain government! ***I pledge not to abuse the power of the office with the use of Executive Orders if elected.***

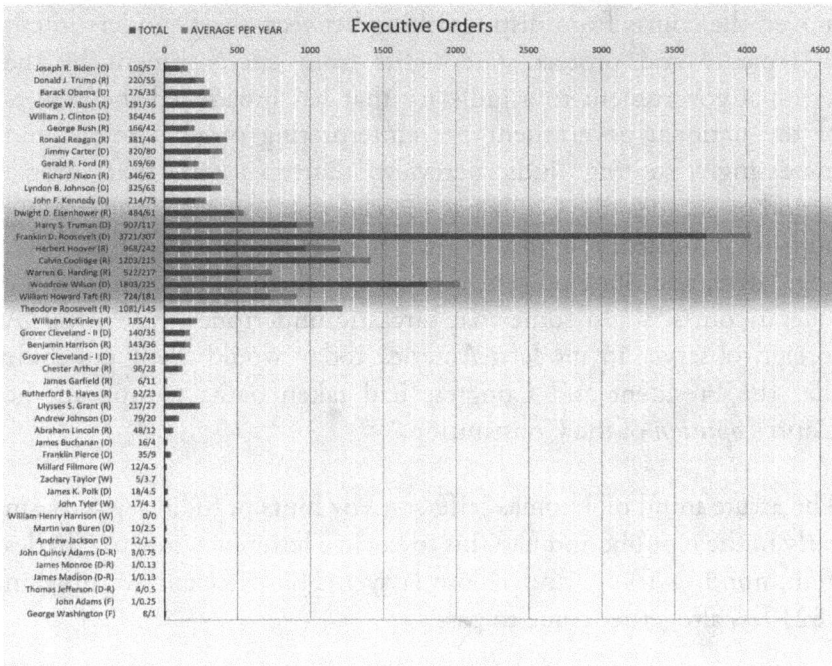

Figure 74: Data from The American Presidency Project, https://www.presidency.ucsb.edu/statistics/data/executive-orders#eotable

The Judiciary branch shall not escape scrutiny in this chapter, albeit there isn't much overlap between the Executive branch (for which I seek election) and the Judicial excepting, of course, the appointment of Supreme Court justices and other federal "Article III judgeships" by the President. History has shown that every president since FDR has appointed on average two supreme court justices (except Carter with zero) and hundreds of other federal judges.[128] Appointments of judgeships that adhere to originalism (the coined term for those who subscribe to the original intent of the Founders) can turn the tide of judicial activism, but the effect is analogous to the helmsman of a large ocean liner. It takes time to reverse the ship's course and the path is a slow, lengthy and gradual change.

Constitutional scholar, historian and prolific writer, David Barton, in his work, "Original Intent" catalogues the events that have moved the courts from distinguishing between the Founders intent to separate and protect state rights from encroachment by the national government to a judiciary that has broadened the powers of the national government by reinterpreting original intent and increasingly exerting "judicial review." Barton asserts that "over a period of decades, the Court has succeeded in completely redefining both the Constitution and its own role. It has usurped Executive, Legislative, and State powers, centralizing them in the hands of the federal courts."[129] In somewhat sarcastic undertones, he writes, "A foreign observer in modern America today would likely conclude that the President and Congress had taken oaths to uphold the Court's *opinion* of the Constitution."[130]

The astute mind of Thomas Jefferson saw hints of judiciary activism early in the republic and had this to say in a letter he wrote to Charles Hammond, a friend and fellow lawyer. His prescient warning in 1821 has altogether come to pass.

> *It has long however been my opinion, ... that the germ of dissolution of our federal government is in the constitution of the federal judiciary; an irresponsible body, (for impeachment is scarcely a scare-crow) working like gravity by night and by day, gaining a little to-day & a little tomorrow, and advancing it's noiseless step, like a thief, over the field of jurisdiction, until all shall be usurped from the states, & the government of all be consolidated into one. To this I am opposed; because whenev[er] all government, domestic and foreign, in*

little as in great things, shall be drawn to Washington as the center of all power, it will render powerless the checks provided of one government on another, and will become as venal and oppressive as the government from which we separated.[131]

In summary, **the Constitution was meant to restrain the federal government.** The ratification would not have occurred if the Framers had not convinced the citizens of the respective states that the proposed national government to be chartered by the Constitution was truly limited in scope. To secure ratification, a bill of rights was promised, and subsequently passed by the first Congress. Those twelve amendments were, afterward, sent to the states for ratification, ten of which were ratified, becoming the treasured Bill of Rights. It is truly disheartening that previous generations of Americans have neglected their responsibility as protectors against the encroaching centralization of power in Washington. If we fail to reverse this trend by decentralizing power, humanity, driven by their fervent desire for freedom, will inevitably resort to the same drastic measures pursued by our founding generation to break free from the tyrannical rule of England. This is a recourse we need to prevent, but we must act today if we are to preserve freedom for our posterity without the expense of bloodshed.

For the past century (on average) more than 40% of the electorate chose not to vote during presidential election years. The figure is more disconcerting during midterm elections: on average more than 55% of the electorate chose not to vote.[132] The midterms are equally as important as presidential election years because it is the House of Representatives whom we elect every two years, and it is the body which more accurately reflects the will of the people. Perhaps they chose not to vote because they have lost hope. Of those who vote today, a large percentage continues to elect representatives that have the mindset that big government is the answer to every problem we face, and the solution is always spend, spend, spend.

We see how that has worked out, over $31 trillion in debt as 2022 winds down, with the resulting inflation that accompanies large deficit spending. To make matters worse, if we don't course correct, the interest on that debt will be the largest federal expenditure, which is unsustainable (see Figure 24 in Chapter 12).

The truth of the matter is that most of our societal problems result from a lack of morality in our 200+ year experiment of self-government. And it's not just a lack of morality among those we elect, but a lack of morality in governing our own behaviors as a society at large. When has honesty, integrity, or virtue been promulgated in communities, schools, or businesses? Sadly, religion (the greatest resource for fostering private and public morality) has been driven out of the public square and this too can be blamed on an overzealous federal government that misinterpreted its role and the Constitution. In the words of George Washington for his last official act as President in the Farewell Address he penned to "Friends & Fellow-Citizens" on September 19th, 1796:

> *"Of all the dispositions and habits which lead to political prosperity, Religion and morality are indispensable supports."*

Is it any wonder that God, the true source of morality, put it into my head and heart that I should run for President? As we circle back to the reason I am running, let it be known and understood that as I continue to depend on God's help and guidance, all things are possible, including restoring our nation back to a sustainable path of liberty, peace and prosperity, if, and only if, we recognize the need to limit the federal government and the barometer ought to be the original intent of the Constitution as framed and espoused by our Founding Fathers.

Chapter 19

AN UNBELIEVABLY BAD YEAR

"The Science of Numbers is in no respect a modern invention. Thousands of years ago the Eastern philosophers and religionists knew and practiced it."[133]

Those are the words of Luo Clement, penned more than a century ago. Today, the "science of numbers" is used in mathematics, technology, the study of the universe, the human body, and not surprisingly, the "divine creator." Patterns can be found in numbers. In Numerology, numbers can be good or bad. In Jewish and Christian theology, the number seven means complete, fullness or perfection.

As for myself, I had little difficulty memorizing numbers and I am delighted when I observe numerical patterns emerge from the arbitrary running balance in my checking account register. When my wife and I walk the neighborhood, we reminisce over the house numbers visible on the mailboxes that correspond to eventful years in our youth, such as, "That was the year I graduated from high school, or that was the year I was born." So, it's no wonder that I'll notice a pattern emerge while looking at numbers and this chapter is dedicated to the number 1913, "a very bad year."

In Chapter 17, we discussed the Federal Reserve System (The Fed), which was signed into law in—you guessed it—1913 (December

23, 1913, to be exact). Our federal government was deceived into passing legislation that was conceived in secrecy by a cartel of some of the world's richest men for the purpose of protecting the larger New York banks. The banking industry, along with The Fed, has the power to create money from nothing, facilitating the Federal government's propensity to spend beyond its means. Excessive deficit spending leads to inflationary cycles. The Fed's power to manipulate the money supply to fight inflation will, in turn, lead to recessions. Both cycles hurt middle to low-income households.

In Chapter 18 we discovered that the 17th Amendment to the Constitution was ratified in, once again, 1913 (April 8th). The passage of that amendment eliminated any power our state governments had on restraining the national government. Since 1913, we can easily observe the expansion of the federal government. As we saw from the spending graph in *Figure 70*, Federal government spending steadily grew from a meager 2 to 3% of GDP during the 12 decades preceding 1913 to 23% in 2022. The combination of these two events of 1913, the adoption of the 17th Amendment, and the creation of the Fed, has been disastrous. ***We now have a federal government that has no restraints, and its loose fiscal policy is facilitated by an unaccountable central bank.*** The major byproduct is chronic inflation—the true reason we have a growing wealth gap. The following chart was created from data taken from the US Census.[134]

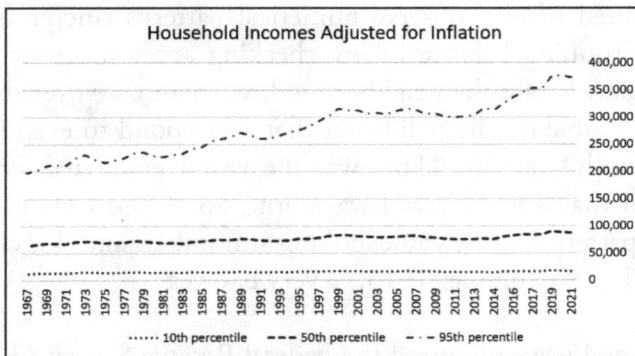

Figure 75: Household incomes adjusted for inflation

If you recall from Chapter 17, the individuals hit hardest by inflation are:

> *"people who get their hands on the money last...those who aren't skilled laborers. It will be the work force that we typically label as minimum wage earners. They will be the biggest losers."*

The dotted line represents the wage growth of the bottom 10% of household incomes, the "biggest losers" from inflation. In 1967 the average income for that bracket was $11,593 compared to $15,660 in 2021, a 35% increase, whereas the top income bracket wages grew 112%. On the other hand, consumer prices rose by 679%[135], hurting all wage earners—the bottom wage earners the hardest. If we want to reverse course in the income gap disparity, we need to restore fiscal restraint on the federal government and return to real money, not fiat, including eliminating fractional reserve banking and limiting the powers of the Federal Reserve Bank, particularly the powers that manipulate the aggregate supply of money. **The Fed and the 17ᵗʰ Amendment were two nails in the coffin for our country.**

There is a superstition that deaths come in threes. I'm not sure where it originated, but it happens often, particularly if you look for it. My uncle died in March of 1999, followed by my father in June and then their mother in August. Superstition or not, it's not surprising that another deathblow to the Constitution happened in 1913.

The 16ᵗʰ Amendment to the Constitution was ratified on February 3ʳᵈ, 1913. It reads,

> *"The Congress shall have power to lay and collect taxes on incomes, from whatever source derived, without apportionment among the several States, and without regard to any census or enumeration."*

This superseded Article I section 9 which states,

> *"No Capitation, or other direct, Tax shall be laid, unless in Proportion to the Census or enumeration herein before directed to be taken."*

The Framers believed direct taxes were onerous and gave Congress the authority to directly tax the people, but it had to be 1) "in Proportion" to the population, or in other words uniform and 2) it was to be used only in extreme exigencies, such as war.[136] As we saw in Figure 70, federal government spending was uniformly low from 1792 through 1913 at about 2 to 3% of GDP. The only time it was above 5% was during the Civil War period when both the Union and the Confederate states assessed taxes on income.[137]

As in most exigencies such as wars (or Covid 19 pandemics) governments might "bend the rules" to suit their needs under the guise of "necessary and proper" that we discussed in the previous chapter. The income tax of the Civil War period under the federal government was unconstitutional because it was not "in proportion to the Census." It levied a 3 percent tax on incomes between $600 and $10,000 and a 5 percent tax on incomes of more than $10,000.[138] Public opposition to the income tax grew after the Civil War and it was finally repealed in 1872.[139]

The use of the income tax to raise revenue for the Civil War was the first time in our nation's history that an income tax was assessed. Although it was finally repealed, sadly, the seed had been planted in the collective mind of the nation and the income tax would be reborn once again. In 1894, as part of the Wilson Tariff Act, the income tax was revived, assessing a 2% tax on incomes above $4,000[140]. It was struck down by the Supreme Court shortly thereafter because it was unconstitutional, it was *"not apportioned among the states on the basis of population."*[141] Nevertheless, the income tax, still, would not die.

"In 1909, progressives in Congress again attached a provision for an income tax to a tariff bill. Conservatives, hoping to kill the idea for good, proposed a constitutional amendment enacting such a tax; they believed an amendment would never receive ratification by three-fourths of the states. Much to their surprise, the amendment was ratified by one state legislature after another."[42]

After ratification of the 16th Amendment, the monster was released and "**_Income tax_**" became a permanent element in American lexicon. The first "constitutionally authorized" income tax was a meager 1% of net income.

Today, there are more than 2700 IRS tax publications and forms, in a variety of languages ranging from English, French and Russian, to Farsi, Gujarati, and Punjabi. Publication 17, the Tax Guide for Individuals, is 139 pages long, with 14 pages of tax tables to help the individual (or couples or heads of households) determine their total tax burden. If they choose the easy route and take the standardized deductions, they might be missing out on qualified tax breaks. In my mind's eye, I can picture the conversations in the congressional committees in their secret chambers as they dream up and write the tax codes, "Let's make the tax code so onerous that we can squeeze out of the masses more money because they don't want to be bothered with the trouble of searching out and itemizing deductions to lower their tax burden."

Filing tax returns has become an industry in and of itself. Before reaching out to a tax professional, an individual may choose to tackle the time-consuming project on his or her own. In addition to Publication 17 above, the individual will need to peruse, at a minimum, 385 more pages of complex tax codes from Publications 463 (45 pages), 525 (43 pages), 529 (18 pages), 535 (57 pages), 547 (24 pages), 575 (51 pages), 587 (35 pages), and 946 (112 pages) with the accompanying "Forms" and Instructions.

Is it any wonder that most businesses and many individuals will hire tax professionals to sort through the quagmire of tax codes to minimize their tax burden?

It is a conservative estimate that the time required for Americans to file their individual income tax returns, amounts to over 2 billion hours.[143] If you add up the time required for all Americans, **including businesses**, to comply with tax reporting and filing requirements, it amounts to more than 6.5 billion hours.[144] Let's put that into context.

The average worker at a 40-hour work week and 4 weeks of vacation and/or holidays spends 48 (weeks) times 40 hours working in a year, or 1,920 hours. If we divide 6.5 billion hours (6,557,902,940 to be exact) by 1,920, we arrive at 3.4 million American workers wasting a year of their lives complying with the tax code. That is a significant loss of human resources that could be contributing to the real economy! The compliance cost in terms of dollars is estimated to equal $313,000,000,000 ($313 billion).[145] To put it another way, the opportunity cost of $313 billion could buy <u>every man, woman, and child,</u> in the combined states of Utah and Nevada, a brand new 2023 Model 3 Tesla (Figure 76).

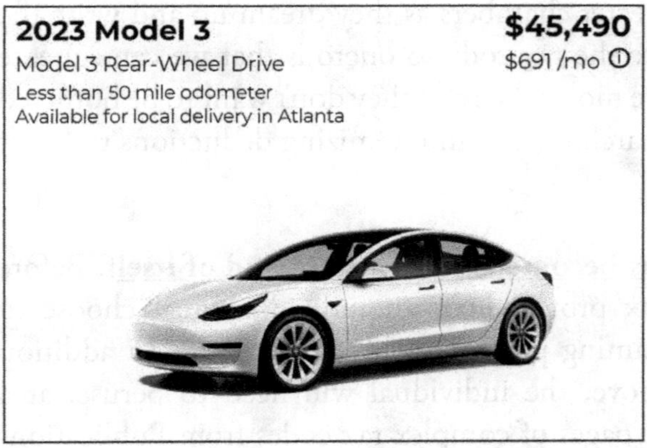

2023 Model 3	**$45,490**
Model 3 Rear-Wheel Drive	$691 /mo ⓘ
Less than 50 mile odometer	
Available for local delivery in Atlanta	

2020 Census data:

Utah population:	3,275,252
<u>Nevada population:</u>	<u>3,108,462</u>
Total:	6,383,714

$313 Billion divided by $45,490 equals 6,880,633 Tesla's—more than enough to buy one for every man, woman, and child in Utah & Nevada—with almost half a million Tesla's leftover.

Figure 76: https://www.tesla.com/inventory/new/
m3?arrangeby=relevance&zip=30152&range=200

By law, your employer withholds from every paycheck, deductions for both the income tax portion you will owe and the FICA payroll taxes. This will amount to 15% or more, depending on your salary and any W4 withholding criteria you meet. If you are self-employed, you pay all the FICA taxes of 15.3% on top of your income tax withholdings.

The government will have the use of your money before you do. But what if they didn't? What if you had the extra 15 to 25% of your money? Let's return to another discussion about money and how it affects the economy. This time, we aren't going to discuss the quantity of money as we did in Chapter 17, but the "velocity" of money.

To understand velocity of money, we need to use a tool economists use for studying macroeconomics, the "Quantity Theory of Money." The Quantity Theory of Money can be written in the following equation:

$$M * V = P * Y$$

M = the money supply (all the money in the economy)

V = the velocity of money (the average number of times a unit of currency is spent purchasing finished goods and services in a given period, usually a year.)

P = the price level of all finished goods and services in an economy

Y = all the finished goods and services sold in an economy, also known as "real GDP"

When we multiply all the finished goods and services sold in an economy by their prices, P * Y, we arrive at "nominal GDP." If the economy remained unchanged from year to year, then the output of all finished goods and services would remain the same and the growth of real GDP would be zero, or constant. If prices change but real

GDP remains constant, then "nominal GDP" would be different. Comparing "nominal GDP" between years doesn't give economists an accurate picture of the state of the economy because it includes prices that often vary. They need to measure "real GDP" to accurately determine the growth (or contraction) of the real economy.

To determine "real GDP," the US Bureau of Economic Analysis (BEA) collects data from other government agencies[146], then its Ph.D. economists and statisticians[147] analyze and determine real GDP. The BEA will publish the official quarterly GDP numbers the month following the quarter, called the "Advance Estimate," followed by two revisions each subsequent month called, respectively, the "second estimate" and the "third estimate" as more detailed and more comprehensive data become available. Annual "estimates" are released in September of each year for the previous 3 to 5 years, but they are far less useful to policy makers and businesses albeit they are the most accurate. While this "real GDP" data is useful, it is not forward looking. Now, let's return to our Quantity Theory of Money equation.

Figure 77: Quantity Theory of Money

P * Y is the production side of the economy, or sellers. For every product or service sold, there is a consumer or buyer. Therefore, the left side of the equation M * V represents the consumers or buyers.

Let's look more closely at V, Velocity. Recall that Velocity is the average number of times a unit of currency circulates in the economy during a given period, such as a quarter, or year. In Figure 78, a unit of currency circulates throughout the economy, purchasing goods or services, 5 times, thus we might

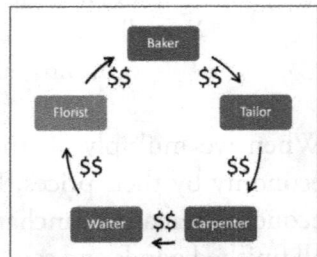

Figure 78: Velocity of Money

say that Velocity equals 5 (V=5). Life is good! Everyone is working and happy! Some economists often assume that velocity is constant. However, there are factors that affect velocity for individuals and the aggregate population.

Savers don't spend as much; so, Velocity of Money is low.

Shopaholics would have a high Velocity of Money.

Figure 79: Variable "Velocity" of money

Let's start by understanding how Velocity can be vastly different between two individuals. As we see from Figure 79, someone who spends all their income would have a higher Velocity compared to someone who chooses to save more of their income. Our Quantity Theory of Money; however, assumes an average Velocity across the economy. For the sake of this discussion, let's assume the average Velocity for a healthy economy is 3. Figure 80 shows Velocity of money as determined by the Federal Reserve. They use the same Quantity Theory of Money equation and solve for V.

$$V = \frac{P * Y}{M}$$

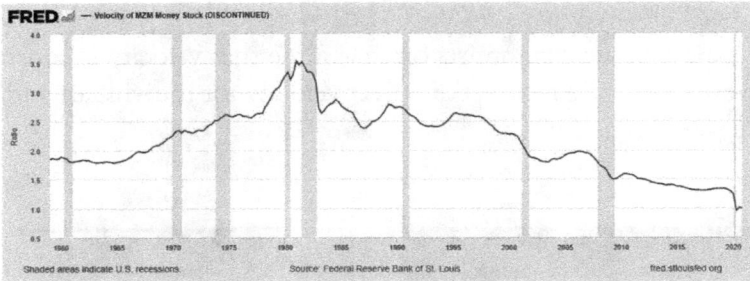

Figure 80: Velocity of Money, MZM, Quarterly

To better understand "velocity of money" let us **assume that the money supply remains constant for several years,** that no new money is created or removed from the total money supply. M (MZM in Figure 80) represents all notes and coins in circulation, traveler's checks (non-bank issuers), demand deposits, other checkable deposits, savings deposits, and all money market funds.[148] If we return to our equation solved for V, we see that V is equal to Nominal GDP (Prices times Real GDP) divided by the money supply.

How does V affect the economy? Recall that Velocity is different for many individuals, some save while others might spend every dollar of their income consuming products and services. Assuming the money supply remains constant, and production of goods and services is constant, what would happen to Velocity if more people saved? The answer, of course, is that V would be lower. If V is lower, what happens to prices if Y and M are constant? They will come down too. Think about that for a moment.

How do sellers entice savers to spend their money? They offer discounts. We often see this behavior from sellers during seasonal sales. As V accelerates (meaning spending increases), so will prices. As prices increase, the behavior of buyers changes once again. They will, of necessity, economize and reduce spending. **We call this the "free market."** Prices and the real economy self-correct without government's help and without a fluctuating money supply. It is government interference and the Fed's manipulation of the money supply that disrupts the real economy causing price confusion, particularly when government programs increase M through the processes we described in Chapter 17.

Let's take another approach and look at V from a different angle, psychology. To understand how psychology affects V which in turn affects prices, we only need to examine the recent historic GameStop bubble in January 2021. To simplify what happened, some institutional investors thought the stock would decrease in value, so they shorted the stock (a process to make money as the stock price declines). A group of savvy retail investors wanted to profit by "squeezing" the institutional investors into losses, forcing them to buyback the stock before their "short selling" turned into substantial losses. The retail investors began buying the GameStop stocks at unprecedented numbers, driving the prices up, not down as the institutional investors had anticipated.

Because the stock price was moving higher, not lower, the institutional investors were losing money; thus, they were forced or "squeezed" into buying back the stocks before they incurred greater losses. The additional institutional investor buying, on top of the large volume of retail investor buying, drove up GameStop stock prices even further. As word caught on quickly, due to the rapid dissemination of information over the internet, FOMO occurred, and a frenzy of more retail buyers were added, driving up prices further.

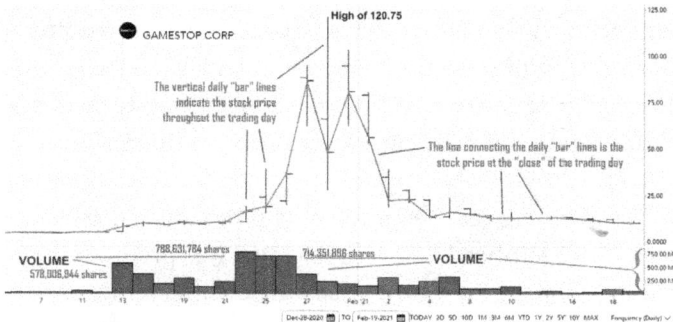

Figure 81: GameStop Squeeze

Eventually, you run out of buyers, and the smarter retail investors knew to sell and take their profits before others caught on. It didn't take long before there were more sellers than buyers and the stock price dropped to previous levels. All this occurred in a little more than two weeks. There were two fundamental psychological forces at play: speculation (easy money) and fear of missing out on the easy money. Velocity was influenced in great part by the two psychological prongs of greed and "fear of missing out" which rapidly drove up the price of GameStop.

A similar pattern occurred with the housing market during Covid, albeit more slowly. As employees began working from home virtually and businesses saw no decline in productivity, those same workers opted to move to locations they found more favorable. Some locations were predominantly more favorable, including metropolitan areas of Phoenix, Austin, and Boise. The increase in demand drove up housing prices in many markets including those previously mentioned. Then FOMO set in, and more buyers came to the market for fear that if they didn't buy sooner than later, housing prices would be out of reach for them. Home builders began increasing production. The Fed's rate hikes ended this bubble and home prices peaked in the summer of 2022.

This bubble had pushed prices higher and faster than the previous housing bubble from 2003 to 2007. The Velocity of money is almost always a psychological function. If people think the economy is doing well, they spend. If they think the economy is slowing or moving into a recession, they will spend less and save, and Velocity will decrease. To further understand the psychological effect that decreases Velocity, we need to examine the "Great Depression" of the 1930s.

The catalyst for the Great Depression is often attributed to the stock market crash of October 1929.[149] The crash was preceded by a decade of economic growth. As FOMO set in, ordinary men and women invested growing sums in stocks and bonds. Seeking greater returns, **individuals borrowed funds** and poured them into equity markets and stock prices soared.[150] Eventually, (as in the case of GameStop), velocity slowed down. When the market ran out of investors, it quickly did an about face as wise investors started taking profits by selling assets. Then, as quickly as the prices rose, they plummeted (See Figure 82).

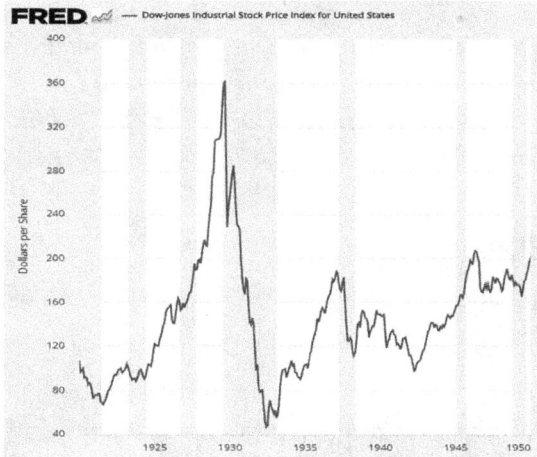

Figure 82: The Great Depression, see endnote 149

The 1930s was a new era in American politics where centralized power in D.C. (including the relatively new Federal Reserve Bank) invited more regulations and manipulations which many economists believe prolonged the Great Depression. Austrian School economist, Murray N. Rothbard elaborates:

> *"The Fed's continuing inflation of the money supply in the 1930s only succeeded in inflating prices without getting the United States out of the Great Depression. The reason for the chronic depression was that, for the first time in American history, President Herbert Hoover, followed closely and on a larger scale by Franklin Roosevelt, intervened massively in the depression process. Before 1929, every administration had allowed the recession process to do its constructive and corrective*

work as quickly as possible, so that recovery generally arrived in a year or less. But now, Hoover and Roosevelt intervened heavily: to force businesses afloat; to provide unemployment relief; to expand public works; to inflate money and credit; to support farm prices; and to engage in federal deficits.

This massive government intervention prolonged the recession indefinitely, changing what would have been a short, swift recession into a chronic debilitating depression. "[151]

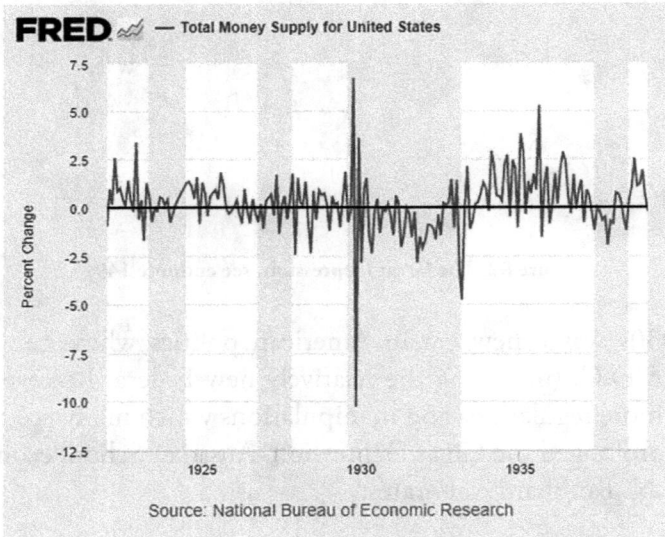

Figure 83: Money Supply shrank from late '29 thru '33

More than 9000 banks shut their doors in the four years from 1930 to 1933, resulting in depositor losses exceeding $1.3 billion.[152] As banks closed, the money supply initially shrank (See Figure 83[153]).

If you recall,

$$M * V = P * Y.$$

As M (the money supply) decreases, either prices or productivity (or both) decrease. Businesses laid off workers and this continued the downward spiral. Unemployment peaked at just over 25% (See Figure 84).[154] As unemployment increased, so did the aggregate mentality of consumer confidence. This debilitating depression did just that, depressed the general mentality of most of America. Pessimism can and does reduce "Velocity" of money with massive force. Even though the Fed pumped money into the economy, high unemployment persisted through the entire decade of the '30s, contributing to chronic pessimism and low Velocity of money.

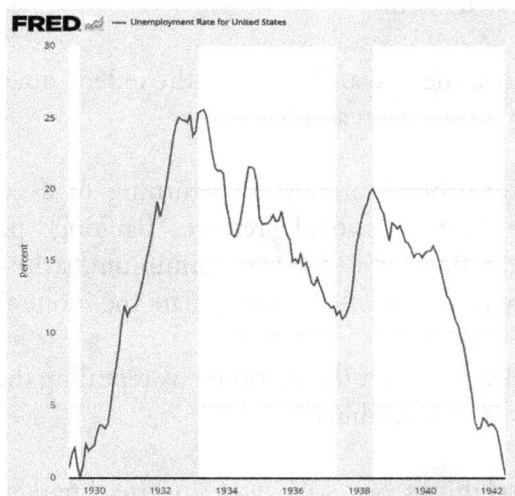

Figure 84: Unemployment, (Endnote 154)

What, then, does "Velocity" have to do with Income Taxes, you might ask? To answer that question, let's propose another: What would happen to the economy if we eliminated the Income Tax by repealing the 16th Amendment?

1. More take home pay
2. Opportunity cost of $313 Billion would be reinvested in "real" economic growth

3. Due to numbers 1 & 2 above, "Velocity" of money would initially increase
4. Significantly reduce the scope and size of the IRS, saving billions

Because we are moving into a recession which, as of this writing, hasn't reached its bottom, American citizens and businesses will collectively struggle as the Fed and the US government will, once again, meddle with the economy as they did during the Great Depression. To restore economic growth, it will be incumbent upon America to correct the ills perpetrated on our nation this past century. It is a commonsense solution I am articulating:

•   Reduce the size and scope of the federal government. Use the Constitution as a barometer.

•   Restore sound money by returning to a gold standard, correcting fractional reserve banking practices and eliminating the Fed, or at a minimum, strip them of their monetary tools which manipulate the money supply.

•   Lastly, jumpstart the economy by repealing the Income Tax (the 16th Amendment).

If we do these things, we will allow the free market to function properly. The free market always self-corrects. America was built on ingenuity, perseverance, and freedom. Those values persist today deep in the souls of Americans. Unfortunately, it has nearly been extinguished by a leviathan federal government with its tentacles reaching into every aspect of our lives. We can rekindle those values, but it will take work. In the next chapter, we will discuss the work ahead of us.

Chapter 20

ELECTING AN INDEPENDENT CANDIDATE

When I was in 6th grade, we lived in Jacksonville, Florida, while my father was stationed at NAS Jax. The Vietnam war was still being waged and battle scenes often appeared on the nightly news. In

Figure 85: POW/MIA bracelet

support of our servicemembers who had been captured or gone MIA, people of all ages wore POW/MIA bracelets. Engraved on each metal wristband was the name of a service member and the date they went missing. I remember wearing mine until my wrist reacted to the alloy.

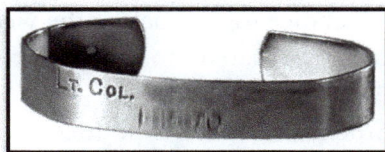

Several years earlier, naval aviator and commanding officer of Carrier Air Wing Sixteen, James Stockdale, had been captured after taking on enemy fire and punching out of his A-4 Skyhawk. He was taken to "Hanoi Hilton," a nickname the prisoners dubbed the prisoner of war camp. Stockdale spent seven and a half years as a POW suffering great deprivations and torture by his captors.

In early 1973, Stockdale was released along with the other POWs. When one learns of his leadership and courage while in captivity, it isn't any wonder he received the "Medal of Honor," the highest military decoration to those *"who distinguish themselves through conspicuous gallantry and intrepidity at the risk of life above and beyond the call of duty.*"[155] Debilitated by the torture he endured, he never returned to the cockpit. Less than a decade later, I had the privilege of hearing him give a lecture to the Brigade of Midshipmen during my tenure at the Naval Academy. James Stockdale was a true American hero during my youth.

A decade after I graduated from the Naval Academy, businessman and patriot, Ross Perot, launched a campaign to run for President against incumbent, George Herbert Walker Bush (Bush senior) and Arkansas Governor and democratic nominee, William Jefferson Clinton. Perot asked Vice Admiral Stockdale to stand in as his *temporary* Vice-Presidential running mate. Ross Perot respected veterans and Vice Admiral Stockdale was an exceptional choice, but Perot didn't change his choice for VP before the vice-presidential debate in October and hadn't prepared Stockdale for the debate.

Stockdale wasn't a politician either and the combination showed during the single VP debate, which may or may not have hurt Perot's chances of winning. I believe, however, that Perot made a major misstep in his campaign which had nothing to do with Stockdale— Perot stepped out of the race.

Like many Americans, I love underdogs and followed closely the campaign of Ross Perot. His message resonated with me, along with 19.7 million other voters who cast their vote for him. Unfortunately for Perot, they were fighting the machinery of the well-organized and well-funded two-party system that may have been responsible for Perot's blunder.

Well into the campaign season, Mr. Perot had accused the Bush campaign of an underhanded plot to disrupt his daughter's wedding and smear her name. He said he dropped out of the race to protect her. This may have been true, but today the reason for his decision to drop out of the race is still not entirely clear. He reentered the race several months later and participated in all the presidential debates, but never fully recovered in the polls. Perot lost the trust and support of many voters because of this hiatus from his campaign. He garnered 19% of the popular vote but was unable to win the majority in any state to receive any electoral votes. Bill Clinton won the election in 1992, ousting incumbent George H. Bush.

In 2016, another outsider stepped into the arena as a candidate, competing with more than a dozen other republican candidates to win the republican nomination to go head-to-head against the first female presidential candidate to win her party's nomination, Hillary Rodham Clinton. That outsider was, of course, Donald J. Trump.

While both Perot[156] and Trump[157] poured millions of their own money into their campaigns, Trump utilized the machinery of the Republican party (including $300 million+) instead of running as a true outsider/independent. Incidentally, Perot spent three times more of his own money than Trump did ($60.8 million in 1992 dollars vs. $18.6 million in 2016 dollars). Trump's decision to leverage other people's money worked, propelling him to the oval office by winning 30 states and 304 electoral votes.[158]

To date, no candidate has won a presidential election that did not belong to a major political party, except George Washington. As a matter of fact, political parties did not exist when Washington took office, nor were they anticipated in the minds of the Framers. Political parties grew into existence during Washington's tenure as President.

It was essentially over the same issues discussed in Chapter 18—how much power should the Federal government have. Thomas Jefferson and Alexander Hamilton were often at odds as Washington's Secretary of State and Secretary of Treasury, respectively. One issue they fought over was whether the Constitution authorized a national bank. Hamilton won out and the Bank of the United States was granted a twenty-year charter by Congress. The Federalists gathered around the ideas of Hamilton while Jefferson attracted anti-Federalists. This was the beginning of the two-party system. It is this entrenched political machinery we need to defeat if we are to limit or restrain the federal government's powers.

When I told a friend of my intentions to run as an independent candidate, he wisely warned me that any organization we build would likely turn into another political party. This would be my greatest concern while building a coalition. As a matter of fact, Perot's "Independent" movement evolved into another political party, "The Reform Party." To combat this, my goal would be to build a grassroots organization for the purposes of educating the electorate about the changes needed while remaining "independent" of "party" or partisan politics.

If we are successful, then the electorate will vote for the right candidates, and we can solve many institutional problems inherent within the government. If we are successful, I believe that many of our economic and political problems will be significantly reduced, if not altogether eliminated. Social problems will likely continue, but there are appropriate solutions that could significantly help, if understood and applied at the community level. Before getting into the nuts and bolts of our grassroots campaign, we need to discuss the Electoral College.

There is an ongoing debate over the "reliability" of the Electoral College. The loudest voices of those who advocate for elimination of the Electoral College are those whose presidential candidate they voted for lost an election even after receiving the most popular votes. Instead, the winning candidate received the most Electoral College votes, but did not win the popular vote. This disparity obviously does not seem fair, so it warrants a discussion and hopefully some lucid reasons for the wisdom of the Electoral College system, ***as intended by the Framers***. So, let's discuss the Electoral College system.

The Framers wanted to determine the wisest process for electing the president. They had a lengthy and often heated debate over this issue. Would it be by popular vote, by state legislatures, by state governors, by Congress, or by the US Senate alone? It was finally decided that the president would be elected indirectly by the people. Each state would select some of its leading citizens as "electors" and they would thoughtfully choose the President. The Framers didn't anticipate political parties, so the runner up would become the Vice President. The 12th Amendment changed the process for electing the President and Vice President to remedy the problem that political parties introduced to the process.

As they debated over whom should hold the power over the election of the President, each process had shortcomings. If chosen by the Congress or the Senators, The Framers thought the President would not be truly independent and this would frustrate the separation of powers they sought to achieve. If elected by popular vote, two major drawbacks concerned them.

The first drawback of a popular vote for the President was the same concern the Framers had over the formula for Congress, the more populous states would have a disproportionate weight for choosing the president over the least populous states. Hence, a presidential candidate could conceivably only campaign in the most populous states and disregard the concerns of the smaller states.

An additional concern expressed at the Constitutional Convention over the idea of a popular vote for President was that, according to Elbridge Gerry of Massachusetts, *the people are uninformed, and would be misled by a few designing men.*[159] George Mason of Virginia expressed a similar concern.[160]

The Framers also had considerable debate over whether the executive branch should be led by one person or several, as well as over length of term and reelection eligibility. They believed that the position was so important and would hold such high esteem that it warranted thoughtful debate regarding every issue. In conclusion, they decided on a single magistrate with a four-year term, no limit on reelection, and a well thought out plan around how the President would be chosen.

The legislature of each state would decide how their "electors" would be chosen. The number of electors would equal the number of senators and representatives each state possessed in Congress, *"but no Senator or Representative, or Person holding an Office of Trust or Profit under the United States, shall be appointed an Elector."*[161]

The idea of Presidential Electors is akin to Representatives and Senators in Congress. We elect Representatives and Senators to fulfill their congressional duty of studying every issue and making wise decisions regarding legislation that will ultimately affect our lives. Representatives and Senators stand in for us to do a job so that we don't have to. We expect them to exercise wisdom in the performance of their duties. In like manner, the Framers expected the Presidential Electors to be some of the wisest, "enlightened and respectable citizens"[162] for the singular purpose of vetting and then voting on who would best serve in the capacity of President.

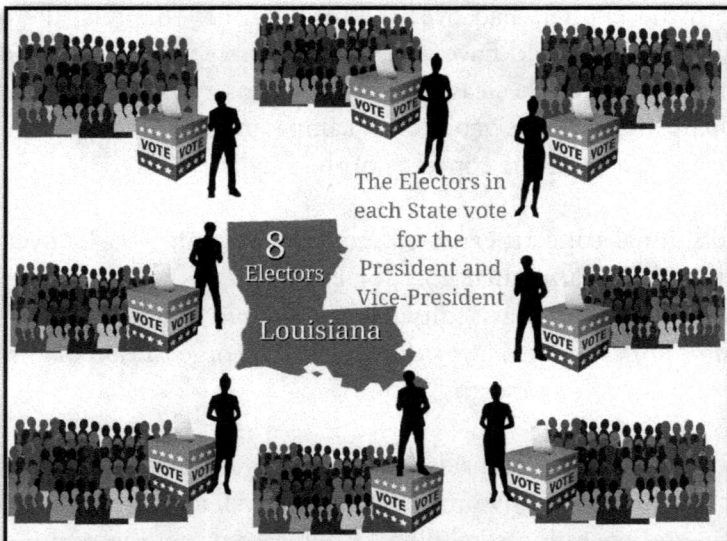

Figure 86: Electors should be "enlightened and respectable."

They left the decision on how Presidential Electors would be chosen to the states' legislatures, but it was anticipated that the people would appoint (or elect) Electors to do the heavy lifting of vetting candidates for President and Vice President, or so the Framers intended. Much like the other problems we discussed in Chapter 18, the Constitution as designed by the Framers, is not followed today, and that includes the process of electing the President.

The process of electing the President and Vice President has evolved into 50 popular votes and the ***Electors no longer serve any meaningful purpose***. This bastardized version is now found in 48 of the 50 states with two minor exceptions, Maine and Nebraska. In the 48 states, each political party candidate has their own set of Electors that, by law in most states, are required to cast their "Elector" vote for their party candidate should that person win the popular vote. For example, in Figure 87 the Louisiana voters will cast their vote for the Presidential candidate and Vice-Presidential running mate on a political party's ticket but will actually be casting votes for the party's respective eight electors.

In 2012, Romney won the popular vote in Louisiana at 57.8%, Trump won in 2016 and 2020 at 58.1% and 58.46% respectively. Winning all Elector votes in a state by a huge margin of popular votes may seem fitting, but when the election is close, the "winner takes all" process can be disconcerting, particularly if there is suspicion of voter fraud.

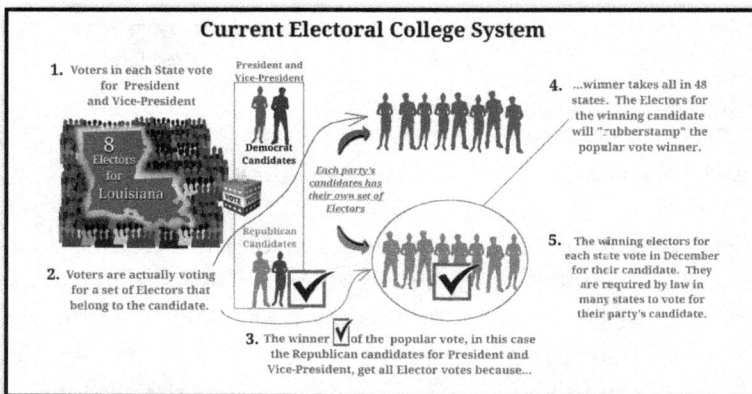

Figure 87: Current Electoral College System

In many "swing states" where the election is close, the "winner takes all" process adds to voter frustration. In 2012, Obama (and the Democratic Party) won all 29 Florida "Electors" even though Romney came close and received 49.1% of the popular votes. In 2016, Trump received all the 29 Electors with 49% of the popular vote. The winner of the popular vote, even if by a small fraction, gets the entire number of "Elector" votes that their state is entitled to. "Electors" are rubberstamping a popular vote in their respective states, and this is entirely counterproductive to the purpose of the Electoral College System. The system has become 48 popular voting contests with Maine and Nebraska having slightly different systems.

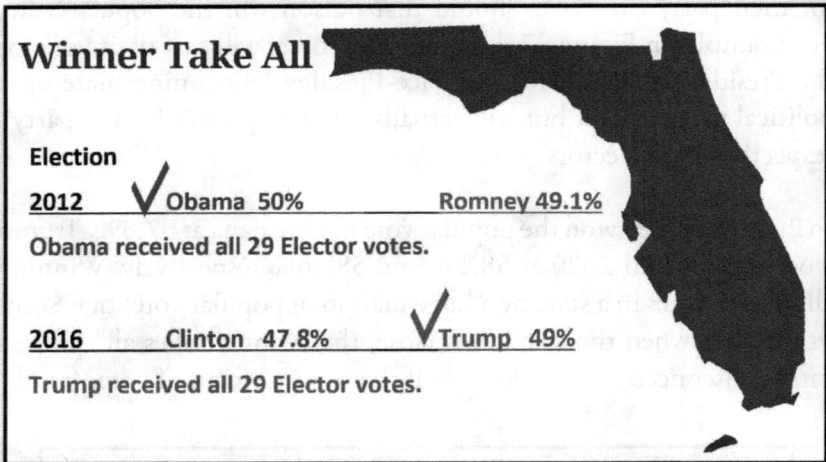

Figure 88: Florida is a hotly contested state for President

It is my contention that **our current process is a product of the two-party system which has hijacked our elections.**

It is my intention to show the wisdom of the Electoral College System as envisioned by the Framers. As you recall, I passionately believe that the God of the Universe spoke to my mind in the winter of 1995 and told me to "run for president." This I intend to do. In the process of running, my plan is to demonstrate the wisdom of the Electoral College system as envisioned by the Framers **_by using it_**.

It is my hope that, by utilizing a pure Electoral College, we can tear down the two-party system and bring to pass a truly independent President, one separate from the major parties, one who possesses a love for country and one who honors the Constitution. If we are to survive as a nation, we need a strong, **independent**, honorable President who has the courage to act according to the best interests of the entire nation, without prejudice to any singular group of people, community, business, or entity within the sovereign borders of our nation.

I have spent the last 27 years often questioning the wisdom of why God would choose me to undertake such a lofty goal. While I am confident I can do as good a job as any president that has been in office these last 27 years, I have had a lot of time to reflect. I have sought wisdom and counsel from some of the most talented people I know. My friend, Paul, from Chapter 6, provided some excellent council and happened to be related to Mitt Romney. Paul was kind enough to forward my letter to Mitt, that I might seek his wisdom too.

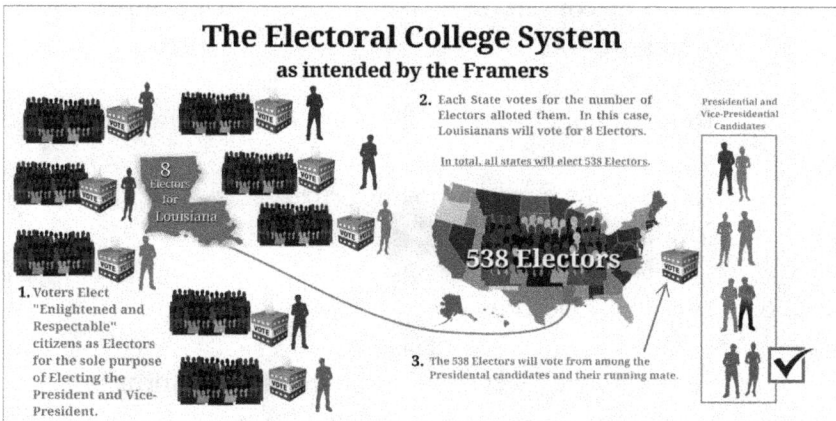

Figure 89: Framers created a pure system.

Yet, with all the council I have received, the guidance I receive from Heavenly Father from time to time is what drives me and strengthens me to go forward. One day I realized that my purpose in running may not be to win, but to provide an opportunity for someone with far more talent and leadership to become president, and I'm not talking about draining votes from one major party candidate so the other can win. I'm talking about something far better. Let me explain.

When I would often reflect on God's commandment to "run for president," I realized that He may have had a different purpose in mind than me becoming president. I've pondered often over what God plans to achieve. After all, many of my experiences in life where I followed a prompting from God didn't turn out as I had anticipated. Sometimes God has a greater, or perhaps different purpose in mind than an outcome we think He wants. So, I've pondered what might be God's desired outcome. I've come up with several.

1. To test the nation's morality

2. To awaken many apathetic voters

3. To stir up conversations about what the Constitution really means

4. To enlighten citizens to the plight of fiat money

5. To awaken freedom loving citizens to take back our government

6. To win the election

7. To restore the Electoral College to its purest form and elect a truly wise and choice president.

I believe that we can accomplish every goal above. Not only do I plan to win, but I also plan to utilize the "pure" Electoral College system so that Americans can nominate other candidates who, for various reasons, do not run for president, but would make an excellent one. To understand this process, I will refer you to our next chapter. Before doing so, I have one question:

Are you ready to help?

Chapter 21

HE WHO FAILS TO PLAN, PLANS TO FAIL

When I served my time in the Navy, each flight required about an hour or two of preflight planning for all aspects of the flight, including reviewing NOTAMs (formerly "Notice to Airmen" which was changed to "Notice to Air Missions" in 2021[163]), weather, fuel requirements, mission requirements, aircraft maintenance discrepancies and anything else that would affect the success of the mission. While serving as an airline pilot, we had a dispatcher who planned our flights and we would review his or her planning, which included all the above except for a mission. Missions in the airline business are all identical: get passengers from A to B safely.

The major difference between the Navy experience and the airline experience is the dispatcher. Because the tempo of airline operations is robust and aircrews fly to multiple destinations any given day, week and month, dispatchers relieve the aircrews of the burden of all the preflight planning.

Aircrews review the dispatcher's work and the captain and dispatcher jointly share in the responsibility of the safety of the flight. Because airline dispatchers plan flights for the same locations and areas of the country day in and day out, they become remarkably familiar with their assigned areas and airports. Aircrew often don't have the same routes in their flight schedules. They often fly into a region or city for the first time, without the benefit of "familiarity." Having the benefit of the dispatcher's familiarity with the region and airports provides an extra layer of safety. The dispatcher is the aircrew's best asset for the success of a flight.

Figure 90: handcart

Planning is critical for the success of any endeavor. As I am writing this chapter, my wife and I have been tasked with an assignment in our church to be pseudo parents to a group of 7 or 8 youth, ages 14 to 18, for an event that lasts three and a half days. The event replicates the Mormon pioneers' handcart trek from Illinois to the Great Salt Lake area. The entire event consists of about 150 youth grouped into "pseudo" families led by a husband-and-wife team affectionately called "Ma & Pa." None of the "family" members are acquainted

Figure 91: Dutch Oven cooking

with each other prior to the event. Each "family" pulls and pushes a handcart loaded with basic belongings for several miles each day. They will cook meals in Dutch ovens and sleep in primitive conditions.

The entire event builds faith, character, and an appreciation for the sacrifices that Mormon pioneers made when driven out of Illinois, to settle in the Great Salt Lake area. The planning for these simulated "treks" takes about a year and past experiences have been overwhelmingly successful in accomplishing the intended goals.

To be successful in any significant endeavor requires proper planning. Running for President as an Independent candidate requires proper planning and there are significant hurdles that need to be achieved if we are to be successful. Let me begin by sharing the process I plan on using.

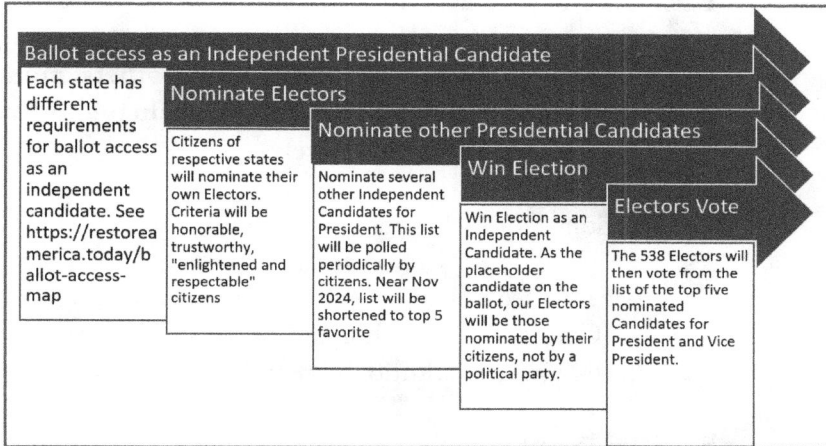

Ballot access as an Independent Presidential Candidate					
Each state has different requirements for ballot access as an independent candidate. See https://restoreamerica.today/ballot-access-map	Nominate Electors				
	Citizens of respective states will nominate their own Electors. Criteria will be honorable, trustworthy, "enlightened and respectable" citizens	Nominate other Presidential Candidates			
		Nominate several other Independent Candidates for President. This list will be polled periodically by citizens. Near Nov 2024, list will be shortened to top 5 favorite	Win Election		
			Win Election as an Independent Candidate. As the placeholder candidate on the ballot, our Electors will be those nominated by their citizens, not by a political party.	Electors Vote	
				The 538 Electors will then vote from the list of the top five nominated Candidates for President and Vice President.	

Figure 92: General Election Plan

I took a course on organizational structures in college and my life's experiences in a variety of organizations ranging from a large corporation, the military, and volunteer groups have all reinforced the importance of a proper organizational structure for maximum efficiency. The most important concept we need to keep in mind is that a group that is too big is inefficient and a group that is too small can be overwhelmed by the responsibilities. A group must be "right sized," just like we discussed in Chapter 15, "Government 101 for Dummies."

Because we are building a grassroots movement from the ground up, we need to recognize there is a final goal, as well as multiple intermediate goals we want to achieve. Our grassroots organization must be right sized for each goal we hope to achieve. We must continually evaluate our goals and reorganize our groups as needed so they remain right sized as we progress through each process of our overall plan. Keeping Figure 92 as our guide, let's discuss each part of the plan.

STEP I. **Get candidate name on the ballot for all 50 states and District of Columbia.**

1. **Each state has its own unique requirements for ballot access as an independent candidate. Some petitions are simple (Tennessee: 275 signatures), others more difficult (California, Texas & North Carolina: approx. 200K, 113K, and 70K respectively).**

   a. Petitions required in most states:
      i. Signed by Registered voters
      ii. Filing fee in lieu of petition for some states (Colorado & Oklahoma)
      iii. Filing fee in addition to petition (Nevada & Utah)

   b. Window of time for petitions:
      i. On average, the window for obtaining signatures on petitions is 6 months, January through June of 2024.
      ii. Texas has a very tight window of 68 days.
      iii. Various deadlines for all petitions, some as early as March 2024, others as late as September 2024.

2. **Ballot access map:**
   https://restoreamerica.today/ballot-access-map
   a. Ballot access requirements are rarely published before September of the year preceding the election (September 2023 for November 5th, 2024, election)
   b. Use this 2020 map as a guide for requirements and planning.

3. **Seek volunteers:**
   a. Seek pledges first, get micro commitments.
   b. Fill positions:
      i. State leaders
      ii. Petition Circulators

        iii. Liaison between Secretary of State over Elections Division
            1. Build rapport.
            2. Stay ahead of deadlines.

4. **Organize by state and ballot access requirements:**
    a. Ballot access requirements are state dependent
    b. Larger petition requirements or shorter window for petitions requires focused attention and greater resources, including volunteers

STEP II. **Nominate Electors**

1. **This should be Step 1 in chronology but is second in importance.**
2. **Ballot access for Independent Candidates requires a list of "Electors" that accompany the name for President and Vice President.**
3. **"Electors" are nominated:**
    a. Seek respected citizens from their communities.
    b. Nomination requirements to be determined, such as a 100 signatures petition.
    c. ***Electors pledge to support the Constitution as intended by Framers, "limited government."***
    d. Need specified number of Electors per state, as per Constitution.
4. **See map for Electors:**
    https://restoreamerica.today/electoral-college

5. **Electors to be voted on if the total number of nominees exceeds each state's Constitutional allotment. For example, if Utah citizens nominate 15 Electors, the 15 names will be periodically voted upon, reducing the size of the list until 6 Electors are chosen.**
6. **Electors shall remain independent of process.**

7. **Electors are bound by state law in 13 states to vote for candidate on ballot if candidate wins popular vote.**
   a. This is a shortcoming of the present system, which we hope to correct.
   b. We want "Electors" to have latitude to vote from the list of presidential candidates we submit to them, _IF_ we win popular vote for the respective state.
      i. The list of candidates is determined by "Step III" below.
   c. Liaison with Secretaries of State to seek and find ways to provide exceptions to "Faithless Electors" voter laws in these 13 states.
      i. This process can begin as soon as possible.

STEP III. **Nominate Presidential Candidates**

1. **America is a great nation with great people and born leaders. We seek to find someone capable of leading and managing the affairs of our federal government.**
   a. Independent, non-partisan
   b. Trustworthy
   c. Proven

2. **We seek to find candidates who possess wisdom and recognize we need to return to limited government.**
   a. Understand the Constitution
   b. Law abiding
   c. Beyond reproach

3. **We will have a nomination process for candidates:**
   a. Nominated by another person.
   b. Nominations must include 100 signatures of people who can attest to the unimpeachable character of the candidate.

4. **Nominees list will increase and be voted upon:**
   a. Nominees will undergo a series of secure, but transparent polls or elections.
   b. Nominees will be "weighted" by each poll or election.
   c. Nomination process will end on or about June 2024.
   d. Subsequent polls or elections will narrow the list of nominees.
   e. The final poll or election will narrow the list of nominees from 10 to top 4 or 5 presidential candidates and 2 or 3 Vice Presidential candidates.

STEP IV. <u>Await result of national election.</u>

1. **Candidate from Step 1 must win majority (270) of "Electors" in general election on November 5th, 2024.**
2. **538 Electors from Step II will not be obligated to vote for candidate on ballot in general election.**
3. **Final list of presidential and vice-presidential candidates from Step III will be presented to 538 Electors from Step II.**

STEP V. <u>"Electors" vote in December 2024 for President and Vice-President</u>

The process described in these 5 Steps is a guide and overview of what we can achieve, electing an independent candidate for President—one not beholden to a political party, nor like Trump, who commandeered a political party to win.

<u>I know that an independent candidate can win, and the numbers bare witness of it</u>. Let's examine some numbers.

The data in Figure 93 was taken from the FEC's report (Federal Election Commission) "Federal Elections 2020."[164] The numbers, bear a striking similarity to Figure 1 in Chapter 1, where Independents at 42% outnumber Democrats at 29% and Republicans at 27%.

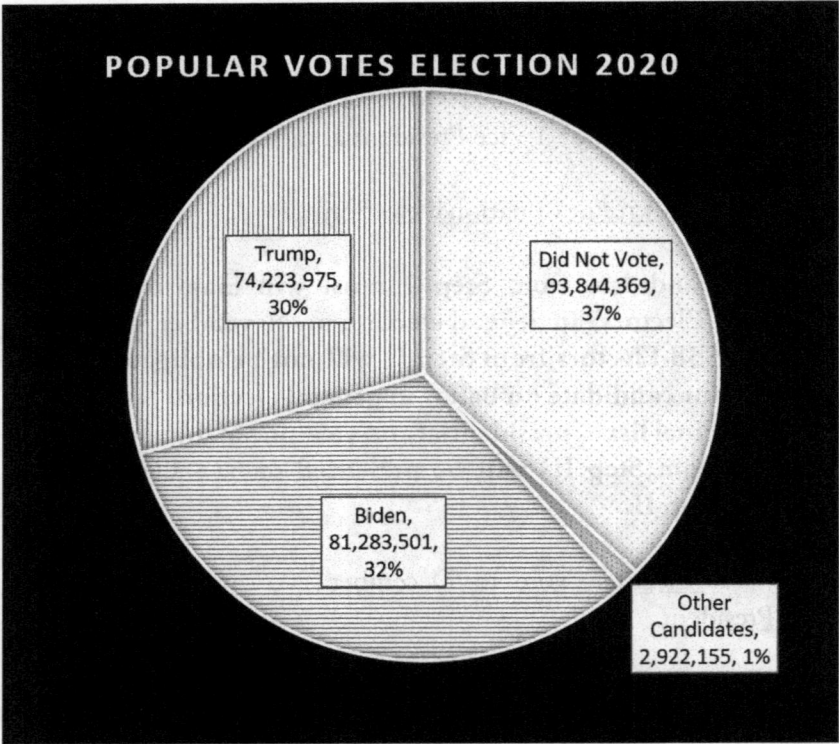

POPULAR VOTES ELECTION 2020

Trump, 74,223,975, 30%

Did Not Vote, 93,844,369, 37%

Biden, 81,283,501, 32%

Other Candidates, 2,922,155, 1%

Figure 93: Election 2020

We can reasonably assume that many citizens who identify as Independents cast a vote for one of the candidates on the ballot. If we conservatively assume that one fourth of the votes cast in the 2020 Election identified as Independents, they will have likely been divided somewhat equally among the 158,429,631 votes cast. Thus, if we take ¼ of 158,429,631 we get, 39,607,407 votes for an independent candidate. Independent voters usually choose to vote for a major party candidate because they often have no other choice. ***Ross Perot proved that a third choice for president can make a difference.*** As a matter of fact, Figure 94 bears a similar resemblance to the 1992 election wherein Perot garnered 19% of the popular vote.

Thus, if a reasonable third choice for independent voters had been available, the vote would have been somewhere between 19% to 25% as Figure 94 suggests.

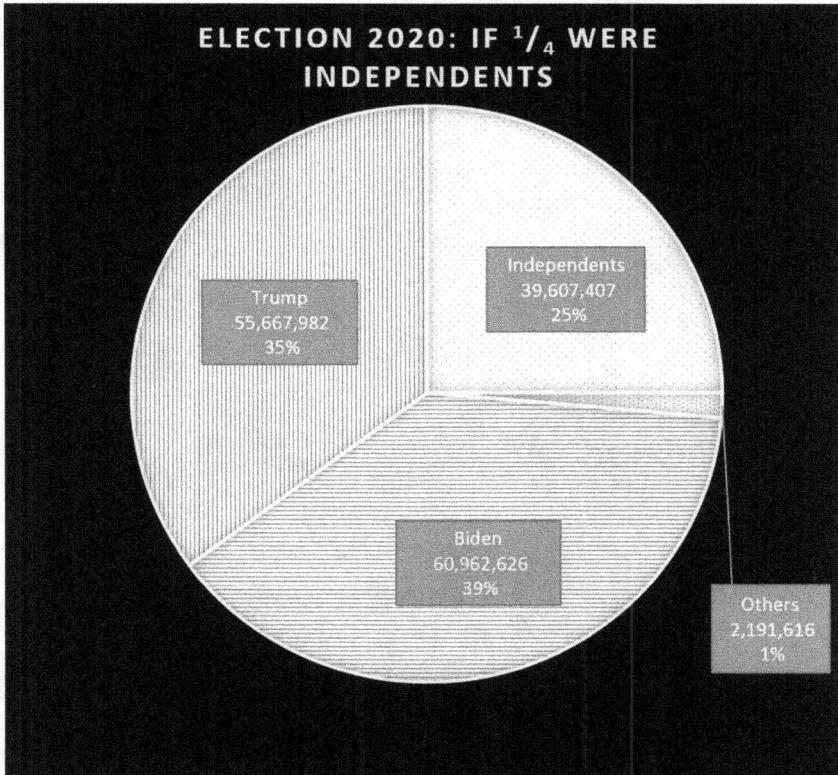

ELECTION 2020: IF ¹/₄ WERE INDEPENDENTS

Trump
55,667,982
35%

Independents
39,607,407
25%

Biden
60,962,626
39%

Others
2,191,616
1%

Figure 94: If ¼ of independents had voted independent

I believe we can give independent voters a compelling reason to vote independent. That means, the actual number of voters in 2020 would have resembled the percentage of voters who identify as Independents (Figure 1 chapter 1), as Figure 95 suggests. Lest we forget, there were approximately 94 million voters who did not participate in the 2020 elections. Why? As we discussed in Chapter 15, voter apathy plays a major role. They have simply lost hope. I believe we can give them hope and a reason to vote because **their vote will make a difference**. If we could persuade just half of those prospective voters to participate in 2024, then the election could look like Figure 96.

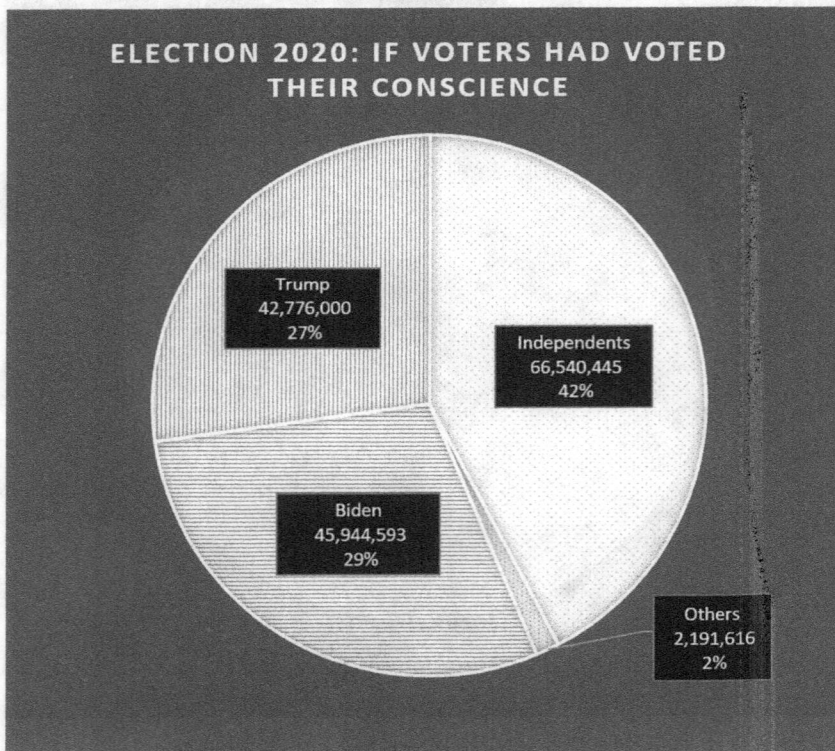

Figure 95: Sample Election -- voters vote their conscience

ELECTION 2024

Republican
42,776,000
21%

Independents
113,462,629
56%

Democrat
45,944,593
22%

Others
2,191,616
1%

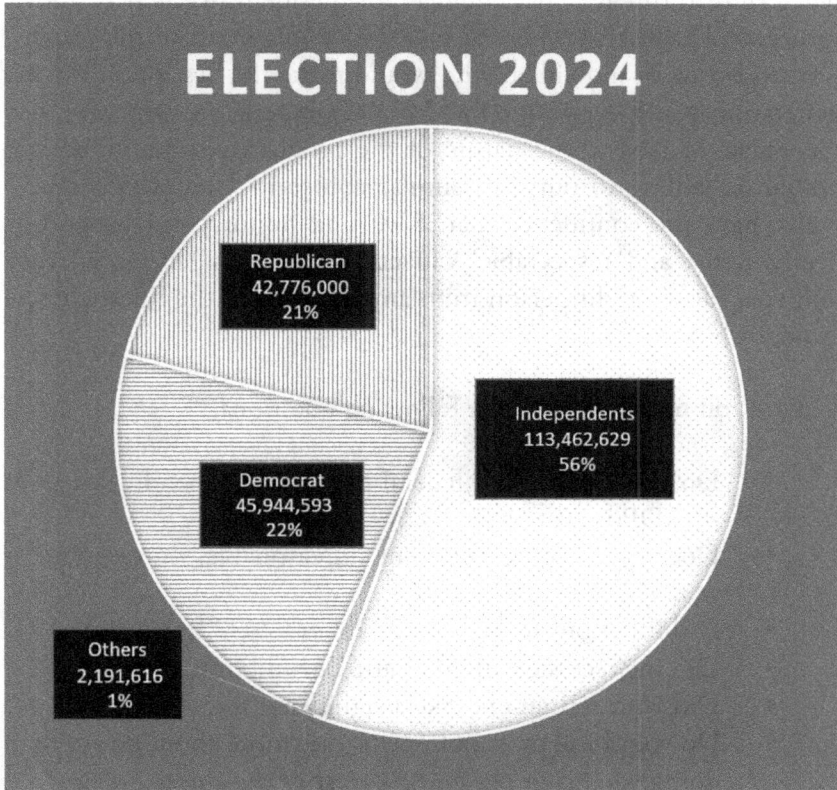

Figure 96: Independent and disenfranchised voters can sway election.

It would be a significant victory for a return to "good government." In case you missed it, I'm not espousing the idea that I would make the best president, nor that I am the best candidate. However, I am wise enough to know there are better individuals in our nation than me who would make an ideal president. My mission in life is to keep the commandment I received in 1995, "run for president." I plan on doing so, but I will require an army of volunteers willing to help. I hope this book is persuasive enough to solicit volunteers, for the reasons I've articulated. We have some serious problems in our nation that we need to correct.

My goal is to run as a "placeholder" for president in "Step 1" above. However, I trust that "Step 3" will find a "diamond in the rough," a true gem of an individual who would make the best president my generation could ever hope for. My only criteria are that they also recognize, as I have, the nature of the problems I've outlined and would be willing to pursue a similar course to "Restore America." I also have the confidence that if we find honorable, trustworthy, "enlightened and respectable" citizens to serve as "Electors," they will vote for the right person from among some of the finest choices America has to offer.

I invite you to ask yourself the following questions.

- Do you believe that federal government spending at 24% of GDP is excessive?
- Does the income tax seem unreasonable, outrageous, or unfair?
- Did inflation throughout 2021 and 2022 hurt you?
- Did the recession of 2023 and beyond hurt you?
- Did your retirement take a significant hit?
- Do you think most politicians care more about power than doing what is in ***the best interest of the entire nation?***
- Did you understand the problem of chronic inflation in Chapter 17 for which our government is culpable?
- Do you believe your liberties are at stake from a growing federal government?
- Do you believe the trajectory of our government to be destructive?
- Do you care about leaving the nation in better shape for your posterity?

If you answered yes to more than one of the above, the next chapter is for you.

Chapter 22

MANY HANDS MAKE LIGHT WORK

It was the night of the biggest fundraiser for our two youngest sons' elementary school. I mentioned in Chapter 11 that I learned a valuable lesson from my wife at this fundraiser. I also learned something that hadn't occurred to me yet. As the head of the fundraiser, I was circulating among the attendees, trying to ensure everyone was having a good time and everything was going according to plan. If you recall, I promoted the event for several weeks as "Springy the Clown" and was dressed accordingly at the event.

We had pizzas provided by the school cafeteria and many people were dining when I realized we had not planned adequately for "cleanup." I turned to a father and asked if he would kindly help us by taking out a trash bin that was full and insert another empty bag. He looked at me with contempt, and quickly dismissed my request. He might have had a legitimate excuse not to help, but it was his look of disdain that surprised me most. I was not used to this behavior.

Most people I associate with are often more than willing to serve others, without recompense or reward. My airline had a long history of hiring people that were service oriented. My associates at church are of similar character. My wife is the same, and we raised our children to help others too.

As I've grown older, I am no longer surprised by those who are unwilling to help. I realize there are people on all sides of the spectrum, those unwilling to help, those who need help, and those who would give the shirt off their back to help. I prefer to associate with the latter. Being service-minded is innate in many people, but it can be learned and is a valuable life lesson. In the Book of Mormon, there is a famous speech given by King Benjamin, encouraging his people to keep the commandments of God and to learn the importance of service. I quote from a portion of his speech:

> *14 And even I, myself, have labored with mine own hands that I might serve you, and that ye should not be laden with taxes, and that there should nothing come upon you which was grievous to be borne—and of all these things which I have spoken, ye yourselves are witnesses this day.*

> *15 Yet, my brethren, I have not done these things that I might boast, neither do I tell these things that thereby I might accuse you; but I tell you these things that ye may know that I can answer a clear conscience before God this day.*

> *16 Behold, I say unto you that because I said unto you that I had spent my days in your service, I do not desire to boast, for I have only been in the service of God.*

> *17 And behold, I tell you these things that ye may learn wisdom; that ye may learn that when ye are in the service of your fellow beings ye are only in the service of your God.*

> *18 Behold, ye have called me your king; and if I, whom ye call your king, do labor to serve you, then ought not ye to labor to serve one another?*

19 And behold also, if I, whom ye call your king, who has spent his days in your service, and yet has been in the service of God, do merit any thanks from you, O how you ought to thank your heavenly King!

20 I say unto you, my brethren, that if you should render all the thanks and praise which your whole soul has power to possess, to that God who has created you, and has kept and preserved you, and has caused that ye should rejoice, and has granted that ye should live in peace one with another—

21 I say unto you that if ye should serve him who has created you from the beginning, and is preserving you from day to day, by lending you breath, that ye may live and move and do according to your own will, and even supporting you from one moment to another—I say, if ye should serve him with all your whole souls yet ye would be unprofitable servants.

22 And behold, all that he requires of you is to keep his commandments; and he has promised you that if ye would keep his commandments ye should prosper in the land; and he never doth vary from that which he hath said; therefore, if ye do keep his commandments he doth bless you and prosper you.

Service to others is a Godly attribute and one that I have found brings tremendous peace to the soul. Jesus Christ, my exemplar, friend, and Savior taught the importance of serving by his deeds throughout His mortal ministry. It is this attribute of service that I am appealing to in this chapter.

The United States of America is synonymous with freedom. Freedom is what defines the soul of our country. People pour across our borders seeking it. My ancestors left their homelands in search of it. Centuries of immigrants from all over the world have come here driven by hopes of achieving it. We must preserve freedom and that requires recognition that the "chains" on the federal government are broken. We must "restore" those chains on the federal government, or we will lose our precious freedoms.

When I shared with one of my friends the epiphany I received, his counsel was to come up with a catchy phrase such as "taking a stance."

Taking A Stance ★★★★★★★★★★★★★★★★★★

I liked it and had plans to use it; however, when I realized we had more to accomplish, "Restore" became my buzzword and I ran with that in my mind. Restore is now the acronym for our platform.

RESTORE AMERICA TODAY

THE CONSTITUTION HANGS BY A THREAD

R-Reaffirm the Constitution
E-Elect Virtuous Leaders
S-Spend Wisely
T-Term Limits
O-Observe God
R-Remember 9-11
E-Embrace the Future

I am confident that there are millions of people who agree with one or more of the following statements:

> Yes, the federal government has usurped powers the founding generation never intended it to have.

> Yes, I understand the problems of deficit spending and inflation and agree it needs to be fixed.

> Yes, I understand our freedom is in jeopardy.

America needs YOU! We need your service! The work to be done cannot be done by one person, or even one thousand people. The work that needs to be done—if we are to hand off our nation to our posterity better than we received it—will require a minimum of one million service-minded people who answered "Yes" above. Many hands make light work and if you become a "million-miler" by volunteering, we can "restore" America.

That's why I bought the following URL:
https://RestoreAmerica.Today

If you visit the website, you will find the same acronym "RESTORE" above. It is the foundation of the work I hope we can achieve. There are many issues that pundits and candidates pontificate about during elections. I don't believe we need to address every issue. In the words of Stephen Covey, we need to put "first things first." Many campaign issues that are discussed are not important to me, nor to many of you. As a matter of fact, I think many of the issues are meant to distract us from what is more important: our federal government wields too much power. In light of this awareness, you will not hear me pontificate over every issue that the media or political parties want to discuss, primarily because many of those so-called issues do not belong within the scope of our federal government's control. Our goal is to return to that fork in the road where we went wrong.

If you recall from Chapter 7, I believe our nation has been on the wrong path for the better part of a century. Maintaining that path won't get us to the destination the Framers sought to achieve for their posterity, namely justice, domestic tranquility, common defense, general welfare, and liberty. We need to make fundamental changes. We need every able-bodied person willing to add their talents to the work ahead, no matter how small the contribution. Your participation will lighten the load because "many hands make light work!"

Chapter 23

A FEW GOOD MEN

Occasionally, Hollywood will produce a movie that becomes a classic, one that you can watch many times and never grow tired of. The lessons and principles found in such movies are timeless. I have my favorites that teach principles of leadership, courage, integrity, compassion, and love. I never grow tired of some of the movies or television productions that teach enduring principles. I chose the above title because it is a classic movie that many readers have heard of. It was produced in 1992, long before many young people today were born, with an all-star cast and superb acting. It is a riveting movie! We need "a few good men" now more than ever! Let me explain.

Every two years, 435 Representatives in Congress are up for reelection. On average over the last 12 elections, only 23 incumbents lost.[165] The following statistics are from the 118th Congress that began on January 3rd, 2023:

Table 1

Number of Representatives	Percent of total Members in House	Have served longer than	Longer than a
193	44.4%	8 years	2-term president
123	28.3%	12 years	2-term senator
67	15.4%	18 years	3-term senator
55	12.6%	20 years	President FDR

Is it any wonder that many are drunk with power? This is not an indictment on all, or even most members of Congress. I believe that many serve with a sincere desire to do what they believe is right. However, most have succumbed to the flawed D.C. culture that has been inculcated for decades: "citizens' rights originate in Washington D.C." and "the federal government has unlimited power." Because of that culture, I would be interested in learning how many of our representatives understand the Constitution as intended by the Framers. Or worse, have they even read it?

We need a "few good men" **and women** who recognize that Congress, along with the President, needs to be reined in. We have an opportunity to make real change, but ***we need to elect at least 220 new Representatives*** to Congress in 2024 who understand the changes I've outlined and have the courage to say "no" to big government.

From Table 1 above, we see that 193 representatives are in their 5th or longer term. 41 more are in their 4th term and will be in their 8th year when Election 2024 comes. Those two groups combined equal 234 representatives, or 54.5% of the House of Representatives. I would be surprised to discover if more than a small fraction understands the "chains" of the Constitution. This group constitutes a good start when deciding who to run against.

At https://spendingtracker.org, you can see how your representatives voted in terms of the cost of legislation over a 10-year window as calculated by the Congressional Budget Office (CBO).

Legislation Status ❷

● Enacted laws

◯ All bills

The data can be filtered to include "All bills" not just those which became laws. Filtering the data for "All bills" gives you an idea of how willing they are to spend your tax dollars. For example, in the 116th Congress (January 3, 2019, to January 3, 2021), 214 representatives voted on bills that would have cost more than $6.2 Trillion over the 10-year window.

Of those 214, 190 were willing to spend more than $9 Trillion. Fortunately for you and me, only $3.2 Trillion worth of legislation was passed during those 2 years, of which more than half was for the Coronavirus response in 2020 (about $2.2 Trillion).

Most of those in Congress have no awareness of the impact of spending money that doesn't yet exist but is created by the process we described in Chapter 17. It would behoove the entire nation if we could vote out of office, at a minimum, the 214 who have no fiscal restraint.

Every year, the CBO publishes a report and in 2015 they warned,

> *"If current laws remained generally unchanged, federal debt held by the public would exceed 100 percent of GDP by 2040 and continue on an upward path relative to the size of the economy—a trend that could not be sustained indefinitely."*

Even the Congressional Budget Office is concerned that our representatives have no restraint when it comes to spending. Sadly, their projection of when the debt would exceed 100% of GDP was missed by 20 years. As seen in Figure 97, published in the CBO's

2021 Long-Term Budget Outlook[166], our national debt exceeded 100% of GDP in 2020.

Federal Debt Held by the Public, 1900 to 2051

Percentage of Gross Domestic Product

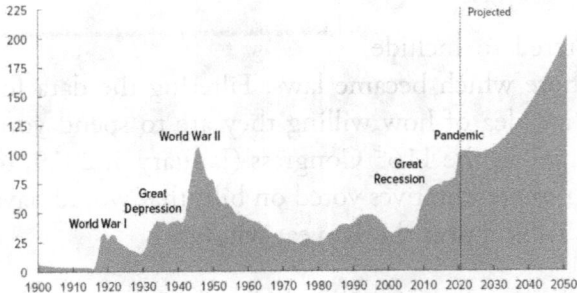

Projected

Growing deficits are projected to drive federal debt held by the public to unprecedented levels over the next 30 years. By 2051, debt is projected to reach more than 200 percent of gross domestic product.

World War II

Pandemic

Great Recession

Great Depression

World War I

Data source: Congressional Budget Office. See www.cbo.gov/publication/56977#data.

Figure 97: Federal Debt Projection

It is time for real change in Congress and while Term Limits would be a good start, I invite at least 220 citizens who understand the need to put our "House" in order, to run for Congress!

Will you be one of those "few good men" and women?

Chapter 24

NINEVAH OR ROME? WE MUST CHOOSE!

As a student of the bible, I find many of the faith promoting stories inspiring. As a Christian, my favorite stories are about the divine character of Jesus Christ found in the New Testament. It is He whom all Christians revere and try to emulate. To dedicate one's life to the service of others, full-time, is something that is still beyond my capacity. My occasional selfish tendencies remind me that I'm very fallible and human. There are many other individuals in the bible, both Old and New Testament, who served faithfully and dedicated their lives to God. Their examples of faith and courage are inspiring. There was one person, however, whose service to God was not quite as virtuous when compared to others. His name was Jonah.

Jonah was a "lesser" prophet in the Old Testament. The book of Jonah was written by an unknown author. There is no scriptural record of any role he played among his own people, the Israelites. Like many ancient prophets, Jonah was called by God to "cry" repentance, not to the Israelites, but unto the people of "that great city" Nineveh (the Assyrian capital) for their "wickedness is come up before me." Assyria was a foe to Israel, so it might explain Jonah's reluctance to go and "cry repentance" unto them. The story is compelling, not because of Jonah, but because it shows that God is mindful of all humanity.

As the story goes, Jonah tried to shirk this responsibility by fleeing in a ship headed to Tarshish. Not long afterwards, the ship encountered a great storm and the mariners all cried unto their god for relief. Upon discovering that Jonah admitted he was fleeing from his God, the mariners asked what they should do to calm the sea. Jonah, remarkably, told them to cast him into the sea. The crew didn't want Jonah's blood on their hands, so they continued to *"row hard to bring it to the land, but they could not: for the sea wrought and was tempestuous against them."*

The story continues:

> *14 Wherefore they cried unto the Lord, and said, We beseech thee, O Lord, we beseech thee, let us not perish for this man's life, and lay not upon us innocent blood: for thou, O Lord, hast done as it pleased thee.*

> *15 So they took up Jonah and cast him forth into the sea: and the sea ceased from her raging.*

> *16 Then the men feared the Lord exceedingly, and offered a sacrifice unto the Lord, and made vows.*

> *17 Now the Lord had prepared a great fish to swallow up Jonah. And Jonah was in the belly of the fish three days and three nights. (Bible: King James Version, Jonah 1)*

God is patient, merciful and loving. He has our best interest at heart, both as individuals and communities. He is constantly giving us multiple chances to learn how best to navigate through life and learn the valuable lessons that only life on this earth can teach us. But humans are selfish by nature. It is this selfish nature that God is trying to help us overcome that we may be more "divine." The selfish side of humanity can bring civilizations to ruin and to self-destruct. We can witness the destruction of civilizations throughout history.

But our selfish nature doesn't prevent God from constantly trying to reach out to us. The story of Jonah continues.

> *1 Then Jonah prayed unto the Lord his God out of the fish's belly,*
>
> *2 And said, I cried by reason of mine affliction unto the Lord, and he heard me; out of the belly of hell cried I, and thou heardest my voice...*
>
> *10 And the Lord spake unto the fish, and it vomited out Jonah upon the dry land.*

God, once again, called Jonah to preach to the people of Nineveh and this time he dutifully obeyed. Upon hearing Jonah's message, word spread throughout the land including the King. They all, from the greatest to the least, humbled themselves, through fasting and prayer, hoping that God might spare them. God saw they were sincere, that they turned from their violence and evil ways and spared them from whatever destruction Jonah had preached unto them.

It is a fascinating story to say the least. If I had not had many experiences in my life where I witnessed the hand of God in the lives of people, including my own, I would say it was a tall tale. However, I'm not so inclined to believe that now. I invite you to reread Chapter 4 to rediscover the handful of experiences where I personally witnessed the hand of God in my life. I will go to my grave with the firm conviction that He is real and anxiously engaged in wanting to help us. We just need to learn how to listen.

Perhaps my mission to run for president is God trying to help us as a nation—to renew the virtues that made our country so successful, to return to the principles upon which our country was founded, to restore the country in which He will continue to bless us. It is up to us. My campaign may just be a test for our nation. Please believe me when I tell you I'd rather be doing something other than thrust myself and my family into the spotlight.

Then there was Rome.

Great civilizations come and go, and the United States is not immune from following the same downward path as the great Roman Empire. We already see in our country today many schisms and problems that were observed during the fall of the Roman Empire. They include:

- Power struggles within government
- Citizens distrust their leaders/government
- Skirmishes and fighting in regions about the empire
- Moral decline
- A culture of violence

While studying the success and growth of the Roman Empire, I found other parallels between the United States and the Roman Empire which contribute to the success of any society. During early Roman history, when the Empire was simply a city on the Tiber River, Romans were conquered by a group called the Etruscans, which introduced Romans to several ideas that helped Romans prosper. One concept was public meetings where citizens could meet to discuss problems. In other words, it wasn't top-down government, at least not yet. Trade was also introduced to the Romans where they learned the value and benefit of trade among the seafaring citizens of the Mediterranean world.

As the Roman empire grew throughout the Mediterranean region (through conquest), the people of outlying towns and cities were encouraged to elect or appoint local leaders. The larger regions, or provinces, were overseen by Romans called governors. Governors, in turn, reported to the Roman Senate, a group of elected officials. This pyramid structure is quite like Figure 29 which we introduced at the end of Chapter 15. Also, if you recall from the Prologue, the Persian leader, Cyrus, who conquered Babylon was "considerate" of the peoples who now fell under his empire. This is an enduring principle—to recognize that the people should have a voice in how they govern their own lives. When governments encroach on this principle, we move towards tyranny.

It is my contention that our great country will self-destruct like the Roman Empire if we do not acknowledge we have growing civil disorder, and the solution isn't more top-down government. As a matter of fact, it is my contention that much of our civil disorder is because we inherently recognize our freedoms are eroding. Solutions to problems do not need to originate in Washington D.C. Governments are often the source of a lot of our problems particularly when we hamstring citizens' lives and livelihoods in ways that restrict or erode freedoms.

We need to ensure that balance is restored, that governments return to the people what has been robbed from them. Additionally, even if we restore good government, it will not solve the social issues that plague our society. I speak primarily of the civil discourse over all issues we choose to pontificate over, especially through social media. It is okay to have differences of opinion. That is how we learn and grow. When we shout down others simply because we disagree, we have set the course towards destroying our nation. It would be my hope that we choose the path of the Ninevites, by examining our own individual behaviors and asking ourselves, "How can I improve my life to be a better version of me?" I have adopted a practice in my life that has served me well for this purpose.

There are two fundamental principles that I use to help me improve myself, to become a better version of me. It involves the use of mirrors. I believe we are born with innate character traits, but we can improve them. I use metaphorical mirrors. When I observe someone who I admire, I try to mirror the same behavior. It takes time to change, but it is possible if we continue to work at it. Mirroring the behavior of people we admire, if done consistently, will become a habit and then it will eventually become who we are. I am reminded of a quote attributed to Lao-Tzu, a Chinese philosopher:

> *"Watch your thoughts, they become your words; watch your words, they become your actions; watch your actions, they become your habits; watch your habits, they become your character; watch your character, it becomes your destiny."*

As Lao-Tzu suggests, the process of "becoming" begins with our thoughts. This is why Christians are encouraged to regularly study and read scriptures, that we may become better people, more divine, by putting good thoughts into our minds. Jesus Christ taught that our actions begin with our thoughts.

The second fundamental principle I use that involves "mirrors" can be found in scripture too and has served me well. However, it is more painful emotionally. I recommend its use, but I forewarn the reader, it is harder to endure. My exemplar, Jesus Christ, taught this principle in his great sermon on the mount (Matthew Chapter 7, King James Version).

> *1 Judge not, that ye be not judged.*

> *2 For with what judgment ye judge, ye shall be judged: and with what measure ye mete, it shall be measured to you again.*

> *3 And why beholdest thou the mote that is in thy brother's eye, but considerest not the beam that is in thine own eye?*

> *4 Or how wilt thou say to thy brother, Let me pull out the mote out of thine eye; and, behold, a beam is in thine own eye?*

5 Thou hypocrite, first cast out the beam out of thine own eye; and then shalt thou see clearly to cast out the mote out of thy brother's eye.

In this scripture, Christ teaches about judgment and hypocrisy. Let me explain how I've used "mirrors" to improve who I am and how it relates to this scripture. My biggest challenge in life has been the negative traits associated with my "Type A" personality, including impatience, competitiveness, and aggression. While there are some valuable traits of the "Type A" personality, such as being self-motivated and goal oriented, the flaws can lead to discord in relationships. Recognizing these flaws and correcting them can and will lead to happier relationships. Unfortunately, recognition is almost always emotionally painful.

When I interact with another "Type A" personality and become irritated or emotionally troubled by their behavior, it is a clue that I have a "beam" as Christ put it, in my own eye. In other words, I am looking into a mirror of my own personality, and I don't like what I see. It is the emotional pain I experience during those interactions that always serves as my reminder, "Chris, you are looking in a mirror." It is my clue that I need self-introspection. Pain is a great teacher and emotional pain is often a clue that I need to look at my own behaviors.

The only person we can change is ourselves. I have observed that people who lack self-discipline, observable by their lack of ability to bridle their own tongue, often seek to use institutions to compel others to conform to their way of thinking. They can't control their own behavior so, to feel good about themselves, they try to control their environment and the people around them. They are often the loudest voices in a debate. If we are to survive as a nation, we need to avoid this tendency to compel our neighbor to agree with us by using government force. George Washington said it best:

"Government is not reason, it is not eloquence-it is force! Like fire it is a dangerous servant and a

fearful master; never for a moment should it be left to irresponsible action."

I have shared who I am and what I believe. I have outlined some of the problems I believe we face as a nation. We need to reign in our federal government, but we also need to discipline our own lives as well. We can survive as a nation; it depends on the course we choose. I choose God and pray that He will give me the strength, courage, and discipline to be worthy of the trust He has placed in me when He called me to "run for president."

ABOUT THE AUTHOR

"You were always content, even as a baby," his mother once told him.

Christopher David Borcik was the 2nd of four children born to David E. Borcik and Lydia Jane Ferguson. Chris' calm, cheerful, and contented attitude has helped him succeed in every endeavor.

Chris graduated from the US Naval Academy in 1982 and distinguished himself from his Navy peers as a frontrunner before departing for a 30-year flying career at a major US airline. Chris also served as an instructor pilot for navigators in the Navy and the B-757/767 for his airline. He has served in multiple volunteer capacities in his community and church.

Chris married his bride of 40 years, Chandra, in 1983, and they are the parents of four sons. Their posterity includes three beautiful grandchildren.

In this book, Chris candidly shares many stories and life experiences that will help you see into the mind and heart of a man who loves people, this nation, and its founding principles.

His wise insights about people, power, money, and politics will leave you pondering, "Will this man be our next president?" When you read this book, you will be convinced he should.

Website: https://RestoreAmerica.Today
Email: chris@restoreamerica.today
Facebook: https://www.facebook.com/groups/873491217714787

APPENDIX

1   Elmer W. K. Mould, *Essentials of Bible History,* pp. 348–49.
2   https://founders.archives.gov/documents/Washington/04-05-02-0316
3   https://news.gallup.com/poll/388781/political-party-preferences-shifted-greatly-during-2021.aspx
4   https://www.flyreagan.com/about-airport/history-reagan-national-airport
5   https://founders.archives.gov/documents/Washington/04-05-02-0316
6   https://www.fec.gov/data/candidate/P80001571/?cycle=2016&election_full=true
7   https://www.dictionary.com/browse/power
8   W. Cleon Skousen, *THE MAKING OF AMERICA, The Substance and Meaning of the Constitution* (The National Center for Constitutional Studies, 2nd edition, rev 1986) p. 401
9   Byron, M. (2022) *Battle of the Monongahela.* https://www.mountvernon.org/library/digitalhistory/digital-encyclopedia/article/battle-of-the-monongahela/
10 https://founders.archives.gov/documents/Washington/02-01-02-0169
11 George Washington Parke Qustis, *Recollections and private memoirs of Washington* pp. 303-304. (Note: This narrative was received by the author from Dr. James Craik who accompanied Washington during the encounter with the Indian Chief 15 years after the Battle of the Monongahela)
12 Ibid. p. 304
13 https://crashstats.nhtsa.dot.gov/Api/Public/ViewPublication/813266
14 https://www.youtube.com/watch?v=kH9-ugh7F2s&list=RDCMUCxM5I-3CoUdjJjhj2_T-eEw&start_radio=1&rv=kH9-ugh7F2s&t=66
15 https://www.cbo.gov/publication/50250
16 https://www.cbo.gov/publication/51580
17 https://www.usaspending.gov/disaster/covid-19?publicLaw=all
18 Pearson, Stephen. "Comparison of Prices Over 90 Years." The People History. https://www.thepeoplehistory.com/70yearsofpricechange.html (accessed 20 December 2022)
19 https://navalofficerrecruiter.com/naval-flight-officer/
20 Human Equation definitions contained herein are used with permission from www.merriam-webster.com/dictionary/human%20equation© by Merriam-Webster, Incorporated.

21 A nautical mile is 1.151 times longer than a statute mile. We use statute miles in automobiles. Therefore, wind traveling at 200 knots is equivalent to an automobile traveling at 230.2 mph (200 x 1.151).

22 https://www.ntsb.gov/investigations/AccidentReports/Reports/AAR8605.pdf, p. 32

23 Ibid. p. 6

24 Government definitions contained herein are used with permission from www.merriam-webster.com/dictionary/government by Merriam-Webster, Incorporated.

25 The birth rate for childbearing years (15-44) in 1800 thru 1970 can be found in "Series B 5-10" on page 49 of "Historical Statistics of the United States, Colonial Times to 1970 Part 1". The rate in 1800 was 0.278 a year, multiplied by 29 years (Ages 15-44) is equivalent to an average of 8 children per woman. Report can be found at https://www.census.gov/history/pdf/histstats-colonial-1970.pdf. Not surprisingly, the rate steadily drops. 1900 was 3.77 children per woman, 3.1 in 1950 and 2.5 in 1970.

26 W. Cleon Skousen, *THE MAKING OF AMERICA, The Substance and Meaning of the Constitution* (The National Center for Constitutional Studies, 2nd edition, rev 1986) p. 45

27 Ibid. p. 44

28 Ibid. p. 44

29 Ibid. p. 44

30 *Federalist Papers*, No. 47

31 https://www.pewresearch.org/topic/politics-policy/us-elections-voters/voters-voting/voter-participation/?_formats=short-read&_regions_countries=united-states

32 https://www.polyas.com/election-glossary/voter-apathy

33 "U.S. population keeps growing, but House of Representatives is same size as in Taft era" Pew Research Center, Washington, D.C. (May 31, 2018) https://www.pewresearch.org/fact-tank/2018/05/31/u-s-population-keeps-growing-but-house-of-representatives-is-same-size-as-in-taft-era/

34 *Federalist Papers*, No. 45

35 W. Cleon Skousen, *THE MAKING OF AMERICA, The Substance and Meaning of the Constitution* (The National Center for Constitutional Studies, 2nd edition, rev 1986) p. 46

36 https://www.churchofjesuschrist.org/study/general-conference/2007/10/good-better-best?lang=eng

37 https://www.churchofjesuschrist.org/learn/conference-center-temple-square?lang=eng

38 https://www.dfas.mil/Portals/98/MilPayTable1971_2.pdf

39 https://aspe.hhs.gov/topics/poverty-economic-mobility/poverty-guidelines

40 Pearson, Stephen. "Comparison of Prices Over 90 Years." The People History. https://www.thepeoplehistory.com/70yearsofpricechange.html (accessed August 18 2022)

41 https://www.eia.gov/dnav/pet/hist/LeafHandler.ashx?n=pet&s=mcrfpus1&f=a

42 https://www.eia.gov/dnav/pet/hist/LeafHandler.ashx?n=PET&s=EMM_EPMR_PTE_NUS_DPG&f=M

43 Ceyda Oner. (April 2023). International Monetary Fund. *Back to Basics: Inflation: Prices on the Rise.*.https://www.imf.org/en/Publications/fandd/issues/Series/Back-to-Basics/Inflation

44 https://www.bls.gov/opub/hom/glossary.htm#inflation

45 Decision of the Reserve Bank Organization Committee Determining the Federal Reserve Districts and the Location of Federal Reserve Banks Under Federal Reserve Act Approved December 23, 1913. Digitized by FRASER found at https://fraser.stlouisfed.org/title/603

46 Board of Governors of the Federal Reserve System (US), M2 [M2SL], retrieved from FRED, Federal Reserve Bank of St. Louis; https://fred.stlouisfed.org/series/M2SL, August 20, 2022.

47 G. Edward Griffin, *The Creature from Jekyll Island* p. 138

48 Ibid. p. 144

49 Ibid. pp. 151-152

50 https://en.wikipedia.org/wiki/Fiat_money

51 https://www.swfinstitute.org/news/89070/what-is-the-cantillon-effect-and-why-its-even-more-important-now

52 https://www.treasurydirect.gov/indiv/products/products.htm

53 © [2023] Federal Reserve Bank of New York. Content from the New York Fed subject to the Terms of Use at newyorkfed.org. Garbade, Kenneth, (August 2014) *Direct Purchases of U.S. Treasury Securities by Federal Reserve Banks.* https://www.newyorkfed.org/research/staff_reports/sr684.html

54 Joseph Wang, *Central Banking 101* p. 53

55 https://fsapps.fiscal.treasury.gov/dts/files/22082400.pdf

56 $468,000 was at the end of Q3 of 2022. Source Data U.S. Census Bureau and U.S. Department of Housing and Urban Development, Median Sales Price of Houses Sold for the United States [MSPUS], retrieved from FRED, Federal Reserve Bank of St. Louis; https://fred.stlouisfed.org/series/MSPUS, August 20, 2022.

57 Joseph Wang, *Central Banking 101* p. 53

58 https://www.usaspending.gov/disaster/covid-19?publicLaw=all

59 G. Edward Griffin, *The Creature from Jekyll Island* p. 167

60 https://www.federalreserve.gov/apps/reportingforms/Report/Index/FR_2900_(Commercial_Banks)

61 Ibid.

62 https://www.iotafinance.com/en/Financial-Definition-currency-drain.html

63 U.S. Bureau of Labor Statistics, Unemployment Rate [UNRATE], retrieved from FRED, Federal Reserve Bank of St. Louis; https://fred.stlouisfed.org/series/UNRATE, August 29, 2022.

[64] https://www.federalreserve.gov/econres/notes/feds-notes/closing-the-monetary-policy-curriculum-gap-20201023.html

[65] Name changed from Civil Aeronautics Authority in 1958

[66] https://en.wikipedia.org/wiki/Airline_Deregulation_Act

[67] Ibid

[68] G. Edward Griffin, *The Creature from Jekyll Island* p. 449

[69] Ibid.

[70] Ibid. p. 24

[71] https://www.cdfund.com/clientdata/222/media/pdf/The-Big-Reset11.pdf p. 26

[72] "Required Reserves" include currency held in bank vaults to meet the withdrawal demands of customers and electronic entries on the books. The "Excess Reserves" and other electronic entries of "Required Reserves" are held electronically in the financial institution's account at the Federal Reserve Bank in their district. There are 12 Federal Reserve Banks, or districts.

[73] https://www.federalreserve.gov/pubs/feds/2013/201311/201311pap.pdf p. 15

[74] https://www.federalreserve.gov/monetarypolicy/0693lead.pdf p. 574

[75] Murray N. Rothbard, *The Mystery of Banking* p. 86

[76] G. Edward Griffin, *The Creature from Jekyll Island* p. 311

[77] Ibid. p. 312

[78] https://founders.archives.gov/documents/Washington/03-20-02-0157

[79] G. Edward Griffin, *The Creature from Jekyll Island* p. 338

[80] Ibid.

[81] Ibid. p. 388

[82] Ibid.

[83] https://www.nber.org/research/data/nber-macrohistory-xiv-money-and-banking. See "U.S. Notes in Circulation, Federal Reserve Banks 11/1914-06/1949"

[84] Ibid.

[85] M2 is the Federal Reserve's definition of an aggregate type of money which includes M1 plus other assets. M1 is the sum of currency held by the public and transaction deposits (both checking and savings) at depository institutions (which are financial institutions that obtain their funds mainly through deposits from the public, such as commercial banks, savings and loan associations, savings banks, and credit unions). The additional assets when added to M1 to make up M2 are small-denomination time deposits (those issued in amounts of less than $100,000), and retail money market mutual fund shares. This is the simplified definition of M2 as found on the Fed's website @ https://www.federalreserve.gov/faqs/money_12845.htm

[86] https://www.fdic.gov/bank/historical/brief/brhist.pdf p. 20

[87] Ibid. p. 21

[88] Ibid. p. 22

[89] Ibid. p. 22

90 Ibid.

91 Ibid. pp.23-24

92 Ibid. pp. 24

93 Ibid. pp. 27

94 Ibid. pp 50

95 https://www.fdic.gov/analysis/quarterly-banking-profile/fdic-quarterly/2022-vol16-2/fdic-v16n2-1q2022.pdf p. 23

96 Ibid. p. 4

97 Ibid. p. 23

98 https://www.fdic.gov/bank/historical/managing/chronological/1991.html

99 https://www.fdic.gov/bank/historical/firstfifty/chapter4.pdf p. 69

100 https://archive.fdic.gov/view/fdic/4000

101 Ibid.

102 Krugman, Paul, *The Return of Depression Economics and the Crisis of 2008 (W. W. Norton & Company, Inc., 2009)* p. 63

103 https://www.gcu.edu/blog/teaching-school-administration/4-qualities-good-teacher

104 Public Papers of John F. Kennedy, 1962, p. 348

105 Ibid. p. 347

106 W. Cleon Skousen, *THE MAKING OF AMERICA, The Substance and Meaning of the Constitution* (The National Center for Constitutional Studies, 2nd edition, rev 1986) p. 19

107 Ibid. p. 46

108 The Writings of Benjamin Franklin, Collected and Edited with a Life and Introduction by Albert Henry Smyth. Volum IX, 1783-1788. P. 569. Letter from Benjamin Franklin to Messrs. The Abbés Chalut and Arnaud', April 17, 1787.

109 US Constitution, Article V

110 https://www.termlimits.com/library/National_Poll_2021-OF.pdf

111 Ballotpedia. (2022, October). Term limits on the ballot: Against limits. Ballotpedia. https://ballotpedia.org/Term_limits_on_the_ballot

112 https://sgp.fas.org/crs/misc/R41545.pdf p. 4

113 Ibid.

114 https://conventionofstates.com/

115 *Federalist Papers*, No. 45

116 *Federalist Papers*, No. 41

117 https://www.ssa.gov/policy/docs/quickfacts/stat_snapshot/index.html?number

118 Randy E. Barnett, New Evidence of the Original Meaning of the Commerce Clause (Georgetown Public Law and Legal Theory Research Paper No. 12-045), p. 862 https://scholarship.law.georgetown.edu/cgi/viewcontent.cgi?article=1855&context=facpub

[119] W. Cleon Skousen, *THE MAKING OF AMERICA, The Substance and Meaning of the Constitution* (The National Center for Constitutional Studies, 2nd edition, rev 1986) p. 401

[120] Ibid. p. 403

[121] Sorman, Guy (2012). *A Brief History of American Prosperity.* https://www.city-journal.org/html/brief-history-american-prosperity-13510.html

[122] General definitions contained herein are used with permission from www.merriam-webster.com/dictionary/governmentby Merriam-Webster, Incorporated.

[123] *THE HERITAGE GUIDE TO THE CONSTITUTION* (Regnery Publishing, Fully Revised 2nd edition, 2014) p. 53

[124] https://www.cagw.org/sites/default/files/pdf/2022PigBook.pdf, p. 2

[125] Gales, Joseph, 1761-1841. The Debates and Proceedings in the Congress of the United States, First Congress, First Session, Volume 2, book, 1834; Washington D.C. (https://digital.library.unt.edu/ark:/67531/metadc29466/: accessed April 8, 2023), University of North Texas Libraries, UNT Digital Library, https://digital.library.unt.edu; crediting UNT Libraries Government Documents Department.

[126] https://www.loc.gov/resource/gdcmassbookdig.theodoreroosevel05roos/?st=pdf&pdfPage=413

[127] W. Cleon Skousen, *THE MAKING OF AMERICA, The Substance and Meaning of the Constitution* (The National Center for Constitutional Studies, 2nd edition, rev 1986) p. 253

[128] https://www.uscourts.gov/sites/default/files/apptsbypres.pdf

[129] David Barton, *ORIGINAL INTENT, THE COURTS, THE CONSTITUTION, & RELIGION*, (WallBuilder Press, 1st Edition, 1996) p. 263

[130] Ibid. p. 266

[131] https://founders.archives.gov/documents/Jefferson/03-17-02-0379

[132] Source of data found at: https://www.electproject.org/national-1789-present

[133] https://upload.wikimedia.org/wikipedia/commons/1/13/The_Ancient_Science_of_Numbers_by_Luo_Clement_ %281908%29.pdf

[134] https://www.census.gov/data/tables/time-series/demo/income-poverty/historical-income-inequality.html Data taken from "TableA-4a and A-4b."

[135] World Bank, Inflation, consumer prices for the United States [FPCPITOTLZGUSA], retrieved from FRED, Federal Reserve Bank of St. Louis; https://fred.stlouisfed.org/series/FPCPITOTLZGUSA, March 6, 2023 (The Annual inflation data for consumer prices was compounded to derive 679%)

[136] W. Cleon Skousen, *THE MAKING OF AMERICA, The Substance and Meaning of the Constitution* (The National Center for Constitutional Studies, 2nd edition, rev 1986) pp. 478-481

[137] Schwab, John C., *The Confederate States of America 1861-1865, A Financial and Industrial History of the South during the Civil War.* (New York Charles Scribner's Sons, 1901) p.292

[138] https://www.irs.gov/newsroom/historical-highlights-of-the-irs

[139] Ibid.

[140] https://www.archives.gov/milestone-documents/16th-amendment

[141] https://www.irs.gov/newsroom/historical-highlights-of-the-irs

[142] https://www.archives.gov/milestone-documents/16th-amendment

[143] https://taxfoundation.org/tax-compliance-costs-irs-regulations/

[144] Ibid.

[145] Ibid.

[146] The Census Bureau and the Bureau of Labor Statistics

[147] Meet the Researchers | U.S. Bureau of Economic Analysis (BEA) at https://www.bea.gov/research/meet-the-researchers

[148] Federal Reserve Bank of St. Louis, Velocity of MZM Money Stock (DISCONTINUED) [MZMV], retrieved from FRED, Federal Reserve Bank of St. Louis; https://fred.stlouisfed.org/series/MZMV, April 2, 2023.

[149] National Bureau of Economic Research, Dow-Jones Industrial Stock Price Index for United States [M1109BUSM293NNBR], retrieved from FRED, Federal Reserve Bank of St. Louis; https://fred.stlouisfed.org/series/M1109BUSM293NNBR, April 3, 2023

[150] https://www.federalreservehistory.org/essays/stock-market-crash-of-1929

[151] Murray N. Rothbard, *The Mystery of Banking* p. 145

[152] https://www.fdic.gov/bank/historical/brief/brhist.pdf p. 21

[153] National Bureau of Economic Research, Total Money Supply for United States [M1490AUSM157SNBR], retrieved from FRED, Federal Reserve Bank of St. Louis; https://fred.stlouisfed.org/series/M1490AUSM157SNBR, April 3, 2023.

[154] National Bureau of Economic Research, Unemployment Rate for United States [M0892AUSM156SNBR], retrieved from FRED, Federal Reserve Bank of St. Louis; https://fred.stlouisfed.org/series/M0892AUSM156SNBR, April 3, 2023.

[155] https://valor.defense.gov/Description-of-Awards/

[156] https://www.fec.gov/data/candidate/P20001558/?cycle=1992&election_full=true

[157] https://www.fec.gov/data/candidate/P80001571/?cycle=2016&election_full=true

[158] Ballotpedia. (2022, December). Presidential election, 2016. Ballotpedia. https://ballotpedia.org/Presidential_election,_2016

[159] The Records of the Federal Convention of 1787, vol. 2. Yale University Press, 1911, pp. 57-58.

[160] The Records of the Federal Convention of 1787, vol. 2. Yale University Press, 1911, pp. 119-120.

[161] US Constitution, Article II, Section 1, paragraph 2.
[162] *Federalist Papers*, No. 64
[163] https://www.faa.gov/documentLibrary/media/Order/7930.2S_Chg_2_dtd_12-2-21.pdf
[164] https://www.fec.gov/resources/cms-content/documents/federalelections2020.pdf
[165] Ballotpedia. (2022, December). United States Congress elections, 2022: Historical comparison. Ballotpedia. https://ballotpedia.org/United_States_Congress_elections,_2022#:~:text=Historical%20comparison
[166] https://www.cbo.gov/system/files/2021-03/56977-LTBO-2021.pdf, p. 6

TABLE OF FIGURES

www.ingramcontent.com/pod-product-compliance
Lightning Source LLC
Chambersburg PA
CBHW061204220326
41597CB00015BA/1346